The Unwanted

The Unwanted

A MEMOIR

Kien Nguyen

LITTLE, BROWN AND COMPANY
BOSTON • NEW YORK • LONDON

First Edition

Library of Congress Cataloging-in-Publication Data
Nguyen, Kien.
The unwanted : a memoir / Kien Nguyen. — 1st ed.
p.   cm.
ISBN 0-316-28664-8
1. Nguyen, Kien — Childhood and youth.   2. Vietnamese Americans —
Biography.   3. Refugees — Vietnam — Biography.   4. Nha Trang
(Vietnam) — Biography.   5. Vietnamese Conflict, 1961–1975 —
Vietnam — Ho Chi Minh City.   6. Vietnamese Conflict, 1961–1975 —
Personal narratives, Vietnamese.   I. Title.
E184.V53 N36 2000
973'.049592'0092 — dc21
[B]   00-057997

10 9 8 7 6 5 4 3 2 1

Q-FF

Book design by Iris Weinstein

Printed in the United States of America

TO MY MOTHER, WHO GAVE ME LIFE

AND

TO FRANK ANDREWS, WHO GAVE ME
A SECOND CHANCE

AUTHOR'S NOTE

The Unwanted *is the memoir of my childhood and adolescence in Vietnam. It springs from my vivid memory of those years and is augmented by the recollections of my mother and my brother.*

ACKNOWLEDGMENTS

Alexandra Bennett and Scott Morgan,
for inspiring me to write my story.
Judy Clain, for giving me a chance to be a writer.
Fiona and Jake Eberts, for believing in me from the first day we met.
Elaine Gartner, for being there.
Michaela Hamilton, for helping me find my voice.
Peter Miller, for your lion-hearted support every step of the way.
BeTi Nguyen, for being my loving sister.
Jimmy Nguyen, for helping me walk the path of memory.
Ilona Price and Jason Goodman, for your generous enthusiasm.
Joann Russo-Tabeek, for feeding me many
free meals at your restaurant, Paninoteca.
Lisa Sharkey, for giving me the encouragement I needed.
Milan Tinan, for the greatest friendship a writer could ask.
Special thanks to everyone at PMA and Little, Brown who has
helped bring The Unwanted *from memory to bound book.*
And especially to Loan, wherever you are. I will never forget you.

The Unwanted

1972

CHAPTER ONE
Nhatrang, May 12, 1972, 7 P.M.

I remember that night quite well. It is my first memory, and the happiest one from my childhood.

The familiar smell of pig roasting on a spit wafted from the kitchen. My mother made cheery noises as she ran from one hallway to the next, giving orders to the help with a hint of pompous confidence. The moist summer air evaporated into a transparent mist all around me due to the kind of heat found only in Nhatrang and only in May. And what I remember most of all is the sense of festivity all around me as the last rays of sunlight disappeared into the ocean, just a few hundred feet away from my window. It was my fifth birthday.

My childhood home, in order to accommodate my mother's passion for living near beautiful beaches, was situated by the water, with the waves murmuring at the foot of the house. The mansion was comprised of three stories and over twenty-four rooms, including at least eight bedrooms. All were furnished with expensive Western furniture thrown together by my mother's own design. And both to give the house personality and to honor my grandfather's last name, Mother named it Nguyen Mansion. From the numerous stories I was told growing up, mostly by my grandparents, I came to understand that my mother built the house during her pregnancy with me, motivated by the idea of having her first baby in her own home. Mother painted the outside of the house the color of eggshells, and, much to her consternation, I always thought the house was just a simple white color that had aged poorly with time. From the main entrance of the house to the front gate lay a large reddish marble pathway that encircled the garden, which housed a kidney-shaped pool. Our gardener, Mr. Tran, had been hired through an agency, and his job consisted mainly of planting and maintaining the many exotic species of flowers around the front part of the house. My mother, in an effort to shield the inside beauty from the outside world, constructed two enormous iron gates, as well as a high barbed-wire fence covered with thick vines, to obscure all within their boundaries. In the old days, I used to play with my toys in the garden while the children playing on the other side of the gate watched me with fascination. According to my mother, those children were either too dirty, or I was too clean, for my association with them. In Vietnam, rich children like myself wore sandals to protect their feet from the dirt and the heat, while poor children like the ones from the other side of the wall ran around barefoot.

That afternoon, before the celebration, much of the activity was centered in the kitchen. I was flying through the crowded rooms with my arms out like an airplane and making buzzing sounds, bumping into people's legs to simulate a crash. My brother and I had made up this clever plan to get treats from the help. Unfortunately, everyone seemed too busy to notice me. In the middle of the main kitchen a group of chefs stood around an enormous table, decorating a gigantic white cake with bunches of red roses, brown vines, and green leaves made from heavy whipped cream and food coloring. On the other side of the room, barely visible in the dark smoke, live fowls awaited their turn to be slaughtered; their frightened cackles rose over the impatient sizzling of the pork. A few steps away, a group of my mother's maids hovered over the busy stove preparing the main courses. One of the women turned on the ceiling fan as her friend strained cooked noodles over the drain. The fog from the boiling water swept up from the pot, adding to the heat in the room.

Looking for a new victim for my airplane game, I spotted a young caterer's apprentice. He was about ten years old and of diminutive size, with dark circles under his eyes. Running through the kitchen with a big bowl of whipped cream, he crashed into me. I knew how fearful our servants were when it came to my mother's wrath. While the boy was making sure I was not injured, I reached into his bowl for a handful of cream. Before he could recover from his shock, I laughed and ran off, lapping the sweetness from my hand.

Upstairs, I decided to take a peek inside my mother's bedroom. She sat regally at her makeup desk, fully dressed in a pale evening gown that glistened under the orange light like a mermaid's scales. Her attention was focused on brushing her long hair, which rippled down her arching back, jet-black and wavy. My mother was not a typically thin Asian woman. She had heavy breasts and round hips, joined by a thin waist. Her eyes, big and rimmed with dark mascara, concentrated on the image before her. Years spent watching my mother gaze at herself in the mirror had convinced me that she was the rarest, most beautiful creature that ever walked the face of this Earth.

My presence startled her. She took her eyes off her reflection, looked at me, and smiled, showing her white, straight teeth. At times I had sat for hours in my mother's bedroom while she confided her beauty secrets to me. I would listen earnestly, not to what my mother said, but to the mesmerizing sound of her voice, always full of wisdom and intelligence.

Her smile faded into a slight frown as she said, "Look at you. What is that all over your face?"

I touched my cheek and felt the remnants of the whipped cream. Licking my fingers, I answered her, "It's for my cake in the kitchen. Can I come in?"

She nodded. "Sure, come in." And then came the scolding. "What a dirty boy, eating in such a manner. Why don't you wait till dinner?"

I sat on her bed and looked at her curiously. Using a small cotton pad, she was pressing white powder onto the backs of her hands.

"What are you doing, Mommy?" I asked.

"I am putting makeup on my hands, darling."

"How come?"

"You are always asking the same question."

"I never remember what the answer is, Mommy."

She paused and held her hands in front of her face, where they stood at attention like two proud soldiers ready for inspection. "I do this because I want people to notice my hands. Aren't they beautiful?"

Along with her fortune, my mother's hands were the ultimate pride in her life. Before she met my father, she had worked as a hand model for a jewelry company. In contrast to her voluptuous body, her hands were long and graceful. Each finger was a smooth cylinder with invisible knuckles and no wrinkles; each nail was defined, extended, well polished, and glossy. She spent hours smoothing the sharp edges of her nails, trimming the out-of-place cuticles, and changing the color of the paint. Not until she was completely satisfied with her hands did my mother apply makeup to her face, a process that would also require a few hours. She said that since her face was not extraordinary, her success would depend on her hands.

As if to prove her point, my mother made sure that her hands were always displayed. They danced in front of her face during a conversation, rested on her cheeks in photographs, or raised her chin when she exercised her power. Sometimes, they daintily held the stem of a champagne glass. Once my mother considered buying insurance for her hands; however, this idea did not meet with approval from my grandfather. I'm sure my mother wished that she had gotten insurance the day I accidentally bumped into her while running down the hallway. The collision broke two of her nails and scratched her fingers, leaving her boiling mad and me with welts on my cheek.

"Is this party for me, Mommy?" I asked as she continued tending to her hands.

"Yes, darling."

"Does it mean I can stay up late tonight?"

"You can stay up a little while after you blow out your candles."

"Will there be any children coming over tonight from my class?" I asked her hopefully.

"No, darling. No other children, just you and your brother. So you can be the star tonight. After all, it is an adult party; you don't want any children here to spoil it, do you?"

"Right, Mommy," I agreed halfheartedly.

I walked to the bedroom window and looked outside. I could see porters carrying cases of Champagne Guy Larmandier into the house. The garden was lit up by multicolored lights, with every shrub transformed into some sort of animal. Next to the pool, behind a couple of rose bushes, a group of musicians tested their electrical instruments. The noise resolved itself into a lively, cheery tune that carried through the thick air. The cooks, maids, and waiters ran back and forth like ants in an ant farm, all lost in their own assignments. The neighborhood children, clustered next to a few adults, gathered around the front gates, staring curiously inside. Should anyone venture too close to the gates, security men would push them away. Over the sounds of celebration, deep in the darkness, the ocean moaned its constant, breathy rhythm.

"When do I get to blow out the candles?" I asked, turning to look at my mother.

"Right after dinner."

"When do we have dinner?"

"When all the guests arrive," she said.

"When will that be?"

"Around nine-thirty." My mother regarded her nails. A pang of dissatisfaction washed over her face as she reached for her bright orange nail polish.

"Can I stay awake after the cake, Mommy?"

"No, darling. After the cake there will be dancing. You are too young to stay up that late. Maybe next year. Now, be a good boy and go play with your brother."

"But he is sleeping in Grandma's room."

"Then go wake him up. Tell Grandma or Loan to dress both of

you." She pushed me out of her room and carefully closed the door without touching her nails.

BY THE TIME Jimmy and I changed into the party clothes that my mother had ordered from the Sears catalog, a luxury that few could afford in Vietnam, the guests had finally arrived. From my grandparents' bedroom, we could hear every noise the people outside made. Gazing at each other nervously, we pressed our ears against the thin wall, listening to the footsteps that ran frantically up and down the hallway. The rich smell of cooked spices mixed with the heavy odor of perfume.

Finally, my mother burst into the room with enough exuberance to burn out a lightbulb. Her off-white evening gown embraced her, gushing down her body like a stream of silver water. Her hair was bound above her neck in a complicated knot, revealing a diamond necklace and two small diamond earrings. She looked foreign, for-midable, elegant as an Egyptian queen. She smiled through her makeup, as she reached for us with bare arms that sparkled with diamonds. We entered her cloud of perfume, and together, hand in hand, we walked into the noisy brightness outside.

The rest of the evening is a blur. I vaguely recall the laughter, the kisses, the food, the stark colors, the songs, and the mountain of pre-sents that filled my room. I also remember the foreign guests with sandy hair and blue eyes, as well as the anxious talk on everyone's lips about the revolution. Jimmy and I were sent to bed immediately after I blew out the candles on top of my gigantic cake. And I was to sleep for three years, banished from my mother's warmth and sent away to school, leaving behind the special night that was supposed to be mine.

1975

CHAPTER TWO

Nhatrang, March 25, 1975

A frightening cluster of explosions jolted me out of a deep
sleep. I jumped out of bed, dimly aware of my surroundings. Through the window, the sky flickered with faint
stars. I wondered if the noises I had just heard were merely a fig-
ment of my imagination.

More gunshots rang out, and terror awakened me with full force.
I groped for my sandals in the darkness, yelping for my mother. A
figure bolted into my room, holding a candle in her hand. It was
Loan, my nanny, who at eighteen was also the youngest maid in our
house. Her hair was tangled, and sleep hadn't completely washed
from her face. In the dimly lit room, she looked bewildered and
shaken. I ran toward her to bury myself in her bosom and inhaled
the soothing, familiar scent of her body. We huddled together in the
middle of the room.

For over a month, gunshots and bombs had been heard all over
Nhatrang. Every day the media had delivered more disturbing
news, until numbness had infected everyone like a plague. People
learned to follow the latest reports with silent and bitter acceptance.
Rumors spread wildly throughout Nhatrang, eating through the
city like a cancer. Since there were no guards, the prison doors
were unlocked; felons trickled out like dirty water, robbing the city

mercilessly. No one dared to venture outside. The streets were deserted, except for an occasional fast-moving car. Locked houses attested to their owners' fear. Television brought us scenes of towns near the war zone, where panicked citizens burst from their doors in the middle of night, carrying nothing but their infants. The refugees, with bare feet and empty hands, rushed from one city to the next, running away from the invisible terror, with no idea of where they were going or what they were fleeing. Finding food became a constant worry, since the markets no longer operated regularly. The city was like a fish dying on hard pavement, hopelessly gasping for air.

Like most people in Nhatrang, we had bolted ourselves inside our home and waited for the horror of war to manifest its fury. So far, only some of its impact had torn through the protective shield of the Nguyen mansion. I recall the first and most awful incident that shook my mother's sense of security: the crumbling of her bank. Since 1968, she had been the co-president of a small privately owned bank in Nhatrang. Half of the bank's assets were in her name, and a rich Chinese couple owned the other half. Late one evening my mother received a phone call informing her that her partners were in Thailand and on their way to New York — with all the cash.

The next day she walked into her office to find herself standing in a deserted, garbage-filled wreck. Outside, hundreds of angry customers were screaming her name, as they fought to get through the locked doors. Mere seconds ahead of the mob, my mother exited the bank through an escape door. She was physically unscathed, but this incident nearly destroyed her defiant spirit.

I watched my mother from the balcony of my bedroom as she walked back to the house. One of her shoes was missing, and a blank stare hollowed her face. Lam, her live-in boyfriend — a man ten years her junior — and his friends were sunbathing by the pool when my mother passed by them, lost in her trance. They stared at her until she disappeared in the house. Only when her feet touched the cold tiles in the living room did she collapse in sobbing howls.

An overwhelming despair engulfed me like a black hole. From my second-floor balcony I began to cry with her, only to realize that a much more ferocious noise was drowning out what little sound I made — the boom of angry, explosive weapons. Down the street, a bomb went off, shaking the ground with vicious force. Now, the same unsettling rumble had hurtled me from my bed and into Loan's arms.

Loan carried me downstairs to the living room to look for my mother, who was hosting a party of sorts. In her search for information, she had gathered together the few officials left in Nhatrang. Sitting in a chair, she was dressed humbly in a traditional Vietnamese *ao dai,* a type of dress with a long skirt split to the waist to form two panels and worn over black pants. My mother was about four months along in her pregnancy, and her belly pushed upward beneath the silky fabric of her clothes. She was in the middle of a conversation with Mr. Dang, the chief translator for the U.S. Embassy.

Mr. and Mrs. Dang were among my mother's important allies. Her heart had no room for any relationship stronger than a detached friendship, and she admitted to me on several occasions that this deficiency was innate to her personality — except that, in her own words, it was not a deficiency but a successful adaptation to life. My mother was simply unable to trust anyone but herself.

The relationship between Mr. and Mrs. Dang and my mother was strictly business. Because of his work, Mr. Dang was able to provide my mother with the latest top-secret news about the nation, the markets, and the key people involved, which included everyone at the party. Thus my mother got her news delivered firsthand, first-class. In return, Mr. Dang got to see the inside of my mother's bedroom, where he was able to confirm that her nightgown fit flawlessly over her shapely body, just as it had been described at the men's mahjong tables.

As for Mrs. Dang, she was always the most significant and interesting guest at any of my mother's gatherings. At that moment, with her half-filled champagne glass positioned dangerously over her large bosom, Mrs. Dang stood a few feet away from her husband, leaning on Lam and another male guest for support. Each time Lam or his friend whispered something in her ear, her exaggerated laughter would break out like shattered glass. Sitting nearby, my mother and Mrs. Dang's husband, lost in their intense conversation, seemed to disregard the tumultuous scene that was happening around them.

"Mommy," I called out from the door.

My mother excused herself and got up to walk over to us. In Loan's embrace, I could feel the tension shooting through the maid's body as my mother approached. Before Loan could say anything, my mother reached out to snatch me away. With an icy stare, she growled almost inaudibly in the maid's ear, "Get out!" She whirled around and returned to her company, holding me in her arms as though nothing significant had happened.

To Mr. Dang, she said, "I am sorry, my son got frightened."

"Well, at this point, madam, he is not the only one," Mr. Dang said with a sigh. "You know, you should get out of here before it is too late."

"Why? What about the Americans? Aren't they helping us?"

Mr. Dang gave my mother the same look he would give to someone who was crazy or just incredibly stupid. "What do you mean by 'the Americans'? They left us long ago. We haven't received any help since 1972. We are on our own, and falling fast."

"But —" my mother stammered, covering my ears with her hands as though to stop both of us from understanding the severity of the situation.

"Exactly my point. You have to get your family out of here soon. The Congs have claimed Qui Nhon City, and Tuy Hoa, too. Only a few short miles through the jungle and they will be here soon."

My mother uttered a small cry. Her hands tightened around my ears, but I could hear the anguish in her voice as she cried, "Dear God, what should I do?"

"I've told you, madam. All we can do right now is run like the wind. As for my family, we are leaving, early tomorrow morning. I suggest you do the same."

"Where should I go?"

"Well, first go to Saigon. At least there, you can always leave Vietnam through the main airport. On the other hand, if the political situation ever improves, you can come back to Nhatrang."

"I have nothing left here to come back to," my mother said. "I lost my bank and all of my money."

Mr. Dang shrugged to emphasize his helplessness. "More reason to leave this condemned place. Please, don't forget to keep in touch with us in Saigon. This is the address where we will be staying." He scribbled on the back of a business card and handed it to her.

THAT NIGHT, even though several guests were still at the party, my mother sent Lam out to rent a minivan. A large vehicle seemed to be the only way for my mother to transport the six of us, including her boyfriend. The moment Lam came back with the van, we rushed to get inside, carrying only a few necessities. As we followed some of our departing guests down the driveway, not a soul in the house knew of our impetuous plan. Most of the servants were already in bed by the time the party began.

Suddenly, from out of nowhere, Loan ran out in front of the van, tearfully begging my mother for permission to come along. For eight years she had been a charming addition to my family, showing kindness to us all, even my mother, who despised anyone beneath her. As long as I could remember, Loan had been one of us.

In her seat, my mother viewed the uncomfortable scene unmoved. However, Loan's cries affected my grandparents, and my grandfather spoke up on her behalf. Confronted with his calm and determined intervention, my mother agreed to take Loan with us.

Once inside, the maid embraced my brother and me tightly. She kissed us with tears on her cheeks before turning to my mother, and bowing down to press her face to my mother's hands. The moment the girl's lips touched her hands, my mother pulled away as if touched by fire. Her face darkened, and her eyes burned at the girl with hatred. With a swift movement that startled everyone, my mother struck a hard blow across Loan's left cheek. The slap sent the girl's head backward to hit the van's steel wall with a cold and hollow noise. Somehow, Loan still managed to keep her head bowed low to the ground.

In the frightful silence, my brother began to cry softly with fear, but no one reached out to comfort him. I was too shocked to utter a sound.

CHAPTER THREE

Saigon, April 1975

I n Saigon we rented a two-story dwelling on a street of French-
style houses. A few blocks away lay the seat of the government,
Doc Lap Palace, where all the Vietnamese presidents had lived.
Unable to adjust to the foreign environment of this new house, my
brother and I ran up and down the stairs, peeking through every
room and observing the busy world outside through the cracks of
the sealed front windows. Neither one of us fully understood why
we ended up there. With the adults in the household lost in their
worries, we were free to roam the place.

Saigon was in chaos. Nguyen Van Thieu, the South Vietnam
president, unexpectedly quit his term on April 23, 1975. Gathering
his personal belongings as well as his assets, he had fled the country.
In an attempt to calm the populace, Congress had appointed Tran
Van Huong to be the country's new president. He, in turn, set a new
record for serving the shortest presidential term in Vietnam's history:
four days. On the afternoon of April 27, at the request of Congress, a
new president, Duong Van Minh, appeared outside Independence
Hall to greet a welcoming crowd. Minh reignited the trust of his
people by making lots of exciting promises. However, like the tee-
tering government, his lofty plans eventually crumbled.

Through the adults' conversations, I learned that my mother had taken us to Saigon with the intention of fleeing the country if and when the government failed. In our first few weeks there she established a web of connections and obtained all the necessary passports and airplane tickets so that we could leave anytime we wanted. However, each time we planned on leaving Vietnam, my grandparents refused to join us. In addition, like the new president, Saigon was still deep in denial of the devastation taking place elsewhere in the country. As long as there were still parties and social banquets, there was hope. Each day we said good-bye to some of my mother's friends as they left. To us, the future did not appear so grim, for there were always more planes coming in, and we had our guaranteed seats on them. We remained in the city and waited.

At home, there was an insurmountable tension between my mother and Loan. The maid tried to keep out of my mother's way, but it was an impossible task, because my mother seemed to be all over the place all the time. Without her bank work to keep her busy, she seemed on the verge of a breakdown. Her erratic behavior got even worse after we received a piece of information from back home via my mother's older sister.

My aunt informed us that since the Communists had claimed Nhatrang on April 2, she and her family had been robbed several times at gunpoint. They had decided to leave the Nguyen mansion after thieves desecrated it and took my mother's Mercedes, her jewelry, and some of the hidden cash.

ON APRIL 28, just before morning broke, my mother heard the report we had all waited for: a panicking voice on the radio reported the coming of the Vietcong. My mother told Loan to go and get me out of bed. Without a word of explanation, Loan took me to the basement, a twelve-by-fifteen-foot hole that the owner had dug under the kitchen floor as a hiding place in the event of war. The rest of the family was already gathered.

In the far corner, my grandmother sat like a statue near a dim light. In her hand she held a string of beads collected from under the Bo De tree, where the Buddha once sat to seek enlightenment. The tips of her fingers moved the beads in a methodical manner. Her eyes were tightly shut, and her lips whispered an inaudible prayer. Next to her my grandfather huddled at the only table in the room, covering his ears, trying to block out the terrifying noises outside. Beside him lay his cane, which he had acquired many years earlier, after serving in the Vietnamese Republican Army as a captain, up until the day a Vietcong bullet exploded in his right hip.

A few steps away Lam lay on a sofa. As usual, his jet-black hair was perfectly combed and blow-dried. He looked alert and relaxed. Deeper in the shadows of the room, my brother stood next to my mother, clutching his favorite teddy bear to his chest. My mother's hair was pulled back in a tight knot, and her face, pale without makeup, appeared stark under the flickering light as she leaned heavily against the door. Her full stomach was visible under her night-gown, and one of her hands lay across her belly as if she were trying to protect the fetus inside. She and my grandfather were in the middle of a conversation as Loan and I entered the room.

"Daddy, we have to leave," my mother was saying. "Please, sir. There is no time left to waste."

My grandfather lifted his head from his hands. His eyes were two dark holes filled with pain, but he shook his head decisively.

"I've told you many times before, and I am telling you again. I am not going anywhere. I was born here on this land. I will die here on this land. So will your mother."

My grandmother continued to pray quietly, her expression unchanged. I wasn't sure if she was paying any attention to the conversation. For her entire adult life, she had never made a move without my grandfather's permission. The fact that my grandfather had decided to stay behind was enough for her.

He continued, "I can't go to America. I don't want to go to any foreign land where I don't speak the language or know the customs.

I'd rather die here by the Vietcong's hands, among my ancestors, than live like a ghost among strangers. You go! Take the children and go. Stop wasting time waiting around for your mother and me. We'll be fine, don't worry about us. I am a sixty-four-year-old decrepit man. No one in this world, not even the worst kind of Congs, would be heartless enough to hurt an old man and his feeble wife. Don't stay here because of us."

My mother was not convinced. "Please, Daddy. Think of the children. You know I can't leave you and Mother here alone, but, if I stay, the children will suffer."

"I am not going anywhere," my grandfather insisted. "Nothing you can say will change my mind."

My mother understood her father's dedication to his country. But she also knew that Vietnam was beset with racism. Through generations of defiance, as they struggled against Chinese, Japanese, and French oppression, this bias had been ingrained in every Vietnamese person. My mother feared what it would do to my brother and me in the future.

Nine years before, when an American civil engineer working in Saigon had hired my mother as a translator, a romance had blossomed between them. I was the result of their brief liaison. My fair skin and curly hair spoke clearly of my father's dominant genes. Perhaps because my appearance made him recognize his own mortality, or because of my mother's irresistible charms, before he left the country permanently, my father emptied his bank account into her hands. The thirty-something-thousand U.S. dollars he left us was a great fortune for anyone in Vietnam. My mother used this money, and her connections, to secure herself a partnership in a bank.

A few years later, she married another American, an officer, and Jimmy, my brother, was born. Jimmy's father left Nhatrang in 1971, with the last of the American troops, to go back home to his own family. He, too, was quite generous. The money he left us helped to pay off the mortgages my mother had on the mansion and provided some needed renovations. My mother also had the tall wall erected around the mansion, which not only shielded the house from outsiders' curiosity but also sealed us up, as if covering something shameful. We were meant never to be discovered.

Now though, my mother realized that no wall on Earth would protect us from being ostracized. The secrets that my mother had tried to protect so desperately were impossible to hide. Hopeless, she knew that we would grow up in an unforgiving society, as neglected as wild rice. Our only hope was to get out of Vietnam and move to a more accepting place. She looked at my grandparents sorrowfully, as she held my brother and me in her arms.

"Daddy, forgive me," she said. "For the sake of my children, I am leaving."

She turned to glare at Loan, and her voice deepened.

"Loan, get the suitcases."

Then she told us, "Go and give your grandparents a kiss goodbye. Make it good. This will be the last time you see Grandpa and Grandma."

We did as we were told. My grandmother dropped her beads on the floor to reach for us. Her tears gushed down her wrinkled face as she kissed us with all of her love. My grandfather's embrace was so tight that it cut off my air supply for what seemed like an eternity. In our ears, he whispered how much he loved my brother and me. Then at last, the embrace broke as Loan reappeared at the door with the suitcases. With her help, we changed into our clothes, packed a few belongings, and headed for the van.

"Take Loan with you. Maybe she can be of help," my grandfather said, pushing the girl toward us.

"What?" My mother stopped in the middle of the room. "She can't come with us. She doesn't have a ticket."

Lam spoke for the first time. "So what? We all know that you are a very powerful woman and that you could move a mountain if you had to. Nobody is asking that you move any mountain; we just want you to take care of this girl instead of abandoning her here. Come on! Give it a try, won't you? For once in your life, do something nice for someone else. Who knows? It might even make you a real human." My mother glared at him as he continued. "Please, I think it could work. Right now, everything is very confusing out there. The police can't possibly check each and every person for passports. Even if they do ask for yours, the way you know people in this town, I am sure we could still sneak her out with us. But seriously, let's be honest. The problem isn't about whether you can or can't. It is whether you want to or not, isn't it?"

"You shut up," my mother said.

"Sure, anything you say, madam." He shrugged and walked away.

"Take her with you," my grandfather repeated. It was no longer a suggestion to my mother, it was a command. "I owe her father that much for the bullet we shared. I promised him I would take care of her, which I have done thus far. I want you to take this responsibility now. Do anything you can to help Loan — for me, please? Besides, she can watch over the kids. And hurry up. Go! Get out of here and save yourselves, all of you, and don't fight anymore, for heaven's sake. If for some reason you can't take care of Loan at the airport, she will come back to me. At least this way, she can fetch some news about all of you for me. Understood?"

"Yes, sir," my mother reluctantly agreed. Before she could change her mind, Loan ran to the van and climbed inside to huddle in a corner. My mother got in last. She looked straight ahead, refusing to acknowledge the girl's presence.

As Lam drove us away, I could see my grandparents' mournful faces pressed against the oval basement window, which was only a few inches above the ground. My mother sat stiffly, her face frozen in an icy mask. On the radio, the same female voice we had heard earlier that morning shakily announced the coming of the Communists. Their arrival was like an attack of locusts in a rice field, fast and uncontrollable.

SAIGON WAS IN its last free hours. The smell of chaos filled the air, and confusion was written all over the faces of the people on the street. Groups of armed convicts were breaking into houses, screaming up and down the streets, and shooting into the sky. Furniture flew onto the street, blocking the traffic. Discarded items were set on fire, either by accident or purposely; the smoke and flames added to the terror. Soldiers ran in all directions, tossing their rifles into trash bins, and stripping off their uniforms as if they were on fire. Some children who had lost their parents huddled on a street corner, crying. Above their heads, fire was consuming a coconut tree, and sparks of flame rained down on them. From the car window, they looked as if they were being burned alive in some sacrificial ritual.

We did not get far. The streets were blocked by hordes of desperate people, all with the same futile intention of getting to the airport. Just as we reached the freeway, a painful truth dawned on us: we weren't going anywhere. As far as we could see, the highway was clogged with civilian vehicles and military tanks. The hellish shriek of panic was dreadful in the hot air. People were abandoning their cars, running over each other, jumping on top of one another, climbing onto anything within their reach in order to move forward. Dead bodies lay in contorted positions, grinning horribly at the living. A few steps away from our van, a pregnant woman lay dead near the sidewalk. Her stomach had been ripped open by many hasty footsteps, and next to her lay her dying fetus, moving weakly under a dark mob of curious flies. A pool of dark blood beneath her dried slowly under the harsh sun. My mother quivered and recoiled in her seat, pulling us closer to her.

All along the freeway, people flowed like water down a stream. The crying of lost children looking for their parents, the screams of people being robbed, the songs blaring from the radio, the gunshots, the wailing of the wounded victims all blended into an incoherent symphony of grief. And like the humidity evaporating in the air, this collective keening lifted higher and higher, mixing with the noxious tear gas in a dark cloud of suffering.

Inside the car, my brother and I were too afraid to make a sound. Lam no longer looked relaxed. His long hair fell over his forehead, which was slick with sweat. His fingers, which held to the wheel tightly, were white at the knuckles. His head shook uncontrollably with each breath he took, and his eyes were opened wide, exaggerating the whiteness of his eyeballs.

Lam let out a loud, frustrated scream, as he pounded the horn in a fury. He turned to face my mother. "We have to get the fuck out of the car," he spat. "This is not going to work just sitting here. You take the children and move."

My mother's lips tightened into a straight line. She grasped my arm, and I felt her fingernails dig deeply into my flesh.

"Are you insane?" she replied. "Look at these people! I am not leaving this car."

Lam leaned within an inch of my mother's face. I could see his jugular veins, engorged with blood like two swollen earthworms, as they stared at each other. At last Lam broke the silence.

"Then give me my damned ticket and my passport. I am sick of listening to you, wretched woman. I am leaving with or without you."

My mother did not respond.

"Now!" he cried.

The scream startled my mother. She shook her head as if to clear it, then reached for her purse.

Lam's eyes followed her hands. "Give me your ticket and passport as well," he blurted. "I am taking Loan with me."

"Why her?" my mother asked.

Lam focused on something invisible on the floor. "She is having my baby."

Loan let out a small cry. My mother ignored her. After exhaling a deep breath, she gazed at Lam calmly.

"So am I. How do you explain this to me? Can't you see that I am also pregnant with your child?" she asked.

"So what? You don't need me. You never did," he said bitterly. "Trust me, you will do just fine."

He yanked the purse out of my mother's hand, searching intensely until he found what he was looking for. In addition to the papers, he grabbed a thick bundle of cash. Waving them teasingly in front of my mother, Lam said, "You just consider this payment for my devoted services."

Behind my mother, Loan finally spoke up. "I am not leaving with you, Lam. I am staying here with the mistress."

He turned to look at her as if she were deranged. Then, his lips pulled back in a distorted smile. "Fine, you stupid servant. Stay. Be my guest."

He picked out my mother's passport and ticket and threw them together with her purse back in her lap. Keeping the money and his own passport, Lam rammed them into the front pocket of his pants. Then, the smile returned to his face. He sank back in his seat, adjusting his clothing, before opening the door to let himself out. Oddly, he turned back one last time to look at us.

"Have a nice life, all of you," was all he said before he disappeared into the crowd.

CHAPTER FOUR
April 28, 1975

After Lam left, my mother sat still for several hours. Her facial expression did not change. Loan held us in her arms as we clustered together on the floor of the van. I watched night fall over the city, while the fire, the explosions, and the screaming went on. As I sat on the steel floor with my hands firmly pressed against my ears, everything seemed to fade away. My surroundings were no longer real to me; it was as if I were inside a silent movie, with a black-and-white background. The soundless, colorless, odorless calmness stayed with me until my mother announced that it was time for us to head back home.

The evening seemed to sedate the nervous city. As we ventured along the dark street, the throbbing frenzy subsided. Most of the streetlights had been broken earlier; and many of them were off due to the lack of electricity. All around us dark shadows were moving through the night. We could not tell if they were looking through the corpses to identify and gather up their departed relatives or if, like hungry wolves, they were simply hunting for treasure. Once in a while, a ray of light splashed across the sky, followed by the rumbling thunder of a bomb, or a grenade, or a rifle, sending a wave of vibration out to the surrounding area.

It was not very far from the van to our home, but it took us a good two hours to get through the congested streets. Cars and trucks were mounted on top of one another in heaps of wasted steel, blocking one road after another. In the house, my grandparents were still hiding in the basement. They saw us right away through the tiny oval window and hurried up the stairs to let us in. In just a few hours, my grandparents had somehow managed to age ten years — strength seemed to have abandoned them entirely.

"Where is Lam?" was the first question they asked.

My mother shrugged. "I'm not sure. We had a fight in the van, and he ran off. He was heading to the airport."

"Bastard!" my grandfather muttered.

"What are you going to do now?" my grandmother asked.

"I don't know." My mother shook her head. "I think we just have to stay here and see."

My grandfather looked at my mother. He spoke, choosing his words carefully, as he did not want my brother and me to panic. "We have been listening to the radio. Saigon is going to give up. The military is about to collapse. The other side is gaining so much power; it seems that nothing and no one can stop them now. Whatever you decide to do, you better do it now. You have only until tomorrow, and the general has advised that everyone stay put since it could get very ugly in the next couple of days."

"After you left, Mrs. Dang phoned," my grandmother said. The string of beads was still moving slowly between her fingers. "She asked for you. You might want to give her a call."

My mother nodded. "Okay, I'll do it right now." She picked up the phone and listened for a few seconds, then slammed it down in frustration.

"The damned phone is dead!" she exclaimed angrily. Turning to my grandmother, she asked, "Did she say anything to you, Mother?"

"Yes, she said something about waiting for a helicopter. She also asked for my passport, but I said you took them all. Then she just hung up. It was at least four or five hours ago."

My mother peeked out across the deserted street. She bit her lower lip thoughtfully. Her hand lay on top of her belly, caressing the silky fabric of her dress as we all watched her and waited. After a long time, she came to a conclusion. Pushing us toward my grandparents, she spoke carefully to them.

"Mother, Father, watch the children for me. I am walking over to the Dangs' house. I will be back in a while."

"Please don't!" my grandmother cried.

"You can't go. It is too dangerous outside. You can't leave the kids here with us," my grandfather added.

From a corner, with her face hidden in the shaded wall, Loan spoke up. Her voice was low, as usual, but clear.

"Madam Khuon, I am still your servant. Whatever you need to do, please use me. With your permission, I would like to go to the Dangs' house instead of you. I can take whatever news you wish to your friends."

My mother looked up at Loan. A flash of astonishment brushed across her face, as if she saw the maid standing there for the first time. She walked over to Loan. Her hand reached out to caress Loan's face, but only the tips of her nails touched the girl's skin. Nevertheless, Loan recoiled from my mother's hand. She looked frightened.

"Are you sure?" my mother asked.

Loan nodded. "Yes, ma'am."

"Then go," my mother said. "Go with my blessing, and hurry back."

The girl walked toward the door, but stopped. Slowly, she turned to face my mother again. With great difficulty and awkwardness, she chewed on her nails and spoke at the same time. However, her words were clear and loud.

"If I don't come back in half an hour, I might be in some sort of trouble. You then can stop waiting for me and start thinking of another plan. Madame Khuon, there is something I have been meaning to tell you but never found the right time. Please let me get it off my chest before I go. I want to apologize to you for what happened between me and Lam." My mother shifted uncomfortably as Loan continued. "I didn't mean for you to find out that way, the night you came into my room, back when we were in Nhatrang. But I couldn't stop it. I never could refuse him. He was too strong, and he was very violent, and he threatened to kick me out on the street if I didn't comply. I never meant to hurt you, madam, not in my life, not as long as I lived under your roof, and I beg for forgiveness before I go." She began to cry bitterly.

"Don't worry, Loan." My mother shook her head. "It is all forgotten. He is gone. It doesn't matter anymore. Just take care of yourself. We all are going to pray for you. We need you to come back to us."

"Yes, ma'am," was all she said before disappearing into the darkness outside.

AN HOUR LATER, Loan kept her promise to us. She returned with one of Mrs. Dang's servants. They were both out of breath from running through the streets. A touch of fear was still visible on their faces.

As soon as they got inside the door, my mother asked, "What is going on? Did they leave? Did you find Monsieur or Madame Dang? Do you know where they are?"

"I saw Mrs. Dang," Loan said, panting. "She was still waiting at home. She has something for you." She took a letter from inside her blouse and handed it to my mother, who grabbed it and read out loud.

Dear Khuon,

I don't know whether I should be happy or sad upon hearing the latest news about you and your family. When I phoned your house and talked to your mother this afternoon, I was under the impression that you were probably on your way to Thailand by now.

Kien Nguyen

Then Loan came in with the message that you had for me. Apparently, you have missed the last flights out of Saigon. I listened to the whole report about the event on the evening news. My heart was torn with mixed feelings. On the one hand, I was happy for myself, since it meant that I am no longer alone, and at least you are here sharing this hardship with me. But on the other hand, I am quite sad for your unfortunate situation. You have suffered a great deal in such a short time. Then again, so have we, darling. Let me tell you what has happened to me since our last meeting, two days ago.

As you know, for some time my husband was trying to get our two sons and me the necessary passports to leave the country. Unfortunately, with respectful thanks to our postal system, my application was the only one that got lost in the mail. As awful as I am feeling right now, I can't possibly blame Dang, since he tried his best to pull any strings while he still could to get me out of this godforsaken place. Yesterday, after my children received their passports, an opportunity of a lifetime fell upon them. They were allowed to leave Saigon on the last U.S. helicopter with some U.S. diplomats, one of which was Dang's friend and confidant for several years. This American friend of his advised us that I shouldn't tag along on the trip, since I was the only one on board without the right papers. I could very well be the cause of troubles for all of them once we got to Bangkok customs. These were important ambassadors, and they took every precaution in avoiding risk for the sake of their own safety. So there I was, standing on the rooftop of the embassy building, watching my own family disappear into the sky, wondering to myself when I would be able to see them again. You, too, darling, are a mother — certainly you can understand how ill I have been feeling since yesterday after the incident.

On a happier note, my husband and children got to Bangkok without any problem and are staying in some shelter, waiting for the next plane to California. Dang has been quite diligent in contacting me via phone, until recently when the entire system went down. He promised to get the same helicopter to come back and get me, soon, in the next few days. I know my Dang. He is a good and able man. I believe him when he says that he is coming for me, so I am waiting and I am not hopeless.

I am writing to you with a proposal that you can't possibly refuse, as I understand more than anyone else does that you don't have much of a choice at this time. Actually, it was Dang's idea, and it is a quite simple exchange. I need an ID, and you need a way out. Together, we can help fulfill each other's task. You can give me your mother's passport, and her ticket to America. Auntie told me over the phone this afternoon that she wasn't planning to go anywhere, so I assume that she won't need her papers anytime soon. When Dang returns with the helicopter, which he will, your family can be escorted with me to Bangkok. From there, I will continue to play the role of your relative until we get to California. Once we get there, you can choose to go your own way if you wish, or you can stay with us as long as you want. In either case, we promise to be the best company you and your children will ever have. Please understand we have to act fast because time is running out. I am sending over with this letter one of my strongest men to guide you back to my place. When you arrive here, we will immediately be heading toward the embassy tower. I have ways to get us all inside. Help me find my children. You are all the hope I have left.

May the Buddha watch over us.

Sincerely yours,
Mrs. Nguyen Dang

After my mother read the entire letter aloud, she looked up at my grandparents and raised one of her eyebrows in the form of a question. No one spoke. Finally, my mother broke the uneasy silence. "So, Daddy, what do you think I should do?"

"Like the woman said in the letter, you don't have much of a choice, daughter. Unless you want to keep the kids here, which I don't think you really want to do. So, if I were you, I would pull myself together and get over there immediately." The bags under my grandfather's eyes seemed to sag lower and darker with each word he said.

My grandmother agreed with him. "You have to give it another fighting chance, as much as you can, while you still can. Take my passport and go."

"What about Loan?" I asked. My own voice startled me as it bounced through the room like a Ping-Pong ball.

"Loan will stay here to take care of us, isn't that right, Loan?" My grandfather spoke for her. His eyes stared right at her. The look expressed more than the words he said.

"Yes, sir," Loan replied. She looked neither disappointed nor sorrowful. Her eyes fixed on the floor and remained there long after we left.

We said our good-byes dispiritedly and walked into the dark with Mrs. Dang's bodyguard. From across the street, the clock on Our Lady's Cathedral struck three times. Getting to Mrs. Dang's house was not a difficult task, as her place was located about two blocks away. It took less than five minutes and a few turns before we were at her doorstep.

The Mrs. Dang who greeted us was not her usual vociferous self, but a subdued, hollowed-out incarnation. Her eyes were red and swollen. Her fingers fidgeted with a tiny, wrinkled piece of tissue, peeling it off now and again from the corners. Her hair was a bird's nest, sticking out stubbornly all over her scalp. There was a brownish stain of some sort across her breasts like a wicked hand, cynically groping her every time she moved.

She grasped my mother's arm, thanking us profusely for coming over. We came inside and sat on the living room couch. Mrs. Dang bubbled with newfound excitement.

"I knew you would come," she said. "You are my last hope, darling. I was praying all night. When I found out that you left yesterday, I was falling apart. I didn't know what to do or where to turn. Then that maid of yours came over, and I saw a ray of hope. Thank God."

She sniffed noisily and wiped her nose carefully on a dirty tissue. As she lifted her head to look at my mother, her eyes, once again, filled with tears. "Khuon," she wailed agonizingly, "my family, my children are gone."

"I know," my mother said. "I am so sorry."

Mrs. Dang tried to compose herself. "I was there, I can't seem to forget it," she said. "On the roof, with my children. The little one, Tuan, was still holding an ice-cream cone. Chocolate! He tried to jump onto my lap. His father and some men pulled him away from me. He knew, you know? He is only three, but he knew what was going on. He grabbed my blouse and screamed, 'Mommy! Mommy!' My heart broke with his cry. His hand, covered with chocolate, stained my clothes." She looked down at the stain in the shape of a tiny hand above her breasts and smiled ruefully. "They took my children away. I fell on the ground. I cried and cried while that helicopter took my children away from me. I just wanted to die. Oh, Khuon. Why is all this happening? When is this nightmare going to end?"

"It is almost over. You should take care of yourself. In a few days, you will be reunited with them," my mother said.

"We've got to go. I don't want to miss Dang when he returns." She got up, hurriedly pacing across the room. "Are you ready? Anything you want to take with you, do it now. We are leaving soon, yes? Sorry to rush, but I can't wait any longer." She clapped her hands at the servants and raised her voice angrily as they ran back and forth to gather her things together. "Let's go, let's go."

THE U.S. EMBASSY building lay directly across from the park. As we expected, we stumbled into a mob of angry people in front of the building. They were screaming in vain at the indifferent and fully equipped Vietnamese soldiers behind the iron gates. We held on to each other firmly as the waves of turmoil threatened to knock us off our feet and away from each other. Mrs. Dang yelled to her bodyguard, the same man who had been with us the last few hours. She handed him a yellow identification card with her picture on it.

"Go get David. You met David, remember? He is the tall blond in that corner right over there. He is the only one in civilian clothes. You can't see his face because it is covered by his headgear. See him yet? Good! Give him this. Tell him in English, not in Vietnamese, to let me in. Make sure you show him this pass. We'll wait right here. Go! Hurry, before he goes back inside."

The bodyguard took the pass from Mrs. Dang's hand, and without any hesitation, forced his way through the crowd. We stepped away from the pavement, huddling together while watching him fight his way closer to the gates. Everyone's eyes were red and swollen from the tear gas in the air. He got the blond man's attention by waving the pass in front of him.

From between the bars, David reached out to take the pass from the bodyguard's hand and he scanned the crowd for Mrs. Dang. Across the street, we jumped up and down, trying to attract David's attention by waving our hands and hollering his name at the top of our lungs. After a while he spotted us, but before he could open the gate and get to us, the soldiers threw more tear gas into the crowd. People fell down to the ground, gasping for air and throwing up.

The military policemen quickly opened the large gates, using the shafts of their rifles to repel the crowd. David and three police officers shoved their way toward us. He took Mrs. Dang by the waist and pulled her across the street. She struggled, pointing in our direction, and screaming at him in broken English. "Take them, too. My friends. Two boys and a *mamasan*. David is Number One. Good. Thank you. Thank you. They come with me. To helicopter. Please."

It did not take David long to understand what she was saying. He signaled the soldiers. One man grabbed my brother; another lifted me up and threw me over his broad shoulders. The last one embraced my mother in his powerful, hairy arms. I gasped desperately for air, but my lungs were filled with poison and they threatened to explode. I could not utter a word, I could not breathe, I could not see anything around me as I was carried through the crowd like a sack of rice. I was scarcely aware of the angry hands scratching and pulling at me from all directions. Instead, I closed my eyes and wished silently for death to free me.

Finally, I was dropped down onto smooth pavement. Someone placed a cool, wet towel over my face, which temporarily wiped away the sting. The knots in my lungs slowly evaporated, and I took a deep breath. Oxygen rushed into me, chasing the ache away. I tried to look around. Although the air was still saturated with tear gas, I could make out the inside of the embassy tower. My brother lay on the ground next to me, crying heartily. But his sobs through his own towel were as weak as those of a hungry kitten. I could hear my mother nearby, consoling him. From a window somewhere above me, a ray of sunshine reflected down playfully at me. Its warm touch stroked my hair, as if it were trying to whisper to me that morning was here at last.

CHAPTER FIVE
April 29–30, 1975

My brother and I spent the next eight hours sleeping in a corner of the embassy lobby, while the adults waited for the return of the helicopter. My mother tried to wake me up for lunch and supper, but in my deep sleep I just pushed her hand away.

When I finally decided to get up, the sun had almost set. Its light soared in a wanton shade of pale orange over the city. There was still a residue of the irksome gas in the air. From my window, I looked directly out on the entrance of the embassy, where I could clearly see the struggle continuing among the soldiers and the people from outside the gates. Only now the crowd had tripled in size and had become twice as restless as in the morning. All were men, since women and children had long given up fighting. A few in the crowd were armed with guns and grenades, but no one dared use them yet, except to hold them up in threatening gestures. The MPs were ordered to keep the gates securely shut, and they allowed no one to enter. I could see a few shiny yellow passes reflected in the light from the afternoon sunset as they were being raised above the crowd. The MPs ignored them.

I ventured up the stairs and out onto the roof, where my mother had told us to meet her right after we woke up. Through the long hallways, I noticed that the building was vacant, like an empty match-box. Everyone else had gathered up on the roof, which was a very lux-urious spot. At one end was a recreational area complete with an outdoor swimming pool, plastic tables and chairs with shades, and exotic plants. The rest of the roof was a smooth, square, solitary plat-form, reserved for the storage and landing of choppers. Besides my mother, Mrs. Dang, and David, there were five American men stand-ing casually by the pool. Their circumstances were basically similar to David's, in that they had stayed behind of their own volition. They were a team of international journalists who had volunteered to record the fall of Saigon. Like everybody else, they had been chased from city to city, watching helplessly as the Communist battalions devoured the land before them, piece by piece. Now, they, too, were at the end of the last road with nowhere to run. The only thing left for them was to wait, either for the helicopters, or for the Vietcong, whichever came first. But unlike everybody else, the Americans seemed untouched by the tide of hysteria. They stood nonchalantly by the pool, perspir-ing profusely from the intense temperature, eating their dinner, and discussing world peace in humorous terms.

By midnight, most of us had abandoned all hope of escape. Nev-ertheless, no one moved. I sat on the floor by my mother, who held my brother in her arms while she settled deep into her own private world. A few feet away and facing us, Mrs. Dang folded her body into a fetal position, with her head clutched between her arms, and stared blindly at the dark space behind me. Every time she heard an engine sound, however faint, she would leap up gleefully, just for a second, long enough to recognize whatever it was. Then she would fall back down to the ground, embracing herself again in the same position. In the thick silence, we counted the chimes from the nearby church each time it struck until dawn came.

That morning of April 30, 1975, outside the gates of the U.S. Embassy building, the mob had grown so large that it spread over ten blocks. From above, the streets looked like a massive hive of killer bees, boiling with rage. We watched in frustration as helicopters from many nations carried out rescue missions in several parts of the city, but none came for us.

Suddenly, as if God had decided to step into the chaos himself, every loudspeaker from every corner of every street simultaneously blared at maximum volume, halting the entire city. A moment later, the familiar voice of President Duong Van Minh rumbled in the air. He tearfully read to his people a letter of surrender, relinquishing Saigon to the Communists. It was 10:30 A.M.

At that exact moment, we realized that two Vietnamese helicopters had separated from the frenzied motion in the sky and were hovering above us. One was disguised with blue-green marine camouflage. The other, much smaller, was a metallic silver in color. Upon seeing them, Mrs. Dang let out a shrill cry. She fell to her knees and cried gratefully to God and the heavens above for responding to her prayers. Soon we were all either howling like wolves saluting the full moon or just shrieking with sheer delight.

The choppers were also catching the attention of people on the street below. As they got closer, the yells from the crowd soared louder. Fists were pounding in the air, and people were screaming with all of their might, "Wait for me — let us in — for God's sake — please —."

As the silver helicopter got about thirty feet away, I could see Mr. Dang standing in its doorway, wearing his properly pressed white-collar shirt and black pants, laughing to his wife triumphantly. He was in his forties, bald and dainty, and quite animated. His head was well hidden inside a military helmet, which was a size too large, making the rest of his body appear smaller. His torso was secured to the aircraft by a seat belt wrapped around his waist. He waved happily and signaled that he recognized us as well. The wind swept powerfully from the propellers to churn the air below like a close-up cyclone, beating each gust wildly on, over, above, and around us. The other helicopter circled at a slight distance waiting for its mate to land on the roof.

Then it happened. From somewhere in the crowd, someone fired a rifle. The bullet tore through the air and struck the side of the helicopter. Then, more guns were fired from the crowd. The helicopter pilot lifted his big bird back up into the sky.

Mrs. Dang ran to the edge of the balcony and pleaded with the crowd. "Do not shoot, please. Stop shooting! My husband is up there." She jumped up and down to make herself more visible. David leaped from under a table to pull her back down. She fought him off weakly, still begging the mob below, "Please don't shoot. Please don't . . . please . . ."

But it was too late. A bullet had found its way to its target. From where I was, I could see Mr. Dang's bright white shirt blossom into a wet trail of red blood, oozing out eerily as he tried to cover it with his hands.

"Nooooo!" Mrs. Dang cried out from the deck.

Mr. Dang faced his wife from up above with a surprised look, as if he were unable to comprehend what had just happened to him. The glimpse between them lasted less than a second before he lost his balance abruptly. The helicopter twirled itself into a half circle, knocking Mr. Dang to the floor, still tied securely by his seat belt. Another hail of bullets hit the front propeller. The chopper twirled in midair, like a sick sparrow, then stopped momentarily, before it plunged down to the quarterdeck below and exploded into flame. The blast blew across the pool, temporarily blinding me.

In an instant, all that was left was a burning chopper lying on its side, dying slowly under the blue sky and hot sun. Above it, the other chopper turned around and disappeared from sight. From the street, the crowd screamed in satisfaction.

"Noooooo!" Mrs. Dang's voice was barely audible. Her knees buckled, and she fell to the floor. Everyone was too shocked to do anything but watch her collapse like a rag doll.

From a far corner below, marching toward the embassy, came the first troop of the Vietcong's military, playing some strange anthem with trumpets and a bass. Their trucks and tanks, concealed under thick layers of dust, roared into the city. On top of these vehicles sat the Red soldiers. Some held up flags, either with the red background and one yellow star in the middle or a half-red, half-blue background, also with a yellow star in the center. Others pulled out banners with slogans scribbled on them. I could make out some of the phrases, such as, "We come in peace. Let's heal the wounds the capitalists left behind. North and South Vietnamese are siblings, we can all stop the fighting now." The music filled the air with happy notes, designed to soothe the tension of those on the street.

David turned to my mother and said, "I am sorry. It is over! The war is over. We can't keep you here anymore. Take your sons and your friend out of this building before it is too late. We are better off here by ourselves, without any Vietnamese. Do you understand me? Get out of here, now. Good luck, and take care of yourselves. All of you."

In a last desperate burst of energy, Mrs. Dang tried to approach the dead helicopter in hopes of finding her husband's body, but to no avail. We were pushed hastily out the door. We held on to each other tightly until we got down to the street. No one bothered to notice any of us as we let ourselves out through the gates, mixing into the stream of people surging everywhere. The Communists marched slowly down the avenue, greeting people on both sides of the street, and handing out little portraits of Ho Chi Minh, together with paper flags, as if these things were small treasures. Finally, they got to the front of Doc Lap Palace. Using their tank as a bulldozer, in one swift motion, they ran down the iron gates while the people applauded and cheered.

Saigon was claimed at 11:30 A.M., April 30, 1975.

CHAPTER SIX
Saigon, May 1975

After the fall of Saigon, my mother took Jimmy and me back to the rented house near the park. For the next four days and nights, we lived in its basement. The floor was dirt; the walls were sandbags. At one end was a small bathroom, which had a dim light. From it ran a cord to the bare bulb that hung over the living area. Because of the frequent lapses in electrical service, candles were our primary source of light. Each day, we huddled on our small futons and listened to the foreign sounds of marching feet and pounding fists reverberating from door to door down the block. Until it was our turn to be tabulated into the new system, we hid like a family of rats during the rainy season.

Only Loan dared to go outside to search for food, gather news, and do errands for my mother. Before leaving, she would cover her body in black garments in order to blend in with the rest of the people in the city. Until she returned home, we would watch for her petite frame from the brim of an oval window a few inches above ground level. The market did not have much to offer. During wartime, no one in his or her right mind would be foolish enough to exchange food for money, for fear of starvation and/or inflation in the future. The markets had always been busy social gathering places, but now they were full of Communist soldiers. Hoping to draw as little attention to herself as possible, Loan never dared to stay long. Although the food she brought back was usually stale and meager, she managed to create tasty rice-and-vegetable dishes, mostly composed of either Chinese spinach or watercress, and flavored by the exotic, fish-based sauces she had learned in cooking school. We were grateful for every bite. Loan would prepare the food in the first-floor kitchen and bring it down to us in the basement.

The news that Loan brought back consisted of rumors and speculation spread by confused and uninformed people. Observations of the Vietcong's activities yielded a few hints for survival. The first and foremost was that in public or at social meetings, everybody had to appear to be a Communist. Any accusation to the contrary would bring instant and horrifying wrath upon the accused. No one trusted anyone, not even family members. Popular fears centered on the new government and its officials; as for the Red soldiers, the majority of them seemed harmless, especially to the children. Nevertheless, everyone was aware that the curfew started every night at exactly nine o'clock, and whoever was caught on the streets after that time would be shot on sight without warning. Reports of these curfew deaths added more terror to the already frightened city.

To make their presence felt throughout Saigon, the Vietcong divided themselves into small groups and spread out. Many eager families volunteered their homes for the soldiers, praying that a sincere gesture would somehow redeem their past sins. The rest of the troops settled into vacant houses, hotels, halls, and schools, or bunked down in the streets.

Inside our new prison, my brother and I became the center of my mother's misery. She had always tried to protect us from the rumors, stares, and judgments that our American features drew. But now the pressures on her were more than she could handle. Hiding in the furthest corner of the cell, my brother and I watched our mother pace like a caged animal. And for the first time in my life, I was overwhelmed with self-hatred, for I realized that I was different and so was my brother, for whom I held a similar and intense dislike. I wanted to pull the fair hair out of my head, scratch off my pale skin, and peel the expensive sandals from my feet. I prayed for something to happen — anything at all, so that the shame would no longer haunt my mother's eyes. Instead, I just sat there, numb with fear, and prayed for time to pass quickly.

One afternoon, after a couple days of hiding, my mother sent Loan to the market to bring back some black dye. Without warning, she swooped over to our hiding corner and seized us with her sharp fingernails, as if she were catching a fowl in its cage. Ignoring our frightened cries, she pulled us along the cold ground into the bathroom. As we kicked and screamed, she poured the dark liquid over us and marinated our blond heads for what seemed a long time. I remember sitting next to my brother in the bathroom, trying to cover my bare chest with my thin arms. Her roughness as she tugged at our hair and her silence burned a panic in us. Both of us were crying from the sting of the dye. She loomed over the two of us with a crazed look in her eyes and pointed her forefinger straight at our faces.

"Listen, you two, shut up! Men don't cry! Remember that." And she added more dye to our hair.

Unable to obey, we could not stop crying. Finally my grandfather ran into the bathroom and struck her face with the back of his hand. Pointing to our reflections in the mirror, my grandfather shouted at her.

"Stop this madness right now. Look at what you've done to your children. Is that really necessary?"

My mother looked into the mirror and froze. Looking back at her were two little faces covered in ink and streaked with tears. We could not meet our mother's eyes. With her shaking hands and crimson face, covered by a mask of hatred, she looked like a monster to us. Shocked by the image in the mirror, my mother began to sob.

She knelt to wipe the stains off our faces with the back of her hands. "I am so sorry," she whispered gently.

The deranged woman who had terrified us was gone, and my mother's voice murmured in our ears. "I can't help you. Nothing I can do can change who you are." She added, "Please don't cry. All of it is my fault. I don't know what came over me. But I promise I will not let anything or anyone harm you two. Not as long as I am still alive."

We all cried on the bathroom floor until there were no more tears left. Later that afternoon, my mother made a decision. After she sent my brother and me upstairs, she announced to my grandparents and Loan that it was time for a family meeting.

From the stairs, Jimmy and I strained to hear the conversation. We could not make out much of what the adults said, but we could hear my grandfather's voice shattering the air. I had never heard him so angry before. "No, I forbid you; it is very dangerous; you are crazy —"

My mother took Loan aside and sent her out into the street, then continued to argue with her parents for another hour. At last, as my mother pushed the door open and stormed back downstairs, I could hear my grandfather's voice chasing after her, filled with indignation.

"Leave Loan out of this. She is too young to make such a decision."

"Don't you see, Daddy? Neither of us has a choice," my mother shot back.

"Then wait till we get back home before you do anything irrational. Please, for heaven's sake, don't make another wrong decision today," he urged.

My mother marched into the bathroom and slammed the door behind her. Shortly afterward, Loan returned. With her was an old woman, whom she told to wait at the front step.

From the window on the first floor, we watched the elderly woman in silence. Standing by the door and clutching a dirty bag between her breasts, she waited for Loan. Her face was seamed by countless deep wrinkles, and her spine bent, forcing her gaze to the ground. Her hair was thin and white. As she noticed us watching her, her face rearranged itself into a smile that was nothing more than a hollow, reddish, toothless depression. To us, she appeared a figure out of a fairy tale, and we half-expected her to bolt through the air with a broomstick.

Loan reappeared with my mother behind her, and they led the woman down to the basement.

"Are you the other one who needs my services, besides this girl?" the old lady asked. "Are you sure you're only three months pregnant? From the look of that belly, I swear you look a lot more —"

My mother turned to hush the woman. The look of concern was quite noticeable on their faces. The visitor stepped into the room to put her bag down on the floor and breathe out a sigh of relief. Seeing my grandparents waiting by the foot of the basement door, she nodded to them in acknowledgment.

Loan introduced the old woman to us. "Everyone, this is Mrs. Tam, the only midwife left in downtown Saigon. She comes highly recommended to us by the people at the market. I told her that we are not from around here, and that we don't know anyone. That is why she agreed to help us."

"Yes, yes, nice to meet everyone. Forget the proper introductions. We'll have to hurry up. I have two more cases downtown, and I have to beat the curfew." Mrs. Tam rushed through her sentences rudely. "Are you two ready for this?" She pointed to Jimmy and me. "What's going on with the children's hair?"

"Nothing that concerns you," my mother answered irritably. "Let me take the children upstairs first."

"No need to. There is nothing here for them to watch anyway. I am just going to give you some herbs to take. Shouldn't take more than eight hours for them to work. And tomorrow, your problem will be all over."

"In that case, let's do it," my mother said.

The old lady searched her bag for two small wooden cases. They had rustic carvings of two golden dragons holding a black capsule and were sealed with sap. She laid them on the floor like two objects of great value.

Looking up to my mother, she said with a trace of concern in her voice, "Madam, I know you don't want me to repeat this question, but the gods give me strength, I can't help it. The job that I do makes your business my concern. Are you sure you're only three months pregnant? Because it looks like you are either carrying triplets, or a special present from the elephant god himself. That girl over there" — she pointed at Loan — "she won't have any problem taking this medicine. See? Her body doesn't even show the pregnancy yet. You, I don't know."

Leaning against the door, my grandfather commented, "My daughter is four months along in her pregnancy."

"I knew it. I must tell you, madam, I don't think this will work in your case." Mrs. Tam shook her head. "Besides, it's too risky."

Again, my mother interrupted the woman. "Never mind about what you think. I don't have any choice, you understand? I can't afford any more children. Just give me the damned medicine."

"Okay, fine." The woman shrugged. "Here is a case for each of you. Inside you will find a black pill. Tonight, eat dinner as usual, and then take the pill at bedtime. Tomorrow morning, the fetus will be shed from your body. Bleeding and pain are normal signs; don't be too alarmed. Any questions?"

"One pill? Do you think that will be enough for me? Should I take more than one?"

"You? I think so. And for the girl? One pill should be more than enough."

"Then give me two extra boxes."

"That is a lot of drugs, madam."

"I don't care. Just give them to me."

"Fine," Mrs. Tam said, sighing. "Anything you say, but of course, it will cost you more money."

"I will pay you in a minute. But first, tell me more about the side effects. Will there be more risk for myself if I take the additional pills?"

"Of course," the woman said, nodding.

"Then for goodness's sake, tell me what kind of risk are we talking about, old crone?"

"What do you think? More pills mean more toxin, which means more bleeding and more cramping. But if you want more drugs, I will do what you ask. However, think about it carefully before you do this, madam. I can't stop you from making your decision, and I can't guarantee whether or not it will work properly. In all of my years of doing this job, I have never given the drug to anyone over three months pregnant; not once, because everybody listens to me, except you. So don't ask me anymore what will happen to you. Because whatever it is, I will not take responsibility. I've already warned you in front of your family. Now, you'll take it at your own risk. Understand me?"

"Khuon —" my grandmother spoke up.

"It's fine, mother," my mother said. "I know what I am doing."

"Really, daughter? Do you really know what you are doing?" my grandfather asked. He looked dejected.

"That will be seventy dong for the four boxes. I am giving you ten dong off for good luck. May the gods help the living," the woman said. She got up and clasped her bag between her breast and her arm.

"Thank you," my mother said, giving the old woman her fee.

No one uttered a word after the old woman left. On the floor lay four wooden boxes, with gold writing scrawled across their covers proclaiming, "O-Kim." Underneath those words was a much smaller inscription: "For women only."

"Loan, take one," my mother said with determination. "Leave the other boxes for me."

"Yes, madam," Loan said.

"Do you want to give this some more thought, Loan?" my mother asked the maid. "You know that it is your right to keep the baby if you wish to do so. And you don't have to do everything I do. I have my own reasons for my actions."

"Yes, madam, I know. But like you, I have my own reasons. I'd like to take the pill."

"Well, good. Looks like you and I are in the same boat together then. Take the pill with you and go prepare some dinner." My mother breathed a heavy sigh. Loan got up to take a box with her and disappeared behind the door. My grandparents withdrew to their usual corner without another word.

"Mommy?" I asked my mother after everyone had left.

My mother jumped slightly before she looked up at me. Her eyes rose as she waited for my question.

"What is going on? What are those little boxes for?" I asked her.

"Nothing that concerns you."

From his futon, my grandfather interrupted her. "What's the matter? Can't you even explain your actions to your own son? Don't do that to him. You owe him some kind of clarification. Explain it however you see fit, but don't brush him off like that. The child isn't stupid."

"Dad, stay out of this," she said angrily to my grandfather and then turned to me. "Nothing honey, everything is fine. Those boxes are for the adults. When I take these pills, they will make me stronger and lighter. They won't hurt me. Understand?"

"Are they going to hurt the baby instead?" I asked.

My mother sank to the cold floor and shook as if a strong current were being shot through her body. Then with a glare, she shot up to grab me by my shoulders and lift me against the wall of sandbags behind me. She bent over so that her eyes were level with mine and spat from between her white teeth, "What do you know about the pills, you nosy little bastard? Listen to me, and listen good. There are no babies inside my body. Everybody thought I was having a baby, but it turns out that everybody was wrong. These are healthy pills for me that will make me stronger so that I can take care of all of you snot-nosed parasites. If you ever breathe any of this to anyone, I'll kill you. Do you understand me? And for the Buddha's sake, don't ask any more questions. Keep them all to yourself. I don't like it when you behave this way."

Unable to speak, I nodded my agreement and felt her grip loosen from my shoulders. The marks of her nails left a red imprint for the rest of the night.

CHAPTER SEVEN

Night overtook us like a skillful thief. There was no electricity in the house. In fact, the whole town was submerged in darkness. Loan descended from upstairs, holding a candle in her hand. Shadows flickered on the wall as she moved across the basement.

For dinner, Loan made a dish of steamed chicken with young bamboo shoots and sautéed spinach. My grandmother refused to join us at the table; instead, she lay unmoving on her mattress, under a thin bedspread. My grandfather ate with difficulty, as if every bite he took was devoid of taste. The rest of us ate quickly and in silence. When it was time for dessert, Loan served a simple yet popular Vietnamese pudding made from sweet bananas and tapioca, but without the usual coconut milk to complete the flavor. Nonetheless, my brother and I found it delicious.

After dinner, my mother disappeared behind the bathroom door, and Loan excused herself to go back upstairs to the kitchen. When my mother returned, she looked paler and more anxious than usual. She sat down on her futon, chewing her nails thoughtfully as we moved cautiously closer to her. Seeing us, she smiled and reached out to grab my brother by his waist. Pulling him to her bosom, she touched his newly dark hair and closed her eyes dreamily.

My grandmother stirred to face the three of us. "How many did you take?" she asked, addressing no one in particular.

"I took them all," my mother replied.

"Oh, God," was my grandmother's moan.

To get my mother's attention, my brother held her chin in his hand and asked her, "Mommy?"

"Yes, darling?"

"When can we go outside and play again?"

"Soon, darling, soon."

"Okay. How do you feel, Mommy?" he then asked.

"I'm fine, and you?"

"I am fine, too, thank you for asking," he answered politely. A moment later, my brother asked her another question with hope in his voice. "May I sleep with you tonight? I don't want to sleep alone."

"Sure, if you like. But why? Your bed is only a few steps from mine."

"I don't know. Sometimes when I wake up at night, I get scared. Can I sleep next to you, Mommy?"

"Anything you want." My mother spoke in monotone. Her eyes were closed. She looked like she was falling to sleep.

"What about you, Kien?" my brother asked. "Do you want to join us?" To my mother, "Can he join us?" His eyes fixed on my face, waiting for her approval.

"If he wants to," she answered with little interest.

"He does, don't you, Kien?"

I nodded. In fact, I dreaded to spend the night alone, awaking in the dark, and thinking of the unknown.

Jimmy and I took our positions, each of us on one side of my mother's mattress. I put my arm across my mother's belly and felt her falling asleep. As I drifted away, I watched the night pass by slowly through the window. On the ground next to our bed, the candle was still burning. Its light danced in the moving air, making strange images on the wall like the coming of hell's angels in the coloring book the nuns used to hand out to us in Sunday school.

Around four in the morning I woke up to the sound of agonizing screams. The basement was submerged in darkness as I jumped up and looked around for my mother. The only light that I could see was a tiny beam escaping from the closed bathroom door. Next to me, my brother was still sleeping, his body curled on one side with his knees bent up to his chin. He was sucking his thumb. I searched for my mother, my fear rising. Before I could cry out, my grandfather slipped beside me. His embrace calmed me down. In the dark, his breath smelled like Jolly Rancher candies.

"Quiet, little one," he whispered to me. "Your mother is fine. Go back to sleep with Grandpa."

"What happened to Mommy?" I asked him.

"She has a stomachache."

From the bathroom, my mother's cries tore through the house. I heard a hollow sound like liquid splattering on the cement floor. Falling noises followed. My brother moved about for a moment. Then his eyes opened wide and he realized that my mother was missing. My grandfather reached out to hold him in his arms, muttering to him the same comforting phrases he had spoken to me a few moments ago. Together in his embrace, Jimmy and I listened to the moaning and yelling coming from behind the bathroom door.

Then we heard my grandmother's voice, thick with worry. "I can't make the bleeding stop. Loan, do something."

Loan said, "Let mistress lie on the floor. Standing up only makes it worse."

"I can't lie down. It hurts too much," came my mother's voice.

More gushing sounds, and something hit the floor.

My grandfather raised his voice with concern. "What is going on in there? Madam, is your daughter well? Do you need my help?"

"No, you watch the children, please. I can manage in here. Just trying to stop the bleeding."

"Well, it is taking too long. I am going to get a doctor," my grandfather said.

"What?" my grandmother replied to him, panting. "Have you lost your mind? It's curfew time; do you want to get yourself killed out there? Please, stay there with the children."

"Oh, God," Loan cried out.

"What is it?" my grandmother asked her.

"My tummy is churning, and it's starting to ache. I think it's my turn now," she said. "Please help me!"

The bathroom door opened, and my grandmother poked her head out. In the candlelight, the bloodstains shined darkly on her hands.

"Help me carry your daughter outside," she said to my grandfather.

He got up from the futon to limp into the bathroom, forgetting his cane. In a minute he reappeared with his back to us, moving slowly backward with my mother's head resting in between his hands. My grandmother faced him, carrying my mother's lower limbs. Mother's body was wrapped in white towels that were dark with blood. My grandparents put my mother on a mattress opposite my brother and me. She turned to her side and curved her body into a fetal position, as my grandmother hurried back into the bathroom to assist Loan.

"Mommy, Mommy, are you all right?" my brother asked. The smell of blood made us dizzy.

My mother ignored us. She buried her head in her hands. Her knees were up, protecting her midsection. My grandfather stood at her feet.

"How are you feeling, daughter?" he asked.

She did not reply. He asked with more aggression, "Are you feeling well? Talk to me."

My mother's face remained hidden. "The bleeding seems to have stopped," she said, "but the fetus is still inside."

"I see. Get some rest then. Don't think too much about it. We can see the doctor tomorrow."

"Maybe," was her reply.

In the bathroom, Loan and my grandmother struggled for another hour. Loan never cried out in pain. We heard her occasional grunting and panting, and finally the flush of the commode.

My mother lay motionless on the mattress for the rest of the night. Her cramping diminished as the night wore on. We could see her body shake weakly under the terry cloth, and blood continued to seep from underneath her. As morning cast its cheerful light on my mother's bed, she startled.

"The drug is no good," she cried out. "The baby is fine. It just kicked me."

I could see the relief wash over my grandfather's tired face. My grandmother sank down to her knees, expressing her gratitude to the gods. My mother let out another scream. Her hand curled into a fist, beating her abdomen.

"What is the meaning of this?" she shrieked. "Damn that stupid hag and her cheap drug. Why me? Why now? Damn you." She hit her stomach again and again, screaming to the fetus inside. "Why don't you get a hint that I don't want you? Why don't you do us all a favor and just die?"

My brother and I watched, unable to utter a word.

For the next couple of days, my mother spent most of her time in bed. Four days passed and finally, the Communists came knocking at our door.

Inside, we all jumped up in terror and held each other, holding our breath, as my grandfather hobbled up the stairs. We listened as the soldiers strode across the floor into the living room. We heard the strange way they talked to each other, with a heavy northern dialect, and we heard my grandfather's voice answering their interrogation. It was not long before he bade all of us come upstairs. My grandmother went up first, carrying the wooden beads in her palms as though they were a talisman. My mother held on to Loan's arm. My brother and I were the last into the living room.

Once we were all assembled, my mother sat on a chair as the

group of men stopped in mid-conversation to stare at us. Their fatigues were old and wrinkled, and the once deep green had turned to a muddy brown. The oldest soldier, a man in his forties with salt-and-pepper hair, pointed a dirty finger at us.

He spat to my grandfather, "Is anyone else still down there? Or are they all here?"

"No, they are all here, sir," my grandfather replied.

"Comrade, go to the basement to verify if he is telling the truth or not," he ordered one of his men. Then turning to us, he asked, "Why did you hide down there all this time instead of coming out and celebrating the dawn of a new era with your country? What are you hiding from?"

"We are just a bunch of women, children, and elderly people. We didn't know what was going on. Please forgive us," my grandfather said.

He shook his head. "That's not an excuse. This is the time to celebrate, not to hide." His eyes swept over us, checking our faces. "Is this your house?"

"No, sir. We rent it."

"Where is the owner now?"

"I don't know, sir. He lived in Cholon [Chinatown] before the event. So much has changed in the last four days. We aren't sure anymore."

"Well, brace yourselves. There will be more changes, as we are in the process of wiping out capitalism from the south. But answer me, why are you here if this is not your home? Where did you all come from? And are you counter-Communists running away from the Revolution?"

My grandfather swallowed a lump in his throat before speaking. "Well, sir. We are from Nhatrang City. We didn't run away. We are here for a reason. You see, Commander, this is my daughter. She is pregnant and because she has had bad complications with her past pregnancies, we took her to Saigon. Because, sir, here she can give birth in Tu Du Hospital. We were just being careful, we didn't mean to run away from the Revolution. The timing was just bad when we ended up getting here."

The commander wrote down everything my grandfather said. He walked toward my mother and studied her. She avoided his stare by looking down at her stomach. She had lost so much weight in the last few days that I could see the blue veins in her thin hands, which were folded neatly on her lap.

"Lady, how are you feeling?"

"I am fine, thank you, sir. Just a little weak from the heat," she replied, not looking up to meet his gaze.

"Can you travel?" he asked her.

"Where am I going, sir?" My mother looked up at him. Her eyes glowed with lament and just a hint of seduction. Usually, this look made men bow down on their knees in front of her. It did not seem to have much effect on the commander.

He answered her coldly, "You're going back to your town. All of you have twenty-four hours to vacate this place. This is the new law from above. The country is finally reunited. Everybody is returning to his or her own home. You, too, have to go back and report to your town leader."

"How are we going to get back home?" my grandfather asked the leader.

"I don't know, and I don't care. It's not my job to find you transportation. However, you all have to leave this place by tomorrow morning. We will return to make sure of that. If you don't leave by then, I have no choice but to arrest all of you. Children and women make no difference to me."

He turned around, signaling for his men. The door slammed shut behind them as they headed toward the next house.

Not until they had all disappeared beyond the front gates did my grandmother turn to her husband and blurt out, "Oh, sir, how are we going to get out of here?"

My grandfather shook his head. Loan, standing behind my mother, cleared her throat. No longer did she look like a shy little maid who was trained to censor her thought before it reached her mouth. These past few days had turned her into a reserved yet intelligent young woman.

"Well, sir, if I might speak freely, here is a thought," she said without raising her eyes. "If the government has thrown us out, they must have done the same thing to a lot of people. How do they leave? We can ask around and find out what these people are doing, and either do the same thing, or join them."

"How are we going to get such information?" my grandmother asked.

"Go to the market," was all that Loan said.

CHAPTER EIGHT

Threw markets facing Saigon River teemed with confused and nervous people. These bazaars stood side by side, separated by a small street that was always thick with soggy mud and unkempt with garbage. The first market sold mainly fresh food, from vegetables to livestock to fresh fish. The second one offered a variety of dried food in large quantities, such as rice and spices, along with fabrics, coals, and firewood. Even though tension permeated the markets' atmosphere, the exchange of goods still took place in an orderly fashion under the watchful eyes of the soldiers. People talked to each other in between purchases to find out information. The buzz of their whispers made it sound as if the air were filled with flies.

It did not take Loan long to make her first contact. By the entrance of the second market, she found a family of five looking for a way to get back to Cam Ranh Bay, a city near Nhatrang. These people had been unable to secure transportation. They were planning on traveling by foot for more than four hundred kilometers through deadly swamps and jungles where a lot of booby traps remained from the war. After hearing their plan, Loan wished them good fortune and pulled us deeper into the market.

All morning we walked through the crowd, searching for a ride. My mother was out of breath, her face pale. My grandfather occasionally fell behind, since his hip bothered him with each step. Each time we stopped in front of a group of people to ask for information, the reaction we received was the same: they all looked at us dumbly at first, then smiled with courteous sincerity. If they knew of an escape, their knowledge would remain hidden behind their smiles before they, too, disappeared into the crowd.

Just as we were about to lose hope, we stumbled upon Mrs. Tam's herbal medicine corner, which displayed baskets of dried flowers, plant roots, and wood chips. She sat behind a mountain of herbs, surrounded by customers seeking a share of her cures. Her voice raised above the noise of the crowd to catch every passerby's attention.

"What are you looking for?" she screamed. "This is for nausea and vomiting. Boil two cups down to one. This one is for inner or outer hemorrhoids. Take it with food twice a day. This one is for the treatment of coughing."

As she spotted my mother, who stared at her with anger, she waved the crowd to silence. Looking at my mother, she asked, "Hey, old dear, where did I know you? Ah, yes, I remember. You are the mean birdie with a knocked-up belly. How are things? You don't look so good."

"Guess how things are," my mother retorted. "Look at me. You sold me your fake herbs, old crone. I am glad I found you here, because I want my money back."

The old woman stood up in between her leaves and barks and pointed a finger at my mother. "Are you crazy, asking for your money back? My drugs are fine; it's you that are fake. Didn't I warn you many times that it might not work? Is it any fault of mine that you all get yourselves knocked up?" She narrowed her eyes with suspicion at my mother and Loan. "The mistress and her servant — you two are sharing the same man, aren't you? Don't lie to this old woman, some gigolo must have grabbed both of you like a pair of chopsticks. By the way, why are you still hanging around town? I thought your pompous behind should be hauled back home by now."

My mother was boiling with rage. No one ever dared to speak to her that way before. She was humiliated as the crowd around her turned to stare and whisper at us. Standing next to her as calm as a lake in the absence of the wind, Loan answered the old woman's questions. "We can't find a ride back home. Do you know of any way, Mrs. Tam?"

"Of course I know." The old woman arched her back. "I know everything about this town. But why should I help that pompous mare? She tickled my angry bone the very first day I met her ugly face, giving me nothing but grief."

Loan then bent down to pick up my brother and me, setting us on her hips. "Then please help these children," she said to the herbalist. "They are innocent. For the good karma of your next life, please find them a way home."

The woman looked at us. Slowly, the wrinkles on her face began to relax as her anger abated. She spoke again. This time, her voice softened. "Two hundred dong for the lead, and five hundred for the tickets. Cash only."

My mother cried out in astonishment. "Seven hundred dong? Are you a blood-sucking thief? Four hundred is all I have. For everything, or you forget it."

"Hey, mad horse, I don't deal with you." The old woman waved her finger at my mother, then she pointed at Loan. "But I'll deal with this child. She is a smart girl."

Loan said to the old lady, "Mrs. Tam, you've heard the mistress. We only have four hundred dong to spend."

"Okay, fine, because of the youngsters." She clapped her hands. "I'll show you a way out. I close the shop at three-thirty. Meet me back here with your money and your suitcases all ready, because old Tam waits for no one."

She returned to the crowd. We stood there, stunned. Then my mother beckoned for us to head home. As we were walking away, I could still hear the old lady's voice advertising her goods. "What is it that you are looking for, sir? How about you, madam? This is the drug that cures all diseases. Take it with an empty stomach, twice a day for one day, and you will be feeling twenty all over again . . ."

AT MRS. TAM'S INSTRUCTION, we met back at her shop at three-thirty, taking with us a few bags of clothing. She was waiting for us. All of her medicines were stored in two hand-woven bamboo chests. Each chest had a long handle, which Mrs. Tam hooked with a wooden cane. And with her shoulder under the pole, she strained to lift her merchandise up off the ground in one breath. Walking toward us and carrying her goods in this fashion, Mrs. Tam threw a small bag toward Loan. She then signaled for us to follow her.

Without looking back at us, Mrs. Tam asked Loan, "Do you have the money with you?"

"Yes, we do. Where are you taking us? And what is in this bag you gave to me?" Loan asked.

"Hold that for later. I am taking you to your ride," was all she said.

We walked for almost an hour, carrying our luggage with great difficulty as the city disappeared behind us. As we moved into the surrounding ghettos, big buildings slowly gave way to tin shacks. Along the banks of the river, which circled Saigon, many of the shacks stood on stilts that rose from the water. At the outskirts of the city, we left the slums behind, and endless rice fields appeared before our eyes, stretching to the horizon.

Just when my mind began to dull, Mrs. Tam decided to stop. In front of us stood a Communist military base, surrounded by barbed wire and open grass fields. We stepped away from the old lady in a panic. A herd of soldiers came out, most of them not a day over eighteen. They held their guns in warning as they saw us getting closer. Many of them recognized the old lady.

To her, they shouted happily, "Mother Tam, how are you? Have you got anything for us?"

My mother was too fearful to speak. She held on to my arm.

Loan asked the old woman, "What is going on? Did we do something to offend you?"

"Relax," the old lady muttered, "I am taking you to your ride. Just pipe down and let me handle things." To the soldiers, she smiled. "I bring you some pork buns, my sons." Turning to Loan, she ordered, "Give the comrades the food, darling."

"What food?" Loan whispered to Mrs. Tam.

"The bag I gave you earlier, give it to them," the old woman whispered back to her.

The soldiers took the bag from Loan's hand. They tore the pork buns away from the oily wrappers and ate them quickly. When the food was gone, they looked at her and smiled. The whitish residue of the bread stuck between their teeth.

"Who are the people with you, Mama?" they asked.

"These fine people are my friends who are in need of a ride to Nhatrang. Are there any troops leaving town this evening that can accommodate them?"

One soldier volunteered the information, "Yes, as a matter of fact, there are. For you, Mother Tam, anything is possible. Platoon three-oh-six is heading to Hue at eight o'clock tonight. The truck can drop them off in Nhatrang tomorrow afternoon. That is, if your friends want to wait right here. You know we can't take them inside the base, right?"

"Right, right. Thank you, sons. Excuse me for a second while I give these people the instructions, yes?"

"Sure, Mama."

She turned to us and lowered her voice. "Look, I found you a ride. These are sweet kids, and they won't give any trouble. Stay right here in one group where they can see you, and don't make any sudden moves, because curfew is coming soon. Now, give me the money."

64

"Where are you going? You can't leave us here like this," my mother said.

"I can't stay with you. I have to get home before curfew. You just have to trust me, lady."

My mother reached into her blouse for the stack of money hidden in her bra. Without letting the soldiers see what she was doing, Mrs. Tam snatched the cash. As fast as it had appeared, the money vanished again.

"Where are our tickets?" my mother asked the old lady.

"Oh, no ticket. Don't worry about it, you are all set."

"I can't believe this. You are cheating us again, aren't you?" My mother swallowed. "You said earlier that it would be five hundred dong for the tickets. But instead, you took us here in front of a military base, before these guns, telling us to wait for a ride that is way past curfew time. How can we trust you in a situation like this?"

"I said don't worry about it. It's all set." The woman spat a stream of phlegm onto the ground. "I am doing you all a huge favor. How dare you question me in such a manner! Do I want to do business with you? Why don't you just shut up before I lose my patience?" She glared at my mother disdainfully.

"How did you get to know these soldiers?" my grandfather asked the old lady, ignoring my mother.

"Get to know them? What a question! I want you to know that they are all my children. I have been raising and taking care of hundreds of these boys in the last ten years, right under your capitalist noses," the woman said, smiling scornfully. "You see, poor folks like myself could and as a matter of fact did get very close to the Vietcong. You might even say that I am one of the Cong's mothers, and many of these fine boys are my babies. Now, if you excuse me, my job here is done. I must get going before it gets dark. Enjoy your trip."

She turned to the soldiers to bid them farewell. Despite her age, Mrs. Tam seemed to have no problem handling the chests on her shoulders. From the top of her lungs, she sang an ode about a hero who died during the war, as she marched down the street and disappeared into the dusty afternoon.

THE MILITARY TRUCK did not leave its base until almost 9:00. Thanks to Mrs. Tam's emphatic recommendation, we experienced no problem embarking. The soldiers pulled us up into the back compartment as the truck prepared to leave Saigon. About forty men were squeezed tightly together in a small area, but they left generous room for my family on one bench against the far end of the truck. We moved together to our seats, trying to occupy as little space as possible. I sat on Loan's lap, while my brother cuddled up between my grandparents. Next to them, in a corner, my mother hid herself in a shadow, clutching her abdomen.

The soldiers smiled to welcome us. Their uniforms were stained with sweat and dirt as if they had not been washed for months. Many of them sat with their buttocks against their calves on the floor, since there were not enough seats. They stared at my brother and me with curiosity. I looked back at them and smiled.

The trip to Nhatrang took more than eight hours. Two-thirds of the way, I drowsed in the arms of a soldier. He played with my curly hair, telling me about his family in the north. He had a little brother on crutches that he had not seen in over five years.

"Pay attention, little guy. I am going to teach you something," he said with enthusiasm, looking at my mother for her permission. She recoiled further into her seat without looking directly at him.

"I am going to recite to you the teaching of Uncle Ho. It is for all of the children in the south, and it tells of five rules. Are you ready?" His eyebrows raised to show his excitement.

I asked him, "Who is Uncle Ho?"

"Uh-oh. Wait a second, little boy." A surprised look flooded his face as he pulled me closer to him. "Who is Uncle Ho? Why, he is Uncle Ho Chi Minh, our savior, our supreme president. His legend spreads far and wide to many nations in the world, and just by his name alone came the destruction of the shackle that, for many years, enslaved our people to the evil Americans and to the phony Vietnamese Republican government. How could you be so unenlightened, little guy?"

My mother mumbled a hasty apology for my ignorance. The soldier nodded as if to express his forgiveness, and continued on with his lecture.

"The first rule is," he began, "*Love thy country. Love thy neighbors.*" Lying in his arms and listening to his voice, I thought of a similar experience that I had had on the beach of Nhatrang. Back then the soldier had been an American who had occupied a military base near my house. One day when I was playing outside with some of my classmates, a voice called out in a foreign tongue, beckoning the children to come closer.

On the other side of the barbed wire, I could see a soldier with a red face and sun-bleached blond hair. He held up a handful of candies, which he used as bait for our company. I came closer to him as my friends hesitated. "Kien," they shouted to me, "come back." Unlike the rest of the children, I was not in the least frightened of the foreigner in front of me. Having attended my mother's parties, I had had plenty of experience with strange people and understood some of their funny language. I took a step closer to the fence.

"Hello, little fellow. Want some candies?" the American soldier asked in English. I noticed a tint of gray in his icy eyes.

I nodded. He gestured for me to come closer, which I did. Through the barrier I accepted his gift. "Nice little fellow," he asked, "do you know how to blow bubble gum?" Again I nodded.

He ran out of the base to the other side of the barbed wire and joined me. My friends stayed away, observing every move we made. The soldier ignored my classmates' aversion as he turned and waved at them.

"Don't you want to share some candies with your friends?" he suggested.

I shrugged. He laughed and ruffled my head. I brought him closer to my classmates, and the candies I had in my hand overcame their fears. We spent an afternoon playing with the soldier on the sandy beach while the sea murmured at our feet.

Before we separated at the end of that afternoon, he asked, "Can I see you and your friends again tomorrow, little fellow?"

I nodded and ran away, catching up with my friends.

The next day, unable to convince any of my classmates to accompany me, I returned to the beach alone. My new friend stood under the coconut tree, holding a plastic bag full of chocolate in colorful wrappers. I ran toward him. He picked me up and threw me in the air, then caught me before I fell to the ground.

I took the soldier to my home and showed him to my grandparents. Upon meeting them at the doorstep, he took off his helmet and bowed his head to salute them, the way Vietnamese people pay respects to their elders. My grandmother made us some lemonade while we sat by the pool. For hours the soldier lay on the grass, folding up yesterday's newspapers into boats that I floated on the pool's smooth surface. At one point, I looked up to see him propped on one side staring into the air.

"Hello, American, you okay?" I waved a hand in front of his face.

"Okay," he replied. His eyes squinted under the sun. "I am just homesick. You understand homesick? I miss my family."

"Family? Oh yes, I know. You have pictures?" I asked him.

"Yes." He perked up. "Do you want to see my family?" He reached into his back pocket for his wallet.

"My family," I repeated after him with my broken English, holding the worn pictures in my hands. Some of them had dark creases, as they had absorbed his perspiration.

"No, *my* family," he said, correcting my poor English. "Not your family."

One by one, he showed me his loved ones. He told me he was from Wisconsin. To me, the name Wisconsin was as strange as the color of his eyes. His parents looked amiable and soft as they squinted at the camera. He also had an older sister who had just gotten married. The wedding picture showed a beautiful woman and her husband laughing on a church's front steps. The bouquet of white roses in her hands matched her dress and the veil on her blond hair. The same picture also showed his younger brother, who was about my age.

"You remind me of my brother, you know?" he said, touching my hair.

"Yeah? Good," I said.

"Uh-huh. His name is Todd. He is a very good boy, sort of like you, very skinny. I miss him very much." He touched his brother's face in the photograph with the tips of his fingers. "Yesterday before I met you by the beach, remember? I was on the phone with Todd. It was his birthday, but I didn't get a chance to sing a happy birthday song for him. He was leaving for summer camp. Anyhow, when I walked outside feeling depressed, I saw you running around on the sand with your bare feet. You look just like a little American boy, you know? I was so happy to meet you. In a way, being with you was like spending time with Todd, except that he talks a lot more than you do."

I said nothing.

"Thank you," he said suddenly.

"For what?"

"For everything, for this lemonade, for being my little friend, for making this place not so alien as it was two days ago."

"Great. Then see you tomorrow?"

"No, I can't. I am leaving tomorrow for combat. I won't be back until a week from Friday."

"A week from Friday?" I calculated loudly with my fingers. "Ten days?"

"Yep. Will you come back to the beach then and wait for me?" he asked.

"Sure. No sweat."

I marked each day with a scratch on the wall in my bedroom. On the tenth day I ran back to the military base, but the spot under the coconut tree was empty. The afternoon went by as I sat alone in the sand waiting for the soldier to return. It was not until the sun dove into the ocean, and my grandmother called me for dinner, that I realized he would not be coming. The next day I returned to the camp only to be disappointed once again.

A week later, while in the middle of a hide-and-seek game, I saw a military truck parked in front of the soldier's base. Its cargo area was piled high with coarse bags made from ponchos, most of them darkened with dried blood. Something prompted me to go closer. I ran to the truck, and the intent look on my face must have convinced the American soldiers to allow me to climb aboard. As though I were dreaming, I reached out for one bag in particular buried deep under the heap. As I touched it, the zipper gave way under my hand, and from the darkness within, a familiar shock of blond hair tumbled out. In my trance, I wondered why I had never asked my friend to tell me his name. Unable to find the courage to rezip his body bag, I jumped from the truck and ran back home. At the doorsteps of my house, I remembered that the soldier had never known my name either.

Now a few years had passed. The Americans were gone. My family was fleeing to a life of danger and uncertainty. And another soldier was reciting Uncle Ho's rules to me. "And the fourth rule is *'Take good care of thine own hygiene...'*" Lying half-asleep in his embrace, I looked up and saw on his face the same expression I saw on countless lonely faces every day. It was the homesick look of the children who were lost in the chaos of warfare, witnessing death and disaster, longing for a meaningful touch.

CHAPTER NINE

I t was six in the morning when we got to Nhatrang. The truck stopped briefly to drop us off. There was barely a moment for us to bid farewell to the soldiers before they continued on their journey. We walked home in apprehension. Nhatrang seemed to have acquired another layer of skin. New flags flew in front of every house. No one was on the streets. The city appeared clean and lifeless, except for the loudspeakers on every corner, broadcasting chapters of the Constitution of the Socialist Republic of Vietnam.

At home, we faced an incomprehensible ruin. The iron gates to our house had been smashed inward, and a trail of garbage and dirt led to the front door. Feces had been smeared everywhere, turning the pale beige face of the house into an obscene brownish mask. Most of the windows had been vandalized. Broken glass lay on the ground, on the patio, and in the dirty pool. The grass had grown like a weed, threatening to cover the front yard. All of the exotic plants had either been stolen or uprooted and left to die on the hard pavement. The tall wall that my mother had cherished had been crushed down to its last brick, and the thick vines that once covered it shared the same sad fate. With each step, we came upon more heart-wrenching surprises. The front doors of the house, expertly carved from rare ebony, had been knocked off their hinges and broken into pieces.

Inside the house, it looked as if a thousand angry horsemen had stormed through, leaving a trail of destruction. We walked through the hallways in shock, stepping on the remains of broken chandeliers and vases. The silence from within the house was absolute, except for the reverberation of our footsteps, echoing from room to room. There seemed to be no one inside.

However, we were not alone. Our cook and two maids had not abandoned my mother's house. When the looters came, they had hidden themselves in the kitchen building, across from the main house, and had remained there since. Upon hearing our voices, they ran up from their rooms, shrieking with happiness as they saw us.

The cook was a woman of my grandmother's age. She had been in my family for more than a decade. We had always assumed that she had no next of kin, for she had never uttered a word about her family. The fact that she never left the house or had any visitors reinforced this comfortable impression. My grandmother used to tell us how the cook had applied for the job, coming in alone one day with a small suitcase. At that time, my grandfather was in the military service, and my grandmother needed a hand in the kitchen. The woman was never much of a talker, but she was a hard worker and a good cook. I did not know her name. My mother taught us to call her Aunt O, because she had a habit of falling asleep by the stove with her mouth wide open, forming the letter O.

The two maids standing next to the cook had come from a large family that lived a few blocks away. Neither had married, and both were in their midforties. Instead of returning to their own home, they had chosen to stay at my mother's place, where they were provided with their own space, a luxury that was not affordable elsewhere. Upon seeing us, they could not stop screaming and reaching out to touch my brother and me in astonishment. They said over and over to my grandparents that they were happy to see us arriving home safe and sound.

Aunt O cracked open a coconut. She poured its juice over a boiling pot of sticky rice as we sat on the floor in the kitchen, listening to the gossip from the two chirping maids. They filled us in as to what had happened to the city since we had left. Convicts who had escaped from prison a few days before the Communists took over had vandalized the house on numerous occasions. After that, looters had come, looking for hidden treasure, and others had come looking for us. Aunt O and the maids were about to give up hope of our return. They imagined that we had fled the country before the fall of Saigon.

In Nhatrang, the Communists had settled in during the last few weeks. Census had been taken, starting with the citizens' voluntary registration. Through the information that they had gathered, the Communists had taken away the first group of men who had held high status in the old government and military. In the middle of the night, the men were taken out of their houses in handcuffs and chains to a top-secret location. Without revealing too much, the government informed the prisoners' wives and children only of the name of their secret camp: a "neo-educational" compound, where they would be enlightened about the superiority of the new order.

The Communists had divided the city into small groups called towns, and even smaller divisions called clusters, or communities, composed of about fifteen families. Each of these communities was headed by an elected official who in most cases either had been brought in by the military or was in the past a spy for the Communist government. The voting was a formality in which everybody came to acknowledge his position.

Aunt O put the sticky rice with coconut topping in little bowls and laid each one down on the kitchen floor in front of us and spoke to my mother for the first time. "You have to go to the community hall and register your family. Do it as soon as possible, if you don't want any more trouble than you are already in."

My mother gazed at her with a puzzled look. "Trouble? You mean they are looking for me? What trouble are you referring to?"

Aunt O shrugged, pointing at my brother and me. "This trouble."

She looked up from us to the window. Following her gaze, we saw the mansion hiding behind a large palm tree. "That trouble," she said to my mother.

My mother kept silent as the cook continued. "Take all of your identification with you, including every piece of paper that you have. They want to know as much about you as possible. And believe me, before you even get there, they already know everything about you and your past."

"Who is our community's leader? Where do I find him or her?" my mother asked.

"Don't ask me that. I think you should go and find out for yourself," Aunt O said. "Just be prepared, that's all. The office is in the community hall."

"Where is the community hall?" my mother asked.

"You know, madam. It used to be Master Kien's school."

My mother jumped. Turning to Aunt O, she said, "Please, don't call us madam or master anymore. In the past month, I have lost everything I have ever had. I am now as dirt poor as everyone else. If you all want to see me live to raise my children, then please stop using those titles."

She got up to leave the kitchen. Aunt O called after her, "You'd better go around town and tell everyone that, and when you meet the town leader, tell him that, too. Otherwise, he will address you as madam. Because that was what you always wanted everybody to call you, remember?"

My mother ran out of the house and disappeared for the rest of the day. As night fell, my grandparents watched the clock and fretted. Unable to stay still, my grandmother walked outside to the front gates and looked up and down the street. Inside, Loan kept Jimmy and me occupied in my mother's room with her stories. Nevertheless, we both wanted our mother. The anxiety mounted and finally, my brother started to cry. A few moments later, I joined him. Loan sat on the edge of the bed, watching us cry ourselves to sleep.

My mother did not come back until the next afternoon, and she was as pale as a sheet of paper. Without saying a word to anyone, she stormed into the house and disappeared into her room, slamming the door behind her. My grandparents ran after her and knocked on the door in vain. Ignoring their pleas, she remained inside for the rest of the day. Later that evening, my grandmother urged me to take a tray of food upstairs to my mother.

I came to her door, balanced the tray in one hand, and knocked gently with the other. A long silence weighed heavily, and then I heard her voice. "Kien?"

"Yes, Mommy. Can I come in?"

I heard her footsteps as she got up from her bed and opened the door. She stood before me with dark circles under her eyes and tangled hair. Looking at me as though I were a stranger, she took the tray. I walked into her room and heard the door snap shut behind me.

The room was a mess. It looked as if my mother had turned everything inside out and upside down. In the middle of her bed, on top of a white handkerchief, lay a handful of her jewelry, gleaming under the light. She set the dinner tray down on her makeup desk, picked up the handkerchief, and tied it into a knot with the jewelry inside. Then she picked me up off my feet and set me down on a chair in front of the broken mirror. She knelt before me. Her eyes stared into mine, dark as black pearls. I could feel electricity racing along the nape of my neck.

"Oh, Kien," she sighed. "There are so many things I want to tell you. I don't know where to start. Let me just begin by saying that from this point on, I can't allow you to be a child any longer . . ."

"Yes, Mommy."

"How old are you, Kien? Can you tell me?"

"In four days I am going to be eight, Mommy," I said to her, thinking that the answer would please her. But she reacted with dismay.

"Oh, God. That's right. Your birthday is coming, isn't it? Kien, listen to me. You are my oldest son. You have to help me. I can't do this alone. Do you understand?"

"Understand, Mommy."

"You have to grow up. I am going to have another baby soon, and I need you to help me. From now on, you can't just cry anytime things get tough, and you can't trouble me anymore. You have to take good care of your brother, and when the baby comes, you have to take care of it as well. I need your help and I need you to promise me. Okay, Kien?"

"Yes, I promise."

"What are you promising to me?" she pressed.

"I promise not to cry, to be tough, to take care of Jimmy and the baby."

She hugged me for a long time. Then she continued, "Good boy. There are two more things I want — no, not want — I need you to understand. Number one: I want you to keep everything you know a secret. Don't tell anyone anything, even if they threaten you. Remember all the dead bodies we saw on the street? If you say anything at all, I will die like them, so will you, and your grandfather, and your grandmother, and your brother, and the baby, too."

"Don't say anything. Everyone will kill us," I repeated.

"Exactly! Number two: guard this for me with your life." She stuffed the handkerchief in my trousers' pocket. "This is all I have left. Without this, we also die. Don't show it to anyone, and don't ever lose it, understand?"

"Why don't you hide it, Mommy?"

"I did. I hid it in your trousers. Just you and I know about this, okay?"

"Okay. How long do I keep it?" I asked her.

"Maybe for a long time. I don't know exactly how long. Every night before bedtime, I will see you in here, and you will show me the handkerchief, so you won't forget and drop it somewhere. Yes?"

"Yes, Mommy."

"Now be a good boy, and go get your grandparents for me. If Loan asks you what we are talking about, what will you tell her?"

"Tell her nothing," I answered her.

She breathed out a sigh of relief, and said to me, "That's my boy. Now go. Go fetch your grandparents."

I didn't have to; my grandparents wasted no time rushing upstairs to meet my mother as soon as they heard her door open. We all sat on her bed as she told us what had happened to her at the community center, where she had gone to register our family.

CHAPTER TEN

Nhatrang, May 11

A unt O was right. The private school I had attended until about two months earlier now housed the community center. The Communists allowed the priests and nuns to stay in the rectory for the time being, but the church was closed down and the school was transformed into a government outpost.

My mother walked into the principal's office only to see, through an opaque glass door, a dark shadow of a man sitting behind the desk. Near the entrance a small table sat against the wall. Behind it, a woman in a police uniform stopped my mother from going any farther. It took a moment before my mother recognized her. Just a few months before, the woman had been a garbage collector. She would come to Aunt O's kitchen through the back door to gather leftovers for her children.

Upon seeing my mother, a look of hatred registered on the woman's face. Her eyebrows rose as she looked my mother up and down.

"I have come here to register my family," my mother said.

"What rock have you been hiding under? It has been over three weeks. Where the hell were you?" the woman asked.

"My family and I got stuck in Saigon. We returned home as soon as possible."

"Liar! You filthy counterrevolutionary. We all know where you've been, what you've been doing." The policewoman grabbed a sheet of paper on top of her desk, then threw it at my mother. "Take a seat, fill out that form if you are here to see our community leader. Do you think you can handle all that without having me repeat it again?"

"I understand, thank you," my mother murmured.

In front of her desk, facing the opposite wall, was a row of seats. Seven people waited to be seen by the town leader, who was alone in his office, assisting no one.

Just as my mother was about to resign herself to a marathon wait, a voice called from behind the door, sending a chill down her spine. It was a voice she knew only too well, as it belonged to her gardener.

"Comrade Sau," he said, "was that Madame Khuon? Tell her to come in. I have been waiting for her."

Inside, my mother's gardener, Mr. Tran, sat back in his chair, with both of his bare feet resting on the desk. The soles of his feet were deformed with calluses and caked with filth. His toenails, infected by fungus from years of working in mud, were ten hard masses of tissue. Not long ago his job consisted of planting and maintaining the many exotic species of flowers in front of our house. Although he had performed his duties skillfully, no one in the family remembered ever speaking with him, except for my mother, and her sole discourse took the form of command.

In most ways, the new Mr. Tran was the same gardener my mother knew. She recognized his rotten front teeth, with the upper incisors erupting downward into his lower jaw, giving his face the look of a sly rabbit. But she could see two big changes in his appearance. The first was the constant, undefeated smile on his face. The second was that he wore no longer a torn shirt but a neatly pressed black uniform.

"Haven't seen you in a long time, Madame Khuon," he said to her as she came in. "How are your plants? Still blooming?"

"Oh — Mr. Tran —" My mother stammered to find words. "I didn't . . . I wasn't informed . . . You can't imagine how shocked I am to see you here. I am so sorry."

He waved a hand in front of his face. "No need to apologize for your ignorance, madam. Just to be here and witness that look on your face is blissful enough for me. How is your garden? How are your plants?" he repeated the question, watching my mother's expression with a keen intensity.

"I have no plants left. Some were stolen. Some were killed. But it is for the best, since I have no use of them anymore. But please, sir, don't address me as madam. I am now just an ordinary woman, while you are the town superior. When you tease me like that, you have no idea how uncomfortable it makes me."

"Actually, I do have a very good idea how it makes you feel; however, I am not here to tease you, lady. Do you know why I am asking you about your garden?"

"No, sir. I am afraid that I don't, Mr. Tran. I know that it was a beautiful garden, thanks to your talent and hard work. No doubt it has always been a masterpiece, and a joy for many people."

"Hah! It wasn't a joy for me! I worked like a slave for your rich and arrogant guests all of those years. I don't care how beautiful it was. All I remember was that the cursed place cost me my sweat and blood, you pretentious mosquito. I asked because I want you to know that it was me who destroyed every damnable tree in that garden of yours." His voice rose with indignation. "Have you any idea how much I despised you and the job that you made me do? I loathed your parties, and your decadent lifestyle, and your arrogant behavior. Day after day, the sight of you in front of the mirror, painting your nails." He spat on the floor. "I just regret that you weren't there to see me and my men destroy your house. It was a lot of fun. Now, before I lose my train of thought, what is it that you want me to do for you today, Lady Khuon?"

My mother sank back into her chair and tried to compose herself. Despite her efforts, her voice quivered. "I had no idea that I offended you so much. I really thought you liked working there. I didn't mean to behave unjustly to anyone. I am so sorry."

"Shut up. Save your crocodile tears for someone else. Just tell me why are you here."

"I came to enter my family into the community."

He got up, picked up a notebook and a pen from his desk, and threw them into my mother's lap. "Very well, then. Take this notebook to the classroom next door and have a seat. Think long and hard before you write anything, because once you start, I will expect you to be thorough. Put down on that paper the longest and most detailed resume that you ever filled out in your life. I want everything I know and witnessed all the years in that house jotted down by those pretentious fingers. Understand?"

"Yes, sir."

It took my mother more than two hours to fill out a ten-page report about her life. When she was satisfied with the content, she got up to return to Mr. Tran's office. Outside, two more people had joined the previous seven who were waiting to meet with him. The policewoman had stepped away from her desk and my mother knocked at his door. He beckoned for her to enter. Once inside, my mother gave him her resume.

Without bothering to read it, he tore it in half. Then he shook his head, pointing a finger at my mother while sucking at his teeth. "Not good enough. Do it again."

"You didn't read it," my mother protested.

"Not good enough. Do it again," he repeated.

It took my mother three such episodes to realize the game he was playing with her. Sitting alone in the classroom, she wrote down her life story, page after page, over and over again. Each time the paper ran out, Mr. Tran would throw her a new stack from behind his desk.

After tearing up my mother's report for the eighth time, Mr. Tran realized that she was no longer intimidated. "You don't learn, do you?" he said.

"I don't understand what exactly you want me to do, sir," she said quietly. "I have been here all day writing, without anything to eat, and I am pregnant. My children are waiting for me at home. If you don't like what you see, please let me go home to take care of them and I will get out of your sight."

"Wouldn't that be convenient for you, Khuon? Is that what you want me to do? Or do you want me to reserve a space for you and your family in the reeducation camp, where you can learn more readily?"

"No, sir. I beg you for your mercy. All I want is to be registered in this town. I want my family to be legalized. I can't help the way I have behaved in the past. But whatever wrongdoings you think I did back then, I committed no sin against the government. I held no position in the old bureaucracy, nor did I ever fight against the Communists in any battle. I am not your enemy."

"Sit down," he ordered. Looking at her as if she were an insect, he snarled, "You are a capitalist, and therefore, you are my enemy."

"I was a capitalist," my mother argued. "But now I have lost all my money, I am a poor, penniless woman, just like everyone else. And I am not afraid to get a clean start."

"What about your Nguyen mansion? Do you still have it?"

My mother did not answer.

He sat back into his leather chair, smiling. "Still consider yourself a poor, penniless woman, Khuon?"

"What do you want me to do?" my mother moaned in defeat.

"I want you to see that as long as you have assets, you and the Vietnamese government are enemies. We are trying to build a country in which everyone will share everything." He leaned close to my mother's face, and she could smell the acidic decay in his breath. "You are standing in our way to the future, Khuon. We have to knock people like you down, so that we can move ahead."

"You want to confiscate the house, is that it?" my mother asked.

"As I understand, Khuon, that house isn't the only property you own. Is it so wrong for us to take away one of your many fortunes if it is the only way to redeem yourself in the eyes of the government?"

Mr. Tran was right. Her mansion was not the only house my mother had owned. Years ago, before she could build her own house, she and my grandparents used to live in a small house on my aunt's property. The house had three rooms. In the front, facing the street, was a three-hundred-square-foot living room. Behind it was another three-hundred-square-foot room, my grandparents' bedchamber. A little storage space in the back had been turned into my mother's bedroom. Since my grandparents had moved into the Nguyen mansion, they brought with them every piece of furniture, leaving that place almost vacant. On the same lot was my aunt's house, where she lived with her husband and fourteen children. Both houses shared a bathroom, kitchen, and well.

On paper, my mother owned that house. The adjacent dwelling was in my aunt's husband's name. The entire complex was located five kilometers away from my old home, surrounded by rice fields and countryside. The idea of returning to live there among the farm animals and her relatives was an overwhelming blow to my mother. She could not help but protest, "That house was built for my parents. I just hold the paper for them."

"Your house, their house, you all are family to each other. What is the difference? We need that big house of yours for our permanent office," he said.

"Why don't you take the small house instead?"

Mr. Tran got up, kicking the chair behind him. "Look at me, you filthy, arrogant ex-Republican traitor. I am trying to make your life easier, but you are making mine more difficult. You don't want to give up that house? Good. Let's see how long you can survive in jail, away from your children. Comrade Sau, get in here, please."

The policewoman appeared at the door with her hands on her hips and a frown on her face. "Yes, Comrade Tran?" she asked.

"Take this counterrevolutionary to the correctional center. Keep her there until it's her turn to go in front of the People's Council. I wash my hands of her. Let the Court of the People judge her crimes exactly the way it did to every other criminal. Good night, Khuon. Have fun sleeping in the Hilton."

My mother clasped her hands in supplication. "Please, I didn't mean what I said. Don't put me in jail. Mr. Tran, please, we can talk about this."

The policewoman grabbed my mother's arm and swung her around. Mr. Tran walked around his desk to meet my mother face-to-face. Waving his arms, he hissed at her, "No more talk! It's time to knock you down, Khuon, because we are moving ahead." He smiled and walked out the door, leaving my mother and the policewoman behind. Once outside, he said to the people in the waiting room, "It is five o'clock. The office is closing now. All of you come back tomorrow morning."

The policewoman did not have a pair of handcuffs. Instead, she used a rope to tie my mother's hands together. She dragged her captive down the street, ignoring the commotion she caused along the way. At the correctional center, after throwing my mother into a cell, the policewoman turned to assign her to the officer in charge. Lying alone on the cold pavement in the dark, my mother feared for her life as well as our lives at home. By morning, she felt totally defeated. But somewhere deep inside her womb, the baby was kicking.

Mr. Tran came to see her in the morning with the same smile tattooed on his face. He looked at her from the other side of the bars and shrugged at her woe.

"Let me go," she begged him. "You can have the house. Let me sign the paper."

"I am not sure I want your house anymore, Khuon." His teasing cut her like a knife.

"Please, let me go. I have responsibilities to my elderly parents and to my young children. They have done nothing against you or the government, Mr. Tran. Think about them, think about the new life inside me, and spare us this time. If I die, they all will die with me."

He reached into the front pocket of his shirt for the keys. As he opened the cell door for her, he whispered in her ear, "It is very wise for you to come to this decision, Khuon. You got yourself a deal — the house for your life. You get out of this town, get away from me. Take your family and make a fresh start someplace else, where no one knows you and hates you the way we do here. Get out by tomorrow or face the consequences. You have twenty-four hours to get ready, understand?"

He turned to the policemen and said to them in an authoritative manner, "Listen up, comrades. I let this woman go because she has shown genuine regret about her wayward, pre-Revolution life by giving up her only possession, her house, to the government. She is a positive example of how forgiving and perceptive our justice system is and always will be. We have successfully turned her from a bloodthirsty capitalist into a productive citizen, and an unselfish human being. We expect her to continue to evolve into a better and more prudent resident in this country. Congratulations to you, Khuon."

She ran away from them as fast as she could and didn't pause until she reached her house.

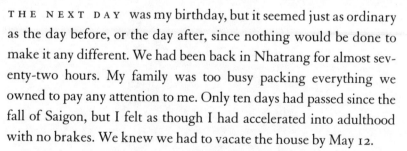

THE NEXT DAY was my birthday, but it seemed just as ordinary as the day before, or the day after, since nothing would be done to make it any different. We had been back in Nhatrang for almost seventy-two hours. My family was too busy packing everything we owned to pay any attention to me. Only ten days had passed since the fall of Saigon, but I felt as though I had accelerated into adulthood with no brakes. We knew we had to vacate the house by May 12.

Just when the furniture was finished being packed and the suitcases were secured and everyone was ready to leave, the front door bell rang.

"The police are here. Kien, open the door to let them in," my grandfather ordered matter-of-factly.

I rushed to the entrance and pulled off the plastic parchment covering the big hole where the door used to be. Standing in front of me was not a team of policemen, but rather an unkempt, tired-looking man. His hair had been shaved off, and his scalp shone under the sun. He had a beard, which covered the lower half of his face. The man looked at me and smiled.

"Hey, Kien, remember me?" he asked. I recognized his voice the moment he spoke. "It's me, Lam, silly boy. Where is your mother?"

CHAPTER ELEVEN

"C an I come in?" Lam asked, standing at the doorway.
I stepped back. He walked in, turning around with curiosity to examine the disheveled garden behind him and the debris that littered the living room. A look of disbelief showed on his face.

"Dear God, what happened to this place?" he asked, but then the answer came to him. "They really wrecked the house, didn't they? Where is your —"

He stopped in the middle of the sentence, as he caught a glimpse of my mother from across the room. A hint of shame washed his dirty face with crimson. He stammered, "Hi, there. How are you?"

My mother stared at Lam through her narrowing lashes. Silently, she folded her arms in front of her chest and leaned back against the wall, unmoved by his discomfort.

He scratched his head with embarrassment. "Thought you would never see me again, didn't you? Well, what can I say? I didn't get away. As a matter of fact, you probably will be very happy to learn about my mishaps, one right after another since that day I left all of you behind." He chuckled. "Damn, what a horrible nightmare. Twice at the airport I almost got killed. But thank heaven I didn't. Sometimes I wonder how a bastard like me could get so lucky. Anyway, I came here today for a reason. I was just wondering to myself if you would find it in your heart to take me back. Maybe in some way, I was hoping that you would be needing me."

My mother's silence was deafening.

Lam's voice trailed off dejectedly. "Or maybe not."

"Get out," my mother said. Her voice was calm, but the hatred was clear in her face.

"Look!" Lam pleaded. "I know you are mad, and I don't blame you. But please try not to brush me away without listening to me first. In the last month, I have been to Hell and back many times over. I don't think I can take much more, not from you or anyone else. But believe me, madam, when I tell you this: I've learned my lesson the hard way. And whatever wrongdoings I did to you, I've been paid back, plus interest. I was robbed. I was beaten. And those sons of the backward Commie whores jailed me for two weeks because I was sleeping in the park. Except for them I don't think anybody else cares whether I live or die. And to top it all off, I spent all of my money, and sold my identification and my passport. I haven't eaten in the last three days and I am very tired. Please let me stay here, at least just for a couple of days."

There was more silence from my mother, and Lam continued. "If you are really going to kick me out, at least feed me something and let me take a shower first. Please?"

My mother did not have time to answer. From outside, we heard the loud noise of trucks, indicating the arrival of Mr. Tran and the policemen. Through the windows, we watched them park their vehicles carelessly on the sidewalk and hurry toward the house on the long and dirty path through the garden. As soon as he saw my mother standing inside, Mr. Tran smiled broadly. His hair was dripping wet and neatly combed to the back of his head like a duck tail, and he was carrying a black nylon backpack across his right shoulder — the Vietcong's style. He gestured for his men to keep up with him as he neared the house.

My mother turned to Lam. "You want to stay here, Lam? Here is a news flash for you: I am no longer the person who could make such a decision. You will need to ask him first."

"Him? Who?" Lam looked confused.

"See for yourself." She shrugged.

Lam eyed the newcomers with puzzlement.

"What is going on?" he asked. "Why are the police at your house? What have you done to this place, Khuon?"

My mother greeted Mr. Tran as soon as his feet touched the edge of the marble floor. "Good morning, Mr. Tran. You are right on time. We just finished packing everything. Do you remember Lam?" Turning to Lam, she continued, "And you, Lam, I don't think you need a proper introduction to Mr. Tran here, but there is something I think you deserve to know. As of today, Mr. Tran, our community leader, is the new owner of this house. So, if I were you, I would be careful in paying my respects to him."

Lam raised his eyebrows as if he wanted to ask more questions, but nothing came.

Finally noticing Lam, Mr. Tran broke out laughing. He walked over to take a hold of Lam's right hand and shook it.

"Oh, don't look so shocked," he said. "I haven't changed that much. Or maybe I have, judging from the look on your face. But you, too, have changed. Good heavens, I almost didn't recognize you. Well, what can I say?" He shrugged, then turned serious. "You have good eyesight, you can see that I am still the same old gardener who watered your orchids and slept behind your kitchen door. The difference is that I am the new owner. Just like the old proverb said, the rivers have their own segments; men have their own moments. I guess now is my moment."

Taking a deep breath, he continued, "Come on you two, don't look so gloomy. Are you still with her?" Pointing at my mother, he winked at Lam. "Now that she is no longer the mighty Madame Nguyen, the smoke-spitting, fire-puffing banker?"

Lam struggled for composure. However, Mr. Tran paid no more attention to him. Turning to my mother, he reached inside his backpack to pull out a stack of paper.

"As for you, Khuon, I took the liberty of withdrawing the deed to your house from the Department of Real Estate. And I want you to know it was not by any means an easy task — just like looking for a pin in an ocean bed. Anyhow, I found it, and there are a few places that I need you to sign and fingerprint, which we can do now. The rest of the legal nonsense I can take care of later. Come on over here by my side, so that I can show you."

My mother walked closer to him. "I'll sign anything you want, but what about my family's proof of registration? I would like to have that before we leave here."

He nodded. "Sure, I understand your worry — nobody is legal until I say so. But fear no more, I got all the papers right here. We'll go through everything by the end of this morning."

He pulled out a thick blue folder. On the top page, the words were typed in bold black letters: "Proof of Existence, Community #4, Unit #125091, Head of Unit: Nguyen, Khuon T."

"This number, 125091," he explained to my mother as his thick finger ran across the cover page, "is your family's number. We don't like to use the word *family*. It's too personal, too alienated from the whole. We refer to each family as a *unit,* like in biology — the single cells that make up the body. A word of advice: you should guard this paper with your life. For the time being, this is your identification. You'll have to carry it with you wherever you go, until our leaders come up with a better system. All of your names will be contained in here, so you need to stay together at all times. When you check into your new community, do not take anyone else in, or allow anyone to leave your unit. Every day after six P.M., curfew time, everybody will have to stay inside, because several nights a week, your house will be searched without any warning. That is the law. When it happens, the police will ask to see this paper and count heads. If they find anyone that doesn't belong, the head of the unit and the extra person will be taken away to death camp. Did you get all that? All right, now I need you to read your new address slowly to me."

As my mother spelled out the new address to Mr. Tran, Loan and the rest of my family walked into the room, watching the scene in silence.

"How many people in your unit?" Mr. Tran asked my mother.

"Sir, am I counting my prenatal baby as one individual?"

He raised his eyebrows. "Don't be stupid. How many people are there in your unit, counting seniors, adults, and children? Forget your belly. You will register that baby at the hospital when it is time."

"Six people. Two seniors, two female adults, and two male children," my mother answered.

From the corner where he stood forgotten, Lam spoke up abruptly. "Seven, including one male adult. Don't forget me!"

Mr. Tran threw a threatening look at Lam, then barked at him, "Do I look like I am talking to you?"

Lam turned bright red, yet he said nothing.

Mr. Tran continued, "The head of this household didn't mention anything to me about any male adult. So I assume that you are taking the liberty of adding yourself into her unit. Is that true?"

Lam forced a smile. "Sir, you know I have been living here for more than half a decade. I am as much a part of this family as anyone else, except you, in this room."

"Are you married to her?"

"No, but I am the father of that child in her womb."

It was my mother's turn to blush when Mr. Tran turned to face her. "Listen, Khuon," he said, "I can't argue with paid boy here, so I'll let it be up to you. What is it going to be? Six or seven?"

"There are six members in my unit," my mother answered firmly.

She wanted to say something else, but Mr. Tran waved his callused finger to quiet her. His eyebrows remained knitted together in thought.

"Hold on a second," he said. "This half-wit may have a point here. There are no males in this unit except for your old father, who may end up in a concentration camp for his past crimes. Even if the government spared him due to his disability, you would not have enough work force for this unit. If I add the gigolo to your group, it will increase your family's strength to almost double. A good idea, don't you think? Oh, well, even if you don't agree with me, someday soon you'll thank me."

And that was his decision. Without giving my mother a chance to object, he jotted down in my family's file the seven names. Soon after my mother signed over the deed of her house, Mr. Tran handed her the folder. Putting the rest of his papers into his backpack, he shifted his attention to Loan. Like a farmer examining a young cow, he gave her a long look of contemplation. When he spoke, there was no hatred in his voice.

"Loan," he said, "you are eighteen years old now, correct?"

"Yes, sir," Loan answered.

"Good, good. Here is a pamphlet I want you to read. It is about a group called The Young Volunteers, a party of young people like you, and I recommend you take a look at it. You can read more about it and at some point if you decide to join, or even if you just want more information, look for your new community leader or me. Either one of us will be happy to assist you with any questions that you might have. The truth is, I've watched you grow up in this house, and I think you have turned into a very smart young lady. With the new change in this country, you can really go far, because it's time for poor folks like us to take charge of our destinies. Promise me that you will read the brochure and do something for yourself and for your country, instead of hanging around here with this sinking ship. There is no law that condemns you to die with these capitalists you once worked for. The days that these people could take advantage of you are over, you understand?"

And he stuffed the pamphlet in her hand. On the way past my mother, he whistled a fast, catchy tune and bobbed his shining head up and down to the music. In the next room, the policemen started to carry our belongings outside. Less than an hour later, we settled inside the truck and it drove away.

I sat back in my seat and stared out the window to take one last look at the place. Through the broken wall and the fallen vines, the house stood empty and ruined under the bright sun. In my mind the snapshots of memory paraded as in a dream. I saw myself running from room to room, laughing as Loan chased after me, her freshly washed hair floating beside us like clouds, smelling like a sea breeze. I relived my mother's endless parties, where people danced by the pool under beautiful lights, and perfumes mixed in the air. My mother's ghost still seemed to be sitting in front of the mirror powdering her hands, with her river of hair cascading down her shoulders.

While these thoughts distracted me, next to me in the truck, my mother held her stomach in her arms, and followed her own thoughts. Were her emotions similar to mine? On the other side of her, Jimmy showed no sign of understanding what was going on. He smiled at everyone, showing his two missing front teeth and watching the streets with thoughtless fascination.

CHAPTER TWELVE

T he truck bumped along for half an hour. When it stopped, Jimmy and I saw our new home for the first time.

My aunt's house faced the dusty street from across a large garden. Built twenty years before, it had a red tile roof and white columns, an odd mix of Asian and European architecture. The windows were trimmed with green shutters, opening outward, on which the paint was so old that it had cracked into thousands of tiny creases, showing the decayed wood within. Only a story high, the house contained six small rooms with white paint and faded red molding on every wall.

The house had been built to shelter a few members of my aunt's family. But as the family grew, it had become too crowded. My uncle asked my mother for help, so that he could build another flat behind the main house. Because of the eternal guilt my mother felt toward her sister for being so poor, she put up the money.

The new bungalow, situated between the kitchen and the bathroom, provided three extra rooms. The two older girls, Moonlight and Snow, lived next to the kitchen, and the three oldest boys, Le, Than, and Nghia, were settled in the two other rooms.

On the left side of my aunt's house stood my new home. At first glance, it seemed impossibly small and primitive. It struck me that the entire place could fit in my mother's old garage and still leave plenty of room for a car. This house, too, was painted white, but it was newer than the others in the compound. At first sight, it looked like a gigantic matchbox, rectangular, covered with a corrugated tin roof, and without columns. Behind it, on the other side of the well, was my aunt's kitchen.

My aunt, her husband, and all of their children ran out to greet us at the gates. Everybody smiled and exchanged greetings as they helped my grandparents carry their belongings inside. Not much furniture had escaped damage at the Nguyen mansion, but my grandparents and my mother had packed as much as they could salvage. Among our reclaimed possessions, the last valuable piece was an ebony altar for my deceased uncle, hand-carved and weighing over one hundred kilograms.

When he was alive, my young uncle was the gem of the whole family, the only son of my grandparents' fourteen children who lived past his eighteenth birthday. He had entered the Vietnamese navy the day he turned nineteen. At twenty-one, he drowned while swimming one morning at the base. The report of his death devastated my grandfather. Coincidentally, I was born across town on that very same day. My grandfather, torn between the bad news and the good news, had taken my birth as an omen, believing that his young son's spirit had returned via my mother's womb. I then became his favorite grandchild.

The altar was given a prominent spot in the new house's living room, which was now being turned into my grandparents' bedroom, with their bed in one corner near the window, and a sewing machine a few feet away. The next room contained three beds for Loan, Jimmy, and me. Next to my bed was an armoire, set against the wall and locked at all times. My mother kept the key. Our bedroom also contained a chest of drawers for clothes. The last room on the back of the house, about ninety square feet, had just enough room to hold a bed for my mother and Lam and her small makeup desk.

While we were moving in, my aunt sat on top of a cardboard box, smoking a hand-rolled cigarette. Her legs in her black nylon pants swung restlessly as she watched my mother making Jimmy's bed from across the room. Some of her children sat beside her. Their dirty faces stared curiously at us.

Clearing her throat, she asked my mother, "Is that all of the stuff they allowed you to take with you? Did you lose the rest?"

My mother nodded, and my aunt responded with a heavy sigh.

"Everything?" she repeated her question. Again, my mother nodded.

"Unbelievable," my aunt continued. "Oh, well, it is too bad, you could have asked me to hold some things for you before you ran off unannounced like your pants were on fire. But since you didn't, I hope you don't mind that I took some things from the house while you were away. Look at it this way, if I didn't, someone else would have. And why can't that be me, your own sister? I don't know what you are thinking, but I don't plan to give any of it back to you."

"What things did you take?" my mother asked her.

"Just stuff." She shrugged. "Mostly for the kids. I don't remember exactly every single thing. Why?"

"Did you find any of my jewelry?"

"Of course not," my aunt snapped. "I didn't even know if you hid any in the house. Don't accuse me of stealing your precious jewels, unless you want me to start a war right here, right now."

"I am not accusing you. I am asking you politely."

"Well, don't even ask me politely. I didn't take your wealth to my house. If anything, I am now taking in your ill luck by living next door to you."

My mother did not say anything more. The silence grew into an uncomfortable tension until my aunt spoke. "More important, what are you going to do now?"

"I don't know. Just start from scratch, I guess."

"I am afraid that you may have to find a more suitable plan, sister.

You are not twenty-one anymore. Besides, no offense, but this time, your half-breed children will definitely hold you back."

My mother stopped in the middle of making Jimmy's bed and turned around to look at my aunt. She lowered her voice. "Would you please modify your language if you are going to talk about my children? You let me do the worrying, since it is none of your concern. And please don't ever use that awful word again in front of the boys."

"Why not?" my aunt insisted. "If you don't teach your kids the facts of life, someday somebody will. And when that happens, the words would not be this sweet to their ears."

"What is a half-breed, Mommy?" Jimmy asked.

Before my mother could answer him, a cousin of mine spoke up. He was about seventeen years old. Sweating from the heat, his face was red and covered with acne.

"A half-breed is a bastard child, usually the result from when a woman has slept with a foreigner. Like you," he said, facing Jimmy as if he were challenging my brother to a duel. His eyes were crossed. The two irises stared angrily at each other across the bridge of his nose.

"Enough!" my mother screamed. "How could you just sit there letting your children talk to us this way?"

My aunt shrugged once again. Her eyes hid behind a cloud of smoke. "I taught my children the freedom to speak their own mind. They aren't stupid, you know." She frowned. "And look who should talk. You, their aunt, have always treated them like dirt. Frankly, I don't appreciate the tone of your voice. You can't talk to us like you still have money, sister. Times have changed."

My mother resumed fixing the bed for my brother without saying another word.

"Listen, maybe you can stay mad at me since it is in your nature," my aunt said, "but I can't be mad at you. You are, after all, my only sister. So, I welcome you to live here. I do want to be straight about one thing, though. You may think that you can choose to live your life whichever way you want. The truth is, it's not that easy any-more, not when we live side by side. What you do will reflect on my family by association. Ah, yes, something else you should con-sider. I'd like you to destroy anything that might link you to the past, because you never know what will come back to haunt you later. Of course, with something like these two big televisions here —" she pointed at my brother and me — "you can't hide them. But pictures and addresses can be very dangerous to keep around. The police come by at night and search the whole block. Think about it! I leave you alone to unpack. Let's go home, children."

She got up to throw her still-burning cigarette out of the window, following it with a hefty spume of expectorates. Her children trailed after her as she left. Loan excused herself to the market to buy gro-ceries, and my grandparents retired to their room. My mother lay down on Jimmy's bed as if exhausted.

Looking fresh and relaxed after a long bath, Lam walked in. His beard was shaven, and his skin was clean. Throwing his soiled clothes in a corner, and still wrapped in a wet towel, he sank to his hands and knees and crawled toward my mother, smiling. She sat up from the bed, looking tense.

"Please forgive me? I am begging you," he said.

He reached out for her foot and pressed his lips against her skin. Like a wild cat, my mother jumped up and kicked Lam in his face. He fell backward and landed on his elbows. Slowly, Lam got up, adjusting his towel while my mother returned to her seat on my brother's bed. His hands folded into a fist as he spat some blood onto the floor.

"Stupid horse," he said. "I would hit you so hard if you weren't big with child."

My mother stood up and arched her back, pulling her blouse up to show her rounded abdomen. "Want to strike me?" she shrieked. "Go right ahead. Hit me right here. Help me get rid of your stink-ing mess."

He pointed his finger at her. "I don't need you. But my name was in the registration, and so I am going to stay here whether you want me to or not. I suggest that you should wise up and learn to live with me, damned woman." He walked outside, kicking a chair that blocked his path.

That night, after my mother locked herself in her bedroom, he crawled into Loan's bed. From where I lay in the dark, I could hear her quiet struggle, as she tried to push him away. After a period of heavy breathing, they exchanged words.

I heard Lam's voice rising with rage. "You did what? I can't believe it. Was that the old hen's idea?"

There was more silence, then he continued. However, his voice was much lower this time, full of regret. "How could you get rid of my baby?" he asked.

"Get off me." Loan spoke in a whisper. "It was not the mistress's decision. It may have been her suggestion, but the choice was mine. I did it for me, so that I can be free from you."

The sound of a slap exploded in the dark. Soon after, I heard Loan jump out of her bed, and her voice penetrated the night. "Hit me again, and I'll report you to the authorities. Follow me to my bed one more time, and I swear to the gods, I'll search for the most painful way to murder you."

Her footsteps pounded toward my bed. I could feel the mosquito net above me being swept away, and soon her warm body slid next to me. Holding me in her trembling embrace, she cried softly in the dark. Back in her bed, Lam lay quiet through the rest of the night.

When I got up the next day, Loan had already left for the market alone. She did not return for dinner. My mother and Lam avoided one another like the plague. Staying in Loan's bed for most of the day, Lam snuggled under the sheet, reading a kung fu novel. My mother stayed inside her room to arrange her nail polish collection.

Jimmy and I ventured outside and saw our cousins playing in the dirt. At first, the boys pretended to ignore us, but it was not long before they ran over to touch us with the same astonishment that they would show to a pair of rare Christmas ornaments.

I learned that my aunt's oldest son, Le, was about Lam's age. He was handsome and a bachelor. His favorite pastime was playing the guitar on the steps of his house. The local girls would stop by every day and listen to his love songs. While he strummed, one of the girls was singing along with him as his mother sat a few steps away, watching with pride in her eyes.

The second son, Than, was my aunt's pride and joy, because he had graduated from college as an electrical specialist. He lived with his new bride, Orchid, in the farthest bungalow in the back next to the bathroom. Every time I walked by his room, I saw him peering at some large piece of stereo equipment through a thick pair of glasses. Than rarely showed interest in anything beyond the work on his desk. Following the wedding, and at my aunt's suggestion, Orchid had given up her teaching job to be an obedient wife.

The third son, Nghia, was the image of his father, and just like my uncle, he had a bad temper and unpleasant appearance. Even his mother was afraid of him. After two years of stumbling around in college, he left school at the age of twenty-four, jobless and loveless, and was again living at home. Nghia shared the second bungalow with his elder brother.

The next two daughters, Moonlight and Snow, had been away at college until that summer, after the fall of Saigon. They now lived in a room that once had been part of the kitchen. Even though the two girls were in their early twenties, which was considered late for marriage, they remained single. The combination of their poverty and their excessive schooling prevented proper suitors from approaching my aunt and uncle for their hands in marriage.

My aunt's next group of children was made up of five boys ranging from fourteen to nineteen who hung around each other like a flock of birds. They were the ones who examined my brother and me in amazement. With rough hands and dirt-encrusted nails they ruffled our hair and pinched our cheeks. My aunt's sixth child, Tri, was known for his reserved and polite manner. The next one, Tin, was the shortest and stockiest. He was the same cross-eyed boy who had defined *half-breed* to Jimmy earlier. He had a job in a factory making rice sacks, but such responsibility did not keep him from behaving like a teenager.

Tin jumped on my back, insisting that I had to carry him across the yard as a part of the initiation into his family. His weight crushed me to the ground. Each time I tried to get up, he would sit back down to shove my face in the dirt. And his brothers would laugh out loud with delight. After a while, when Tin realized that I was too weak to carry him, he changed his demand. Now he directed me to crawl on all fours from one end of the garden to the other, underneath his three younger brothers' outstretched legs. While I made my slow, painful way, the boys loomed above me, spitting on my back and poking my backside with sticks to force me to go faster. A few feet away, my brother was sharing my fate. But the moment he was hit with the sticks, Jimmy cried out to my grandparents for help. Fearing my grandfather, my cousins left him alone.

Nhon, my eighth cousin, was skinny and tall. His body reminded me of the shape of the bamboo tree. Hieu and Hanh were my ninth and tenth cousins, and were around my height and of similar build, even though both of them were at least two or three years older than I.

Underneath a rambutan tree that had bright red spiny fruits covering its thick branches, my brother joined my aunt's last four daughters and watched the scene in silence. The oldest girl in this group, Pink, was my age. Next to her stood the twins, Cloud and Wind. The youngest, Proud, was my brother's age. In fact, their birthdays were only two days apart.

Inside the house, my mother did not see us come running from the outside, looking like two rag dolls with torn clothes and bruises. My grandmother took Jimmy and me to clean up by the well as my cousins stood around and watched without making a sound. Afterward, my grandfather took us to the local public school, a few blocks away, to enroll us in summer school. I was assigned to third grade, class 3C, with Pink and Hanh. My brother would be in the first grade, class 1A, with the twins and Proud.

CHAPTER THIRTEEN

C an anyone recite for me Chairman Ho's teachings?" my teacher asked, looking at no one in particular through her thin-rimmed glasses. Her hair was a tangle of big curls, spilling down to cover most of her face, except for the shiny tip of her nose and two thin red lips. Her skin was oily and dotted with tiny red pimples. Behind the desk, her body, at least two sizes too small for her uniform, sat up straight in her wooden chair. On the blackboard, her name was written in white chalk. "Miss San," it said. It was the first day of summer school, but the sun had already cooked the classroom to baking temperature.

From the last row, I raised my hand in the air with hesitance, and several pairs of dark eyes turned to stare at my face with curiosity. To my surprise, no one else in the class seemed to know the answer.

"Yes?" the teacher acknowledged me. As she looked straight at me, I noticed that one of her irises floated upward to hide behind her eyelid. Looking out that socket was the back of her eyeball in an almond shape, staring blankly at my face.

I stood up from my seat and recited the verses I had learned from the northern soldier on the military truck after the fall of Saigon.

Love thy country. Love thy neighbors.
Be a good student. Be a responsible worker.
Get along with thy friends. Keep in line with the law.
Take good care of thine own hygiene.
Humble. Honest. And courageous.

"Excellent." She clapped her hands together. Droplets of sweat fell from my forehead to the desk below, vanishing quickly into the wood's rough surface. "What's your name?" she asked me.

From somewhere in the room, before I had a chance to answer her, a voice mumbled, "Half-breed." The rest of the children laughed.

"Silence," she said to the classroom. Turning her good eye in the direction of that sudden outburst, she remarked, "That is a horrible thing to say to one of your classmates. You children should be ashamed of yourselves."

Studying the wet spots my perspiration had made on the desk, I decided at that moment that my teacher was one of the loveliest persons I had seen in this new town.

Despite the ridicule, I received a red neckerchief that day — the first boy in my school to be granted such an honor. My teacher said that it signified my commendable behavior as one of Uncle Ho's good children. I was to wear it every day on my shoulder, until its color faded. Then, and only then, would I become the perfect citizen the country had long waited for.

That night, when it was time for dinner, my grandparents realized Loan's absence and began to search for her in panic. She did not return home until after the curfew. In her arms, she carried a large cardboard box, which she set outside before entering the house.

Loan walked up to my grandfather, who sat in his favorite rocking chair reading a book about Zen Buddhism. She knelt before him. My grandfather stopped reading to look at her. His eyeglasses slid down to the tip of his nose.

"Uncle," Loan said, touching the soft fabric of my grandfather's pants with her hands. "May I have a moment of your time, sir?"

He nodded. "Tell me what is on your mind, little girl."

"I came with a purpose in mind — to bid you farewell, sir," she said quietly.

Everybody in the room looked at Loan with surprise, but no one said anything. We all waited for my grandfather to respond. Closing his book and setting it down on the floor, he spoke in a voice that seemed sad, but contained no trace of astonishment. "Where are you going?"

"Uncle, a couple of days ago, Mr. Tran gave me a pamphlet about an organization called The Young Volunteers," she explained. "It got me thinking about my future. So, this morning I went to the Community Center and spent the whole day there, meeting with some of the comrades and getting to know more about the assemblage. I found out that the group's main purpose is to enlist young people all over the country to aid the armed forces. The group is basically a supportive branch of the military. Although there are no more battles to fight, the country needs a lot of help to clean up the damage that was done during the war. I figured since I am a cleaning maid, this sounds like a job for me, so I signed up. It only takes three short years out of my life, but in the end, my resume will have a good recommendation by the government."

From the door, Lam interrupted. "Oh, God, she is talking crazy." He took a step toward her. "Yes, you! You are crazy, Loan." Then he turned to my grandfather. "She will do no such thing. Stop her, Mr. Nguyen. Stop her from making a fool of herself."

Loan resumed her conversation with my grandfather as if she did not hear Lam. "I did join the corps, Uncle, without your permission, but there wasn't time to ask for it. I am leaving tomorrow morning. The group sent everybody home tonight to pack and bid farewell to loved ones. I don't have any relatives left since my father died. I only have you. Uncle, even though you would never admit this to me, I know you blame yourself for what happened to my father. Both of you may have been hit by the same bullet, but he was the one who got killed and you were spared. So what if that was how it happened? You have done nothing but good deeds on my behalf since the first day I came to this family. I beg of you, no more guilt. I want you to know that I understand. You don't owe him or me anything because it was fate that killed my father. I also want to thank you from the bottom of my soul. Uncle, I am saying good-bye to you now, because I have to leave at three in the morning. Thank you for loving me all these years. Once my term of service is up, I will be back to see you again."

My grandfather took Loan's hands in his and blinked several times. "I understand, little girl," he said. "Promise to take care of yourself, and stay out of trouble?"

"Yes, sir. I will."

They hugged each other; however, the embrace was short and spiritless. Turning to my grandmother, Loan smiled. Her fingers touched the wrinkled skin of my grandmother's face with tenderness.

"Take care, Auntie. I love you," she said.

"Do you know where you are going? Can we write to you?" my grandmother asked.

"I don't know much about the future, Auntie," Loan said. "I was informed only that we are heading to Hue, on foot. We will stop along the way to help people build new houses, pushing the jungles back to gain more land, and clean up the debris from the war. This will be a challenging experience for me, and I am afraid that I won't have a steady address for quite some time, Auntie. I will write regularly, though."

"Sounds like you have everything planned already." My grandmother chuckled. "But I have no doubt about your abilities. You are a good girl, Loan. Come back to us soon."

She turned to my mother, who stood in the middle of the room. Loan's eyes avoided my mother's stare to look at the floor. My mother broke the uncomfortable silence between them. "To set the record straight, I never asked you to leave the house, Loan. I just want you to know that."

"Yes, madam, I know. I never wanted to leave either, especially now that your baby is coming. But I have my reasons for leaving. Please take care of yourself."

"Don't leave because of Lam." The light reflected in my mother's dark eyes as she glared at her boyfriend.

Loan turned to Lam and said in a low tone, "Good-bye, Lam. Take care of my mistress, and treat her well, because she is having your child. If you wrong her, I will make certain that you'll pay for it when I come back, and that is my solemn promise. Don't interpret it as an empty threat. You and I should never have been together in the first place. I may have had no choice in the past, but as for the present and the future, I choose to leave so that you can stay."

He did not reply. Instead, a corner of his lip twisted into a disgruntled smile.

Loan turned to look for my brother and me. She knelt down, beckoning us to walk into her outstretched arms.

"Look at you," she whispered to me, touching the bruises on my face. "What did you do? Get into a fight? I just leave you alone for one day, and you are already getting yourself into trouble? Listen to me, I won't be around anymore to take care of you. You have to take care of yourself and your brother. Help your mom with the baby when it comes, yes? And most importantly, don't forget me."

"I won't, Loan. I'll miss you," I told her.

"I know, sweet angel." She smiled. "I got you a present for your birthday. Something sensible for you to practice your skill before the baby arrives. Want to see?"

I nodded. She ran outside and returned in a moment holding a cardboard box in her hands. Then she lowered it to my eyes' level. There was no cover on top of it. Jimmy and I both looked inside and saw a puppy, huddled in a corner and looking up at us with large, black eyes. Its body was covered with short, brownish fur. It had droopy ears and a nose that was so wet on its short snout it shone like a brand-new button. Upon seeing us, the dog cried softly. I was so excited that I kissed Loan all over her face.

"Go ahead, touch her," Loan whispered. "She is yours, Kien."

I reached inside the box and touched the puppy. Its fur felt like velvet. Then I picked it up and held it close to my chest, feeling its heart beat wildly. The dog looked up to lick my nose; and that simple act created a bridge of trust between us. I looked down at the puppy's face, resting against the thin fabric of my pajamas, and a feeling of calm swept through me.

"She is two months old, Kien," Loan said. Her voice seemed far away, since all of my attention was devoted to the small creature I held in my hands. "I have good news and bad news for you," she continued. "The good news is that she is weaned from her mother, so you can feed her food, starting tomorrow. The bad news is that she has a slight birth defect. As you can see, her front paw is deformed. She can only walk on three legs. I picked her out for you because she needs a lot of attention, and that is going to be good practice for helping out with the baby, Kien. Think of a nice name for her, will you?"

Turning to my brother, she said, "I didn't forget about you, Jimmy. The puppy is partially yours, and you can help Kien take care of her. You are still too young to have one on your own. So for the time being, you have to learn how to share."

Jimmy nodded, his eyes fixed on the puppy.

Loan then asked my mother, "Madam, is it fine with you that the children keep the dog? I am sorry for not asking you first, but I do want to leave them something to remember me by before I go."

My mother nodded hesitantly. A thought flashed through my mind, and I told Loan, "I have a name for her, Loan. I want to call her Lulu."

"Lulu is a beautiful name," Loan said. "Where did it come from?"

"She looks like Lulu."

"The British singer?"

"Yes, I like her songs very much."

"Okay, Lulu it is. Maybe someday this dog will learn to howl *To*

Sir with Love for a living," Loan said, and everybody laughed except my mother.

That night, Lulu slept inside her box next to me, her body curved into a half circle, her nose hidden in between her paws. The next morning when I woke up, Loan was gone.

CHAPTER FOURTEEN

Every day at five in the morning, before any activity could begin, the adults in my neighborhood were required to come out of their homes and salute the flag, while a loud-speaker played the national anthem. Afterward, the Communists held meetings at different houses in the vicinity. The agenda at these gatherings usually involved the teachings of Karl Marx, or the reading of Communist poetry, or the examination of each individual's behavior toward Communism. Sometimes, instead of the usual "new-education" meetings, the town's citizens formed groups, walking from door to door to pick up trash until every street in town was clean. Today, it had been decided, would be the investigation day. And since she was the newest person in town, my mother was the target of a group discussion.

In front of a crowd full of sleepy faces, my mother was directed to speak about herself, not as a form of self-introduction, but in a confession of her past sins against the Communist party and the new government. Standing alone onstage with a microphone in her hand, my mother rushed through the major events of her life, trying to convey enough sincerity to keep herself out of trouble. She acknowledged her guilt and ignorance during the Republican era, and praised the enlightened attitudes she had since learned. Her Communist vocabulary had improved a great deal through her encounters with Mr. Tran, and she incorporated his words into her speech, maintaining her eye contact with everyone except Lam. He sat among a group of men, acting as inconspicuous as possible.

When my mother had finished, the community leader stepped up to the podium. Unlike Mr. Tran, who had earned his position through spying, the new leader was a high-ranking officer in the Vietcong's military. He was in his early fifties, with thin silver hair and a catchy smile. He had spent the past ten years of his life in the Truong Son Mountains, trekking the Ho Chi Minh trail. Rumors had it that he was now waiting to be reunited with his wife and children.

Taking the microphone in his hand, he said, "Thank you, Miss Khuon. What a story! Does anyone care to give any feedback? It is time for some constructive criticism, so without further ado, let's start. May I remind you that each time anyone among you makes a statement, he or she will earn a point toward community work."

A man stood up. My mother recognized him as one of her regular customers at her bank during her pre-Revolutionary days. A chill shot through her, since his appearance conjured up in her mind the hundreds of angry customers who had confronted her only a short time ago. As for the man, earning up to thirty points would exempt him from a day of volunteer work in the jungle; however, he also understood my mother's capacity to hurt him, through her knowledge of his past business affairs.

He cleared his throat and said, "It was a sincere story, told from the heart. But are you leaving out any details? I want to know more about your personal life. Do you have any children? And how many? Have you been married?"

The Communist leader looked at my mother, waiting for her reply.

"Well, to tell the truth," my mother began, mechanically touching her stomach through her blouse, "I have never been married. I have two sons, and a new child on the way."

"Tell us about your sons," a voice said. It belonged to a woman who lived in a farm a few blocks away from my house. She was the wife of the town butcher.

"What do you want to know about my sons?" my mother said. "They are still very young."

The butcher's wife stood, looking up and down at my mother. Then she blurted out, "I've been watching you since you moved into this neighborhood. I don't need you to tell me how old your children are. What I want to know is the nature of their ethnicity. Are they half-breeds or not? Because if they are, it is an issue to us."

"Yes, they are." My mother swallowed.

"Then how did you get these children — through a catalogue?"

"I got them the same way you got your children, through intercourse, of course." My mother's answer stirred up a round of laughter in the crowd.

The community leader warned my mother, "Behave yourself, lady. This isn't a nightclub."

The butcher's wife turned bright red but was not giving up. "Under the Imperialist government," she said fervently, "there are two possible ways for a person to have had mixed-blood children: through prostitution or through adoption. You have admitted earlier that fucking was how you got them, so you must be a hooker." She ended triumphantly, looking around the audience for affirmation.

My mother swallowed again. She knew at that moment she had to make up her mind about her past status before these strangers. They wanted to label her so that later, they could justify any action taken against her. What was the lesser of the two evils she could admit to — being a lowly prostitute or an arrogant capitalist? To the new regime, capitalism was considered the higher crime. Fifteen seconds dragged by before she could speak. Finally, with the crowd's full attention, my mother nodded in agreement. "Yes, I was," she said. "A prostitute is exactly what I was. And I am utterly ashamed of it."

"If you had any shame," the butcher's wife criticized, "you

wouldn't admit it in front of everybody. I think you would find a way to be rid of the bastards. In fact, you could very well get an abortion right now if you wanted to."

"Who are you?" the leader asked the woman. "Give me your name so I can give you a point."

From the stage, my mother spoke into the microphone as she pointed her finger into the crowd. "If you ask the man over there, you'll find out that he is responsible for the baby inside me. It was not from a foreigner's seed, and I was not getting paid sleeping with him. Can I then keep this bastard child?"

No one answered her; however, the crowd's attention turned to Lam.

"Come up here. Tell us your story," the leader said to Lam.

CHAPTER FIFTEEN

Whenmy mother returned home from the meeting, she was in a cranky mood. Lam looked as though someone had let the air out of his body. A disgusted look appeared on my mother's face when she saw Jimmy and me lying on the floor with the puppy.

"Get that filthy beast out of here," she told us. "It's got to learn to stay outside."

"It is too young to stay outside," my grandfather protested.

"I don't care. Take it out for a walk."

I took Lulu in my arms and, with my brother behind me, hurried away from my mother's sight. In the front yard, we walked back and forth, with Lulu hopping between our feet. A moment later, Tin, leading his brothers, stopped us.

"What in the devil's name is this?" my cousin asked, pointing at the puppy.

"She is a present from Loan," I told him. "Her name is Lulu."

"Let me see." He pushed me aside to pick her up. Lulu let out a yelp as his hands tightened around her midsection.

"Please don't hurt her. She can't walk very well," I begged, reaching under his fingers to take her back.

He held the dog high up in the air, out of my reach. His brothers laughed as I jumped up to try to get her. He turned around to face them, swinging her back and forth and laughing.

"Hey, Nhon and Hieu, run back and catch the crippled dog," he yelled out to them.

I screamed for my mother. My brother began to cry. I watched my dog dangling in his hands, fearing that my voice was not loud enough for my mother to hear. Suddenly, the front door flung open, and the stern voice of my grandfather roared behind me, "Tin, give Kien back his dog. Now!"

Tin froze in the middle of swinging Lulu. I ran to him and peeled her from his clutches. My aunt and uncle rushed out of their house. My mother also appeared, looking annoyed. My aunt looked at her son, then pushed her hands against her bony hips. A hand-rolled cigarette dangled at one corner of her lips.

"What in hell did you scream like a girl for?" my aunt said to me. "It is just a stupid dog. And you too, father. You don't have to yell at my sons to defend him. They are all your grandchildren; you don't always have to pick sides. If you don't want my children to play with your precious grandchild, just say so. But don't yell at them."

My mother walked toward me with a look so dark and severe it paralyzed me. She whacked my face with her open hand. Stars exploded into a thousand specks in my head. "It is about this dog again," she shrieked. "Why is it, Kien? Why can't you just get along with your cousins? Why do you have to make things so difficult for me?" She kept on yelling. "Don't you understand the stress that I am under; or do you ever consider that I might not be able to take it anymore?"

My grandfather shouted at my mother, "Don't hit him! It is not his fault. He was just playing with his brother. Don't take your anger out on your son. Let him be."

My mother walked toward my cousin and touched his head gently. "Don't mind Grandpa," she told him. "He is old, and he doesn't mean to yell at you, okay? And forgive your cousins. They are just bastard children. And maybe you don't believe this, but trust me, these weaklings can't possibly harm you or your family, so you can stop hating them."

My aunt pulled her son away from my mother's caress. She pushed him toward her house, threw my mother another sneer, then disappeared after him.

My mother turned to face me. "Don't you dare cause another scene today," was all she said to me before she went back inside.

I sat down on the ground, hugging my dog, and instantly forgot the awful pain my mother's hand had left on my face. Jimmy knelt on the ground, watching me with concern. A tear still remained in his eyes, but he was already laughing. Lulu lifted her little snout. Her tongue found the red mark on my cheek and licked it. On the front steps, my grandfather shook his head. He sat down on the stoop, watching us through the rest of the morning.

That afternoon, after waking up from a nap, I couldn't find Lulu. I jumped up from my bed, expecting to find her with my brother. Instead, I found him alone sleeping on his bed. I searched every corner in the room, but she was nowhere in sight. My mother stood at the door, looking at me calmly. My frantic search seemed to annoy her, because after a few minutes, she said quietly to me, "If you are looking for that dog of yours, you can stop now. I gave it away."

I searched her face for an explanation. "What do you mean?" Then I understood and I stammered, "Why, Mommy? I was good. I didn't get into any more trouble. Why would you do something like that? Who did you give my dog to?"

She did not answer me, but someone else did. From outside, I could hear a faint yet familiar cry — the sound of my dog. I ran to the window and saw my cousins playing in their garden. Tin grabbed the back of Lulu's neck in his hand. Her paws were dangling in the air.

"No," I screamed. Tears flowed from my eyes. My chest felt so tight that I could barely breathe.

Tin looked up to grin at me. He pulled the dog up close to his face, ignoring her yelps as he called out, "Watch me, half-breed. This dog is mine."

My knees were weak as I turned to my mother, "Please, Mommy. Get her back. Please. I beg you. I'll do anything you want, just get her back."

"Get away from the window. She doesn't belong to you anymore," my mother said.

I heard my aunt's sour voice raised to her children. "I don't understand you boys. Why did you insist on getting that lame mutt? It doesn't even walk straight."

Tin answered his mother, "We are using it for football, Mother."

From the window, I could hear his every word, cutting through me like a sharp knife.

"Get rid of it." His mother laughed.

I screamed out with fright. Looking at my mother as my last hope, I cried, "No, don't let them kill her, Mommy."

"Shut up," she shouted at me. "You have lost so much more than that, but I never saw you drop a tear. Why do you cry now? And for what, a stupid dog? Get away from the window and toughen up." She turned her back to me.

Outside, Tin threw my Lulu into the air. Her little body flew upward. Before she could land on the ground, he aimed a kick at her side that tossed her across the garden toward one of his brothers. The puppy did not make any noise. His punt knocked the air from her lungs with a hollow sound. A trail of her vomit flew through the air like splashes of white paint.

I ran out the door, pushing past my mother, no longer caring about anything but my dog. My mother grasped me by my upper arm, pulling me back. "Stop!" she screamed, and began to cry.

My grandparents appeared by the entrance of their room.

"Look what you've done," my grandfather said. "Why are you destroying him?"

"Daddy, you stay out of this." My mother wiped her eyes with the back of her hands, sniffing loudly. "You are wrong, I am not destroying him. I am teaching him to be a man. There is a difference in how we view things, so please, leave us alone."

From outside, the sound of Lulu's body being kicked back and forth became duller and further away, until it disintegrated among the laughter of my cousins. I fell on the floor, exhausted.

Long after everybody had left the room, I still lay on the floor. My mind was clear of all thoughts, except for an image of a green field, with nobody, no scent, and certainly no sound. I envisioned myself running barefoot on the soft bed of grass, feeling the sun's warm touch all over me. It was Jimmy who snapped me back to reality.

"Kien, get up. Mommy wants you," he said with concern. "It's time for dinner."

I remained quiet for a while, feeling the grass withdraw from under me until there was nothing left but a hard floor. Jimmy tugged at me to get up, offering a helpful hand. My thoughts returned to Lulu, to her wet nose, her warm breath, and her soft tongue each time she licked my face. Tears flooded my eyes, and the anger coursed though me once again, making me straighten up. Reaching for a lantern on the nearby table, I walked outside and into the garden.

My brother ran beside me, pulling at my arm. "Kien, where are you going? Come back. Mommy is going to get mad again."

"Leave me alone, Jimmy. I don't care anymore." I told him.

"What are you doing? Where are you going?"

"Looking for my dog," I answered.

"She is dead, Kien. I saw Tin throw her body in the trash."

I turned around and clutched his shoulders. "Where? What trash?" I demanded.

He pointed at a place out in the garden, a dark corner filled with dead leaves that my uncle reserved to fertilize his garden. Above it grew a large guava tree, with black and torturous branches reaching out against the sky. The vine behind the tree had grown into a thick web of greenery that allowed no light to penetrate. In the dark, the tree had become a monster in disguise, with clawed hands and webbed feet, guarding the ground. Fear did not prevent me from venturing closer. Behind me, my brother jumped as my mother's voice called out to us from inside the house.

"Jimmy, get inside, please," I told him. "Don't get in trouble because of me."

"I can't go back alone," he said. "I am staying here with you."

"She will beat you if you don't listen to me."

Jimmy bit his lower lip but somehow decided to stay with me. I walked further into the garden. From where we stood, I could see my mother's silhouette against the window frame. She made no attempt to get us back inside.

CHAPTER SIXTEEN

The night was cool. My uncle had watered the garden, and the dampness from the ground saturated the air. From between the branches, the sound of a bird's wing fluttering in its sleep tickled the night. To Jimmy and me, the sound became the panting of some vicious monster, lurking behind the bushes. We walked forward in the dark, holding each other's hand. The lantern burned weakly in front of me, showing just a few feet of ground. I could hear the sound of my cousins quarreling at their dinner table, and their mother trying to quiet them.

When we came to the heap of dead leaves, I searched for my dog's remains while my brother stood next to me, holding the lantern in both hands. It did not take me long to find Lulu, half-buried under the leaves. In the flickering light, I saw her lying on her side with her mouth open. Even in death, she had a look of surprise on her face. One of her eyes was smashed cruelly into her head, darkened with blood. Blood also was visible from other orifices, running down her body like black paint. Her deformed paw was pulled across her snout, as though she had tried to protect herself from the assault. The rest of Lulu was wet with some unexplained fluid, possibly her urine, or her vomit, or even the water my uncle had sprayed on his garden.

I picked her up with both hands, ignoring the slime my fingers came in contact with. Death had kissed her long and hard with its frozen lips, and her body was stiff. I held her in my arms, hoping the warmth of my body could bring her back to life. Ignoring my brother's presence, I wept uncontrollably. With Lulu in my arms, I walked toward the front lawn. I had chosen a burial site for Lulu — a strip of land under the cherry tree overlooking the street.

My brother followed me without speaking. As soon as I picked up a small shovel to dig into the soft earth, he took a spade and began to help me. An unexpected noise behind a bush startled us both.

"Who is it?" I shrieked out in fright.

From behind the wall that separated our property from the one next door emerged a boy about my age, hiding his hands in his pockets. In the dark, I could see the outline of his face, directing a curious glance in our direction.

"Nobody." He stepped out into the light, and I could see him. Most of his face was hidden under the long strands of black hair. An extra-large T-shirt wrapped around his thin body and extended down to his knees like a muumuu. He was barefoot. Cocking his head to one side, the boy asked, "What are you two doing?"

"Burying Kien's dog," my brother answered.

"Really? Can I help?"

Jimmy looked at me, and I nodded my approval to the boy. He was the only friendly person I had encountered in a long time, and the urge for a friendship prompted me to want to accept him.

"Let's go open the gate," I told my brother.

The boy waved his hands to decline my offer and said, "No need to, I'll just climb over the wall." He continued matter-of-factly, "I did this a million times before your family moved here, usually to steal your uncle's guavas."

He proceeded to scale the tall wall like a monkey. He leaped over the barbed wires on top, dangling in the air for a moment before jumping to the ground on my side.

"How do you know that man is my uncle?" I asked him as he got up, brushing the grass from his clothes.

"Everybody knows everything around here. Besides, I have been watching. I saw those bastards kill your dog."

Tears once again threatened to blur my vision. I made no comment to his remark and resumed my digging. The boy took the small shovel from my brother's hand and began to scoop aside the grass. His digging, much like his wall climbing, was a lot faster than mine. I could feel his intense gaze silently studying the two of us. His almond-shaped eyes, like two black holes dotted with fire, sparkled on his face.

"What's your name?" I asked him.

"I am called Duy. You are Kien, correct? I heard Miss San call your name earlier in school. I don't know if you remember seeing me there, but we are in the same class. I sat by the window. Nice poem, by the way." Again, I made no comment, and he continued, "Anyhow, nice to meet you."

"Likewise. This is Jimmy, my brother." Jimmy looked up with a grin.

Duy leaned closer to me and whispered, "For a son of a capitalist, you sure know a lot about the Communists. Where did you learn the teachings of Chairman Ho? Wait! Don't tell me! I don't want to know." He paused, then switched to a more sympathetic tone. "Don't feel bad about your cousins. They are a bunch of jerks. Nobody around here likes your aunt's family either. My dad says that they're definitely low-class minions. Someday, me and my brothers will find a chance to kick their asses. You are different than them, which I like. If you want to, you and your brother can come over to my house sometimes. I have a dog. He really is a lot of fun, you'll see once you play with him."

"What's the name of your dog?" my brother asked.

"Goofy."

"Goofy?" my brother repeated, laughing. "That's a funny name."

"Funny name for a funny dog," Duy replied.

By now, the hole we were digging was deep enough to fit Lulu in. I put the shovel aside and sat on the ground beside her. Taking my time, I touched her one last time before I set her into the soft earth. We watched in silence as the dirt began to cover her little body, bit by bit, until she was out of sight. Duy laid back the grass to cover the ground above her grave.

"Thank you very much," I muttered to him.

Duy shifted on his feet. "I should get going. It's almost curfew time."

"Don't you want to get some guava before you go?" I asked him.

"No, not tonight. Someone is watching us. Got to go. Good night, and see you in school tomorrow. Ah, Kien, now that you know I am in your class, for heaven's sake, please hang out with me instead of spending all day around the schoolyard by yourself, will you?" He rushed through his sentences, and before I had a chance to reply, he leaped over the wall and vanished into the night.

As Jimmy and I neared the back door to our house, a thin whistle, coming from the foot of my uncle's house, stopped us in our tracks. A shadow by a column waved, beckoning me closer. I recognized the petite frame of my aunt's eldest daughter, Moonlight. My earlier experience with her brothers prompted me to walk away, but my curiosity overcame that impulse. I turned to my brother.

"Go inside, Jimmy. I'll be right back," I ordered him. Before he could protest, I pushed him through the back door and ran over to meet Moonlight. She sat on her buttocks, with her legs folded against her chest so that her chin could rest on her knees. The light from the window barely kept her thin body from blending into the surrounding blackness. She coughed slightly, using her hands to cover her mouth in a polite manner.

I walked in front of her. "What do you want?" I asked as aggressively as I could.

"Nothing," she said. Her lips trembled as she spoke to me. "I have been watching you, Kien. I saw you bury your dog. You must feel terrible about what has happened. I want to apologize for my brothers. They were very mean to you earlier this afternoon, weren't they?"

I didn't know how to answer her. She patted the ground beside her and said, "Sit down."

I did what I was told.

"Do you know my name, Kien?" she asked.

I nodded. "Anh Nguyet."

"Yes. But do you know how to say it in English?" she asked.

I shook my head and she smiled. Her hand stroked my head. "Moonlight. Doesn't that sound pretty?"

"Yes, very pretty," I agreed.

"I want you to call me Moonlight from now on, the way my friends used to back in college," she said. Her hands returned to cover her lower face, muffling her mouth so that she spoke as though she had a mouth full of food. "I saw a boy with you earlier. Where is he?"

"He went home," I replied.

"Did he tell you why he didn't steal any guava today?"

I shook my head. "He said someone was watching him. He might have meant you, cousin."

"Moonlight," she corrected me.

"Moonlight," I repeated.

"Did he mention anything about his brothers to you?"

I decided to be straight with her. "He said that someday his brothers will beat your brothers up, because everybody thinks your brothers are a bunch of bullies."

Moonlight laughed and again ruffled my hair. "No kidding, he said that to you? I doubt that would ever happen, though. We have been neighbors for many years, but I never saw those boys start a fight."

"Why not?" I asked.

"Because . . . Oh, forget it! You are too young to understand." The grown-up emphasis in her voice dismissed me.

"Try me. I understand lots of things," I said proudly.

"Oh, yeah? Maybe you can understand, but can you keep a secret?" she asked.

I nodded and waited impatiently.

"Be careful," Moonlight warned me. "If you speak to anyone of what I am about to tell you, my brothers will come looking for you. And I promise you, you will be reunited with Lulu soon after."

"Moonlight, I won't tell anyone, I promise. Not even Jimmy," I answered her.

"All right then, here it goes," she began. "This story involves that little boy's big brother and me. We have known each other for a long time. His name is Ty Tong." Her head tilted to rest against her knees, and her arms wrapped themselves intimately around her ankles. She looked up to the clear sky and went on in a whisper. "We grew up together, Ty and I, and seven years ago, he began to court me. It's a secret. My family must not know about this, do you understand?"

"Why not? They don't like for you to date him?" I asked her.

"No, but it is a little more complicated than that," she said. "Before the fall of Saigon, his family didn't want him to marry me because they were rich and we were poor. Ty Tong is also their first born, so they thought he should get for himself a strong and fertile wife. I am sick with tuberculosis, so that is another reason for his parents to be against the relationship. Now, after the Communists took away everything they had, it was my family's turn to look down on his family." She stopped, losing herself in her thoughts.

"Can anything be done?" I asked.

"I don't know. The fact is, his father held a very high rank in the Republican military. Everyone thinks they have bad résumés, like you people. My dad doesn't want me to get involved with a guilty party like him. It is bad enough that the whole town knows we are related to your family. So, it is understandable that I am now forbidden to see him," she said, rubbing her face against the silky fabric of her pants.

"What is wrong with my family?" I asked her.

"Nothing," Moonlight replied immediately, then added, "except that you remind everyone of the past. The odd appearances of you and your brother, and the way your mother has made her money through her association with the foreigners. Everyone in your family is a capitalist."

"Your father, too, has fought in the Republican Army," I argued.

"True, but the government knows that he was just a low-rank enlistee, working in an office. He never killed anyone in battle. It's not the same. Compared to most people in this town, we belong to what is called the lowest working class in the south."

She looked at me through her eyelashes. "Listen, I don't make up these rules, so don't waste your time arguing with me. Besides, why should we fight? If the situation were reversed, you would treat us the same way. That's life, Kien. Let's be friends, because I want you to help me."

"Help you? How?"

"You know Duy Tong. If you hang out with him, you can meet his brother easily. You can give Ty my messages, yes? If I could ask any of my brothers or sisters to help me, I wouldn't trouble myself to ask you. But I know they would refuse."

"What message?" I asked with a pang of nervousness.

"Right at this moment, I am not sure. Maybe some notes, or some presents, that sort of things. I don't know yet, but when I do, will you deliver them for me?"

She looked at me with hope in her eyes. There was also something else I detected on her face — a sense of helplessness. I found myself promising her what she needed to hear.

"Good." She reached out to hug me, and her long black hair fell over my face. "Thank you. You are my sweet little blue bird. I will do my best to keep my nasty brothers away from you and Jimmy."

I watched her disappear behind the heavy doors before I returned to my house. On the floor, next to a lantern was a small portion of food my grandmother had left for me. My mother had locked herself in her room; however, she was not asleep. I could hear her sniffing from behind the shut door as though she had a bad cold. Jimmy lay on his bed staring at me. I climbed under my covers, ignoring the dinner on the floor. Before long, I was asleep.

CHAPTER SEVENTEEN

That summer of 1975 brought more rain than the land could absorb. Swampy water accumulated all over the city, creating fertile breeding conditions for insects that spread diseases at a rapid rate. Malaria, dysentery, and tuberculosis were rife. In an attempt to contain the problem, the Communist government assembled a health-care system in which everybody was trained to take care of himself or herself. Three times a week, a group of nurses would set up a table outside the community center to dispense a dose of quinine for everyone as a safeguard against malaria. Fortunately, my village had yet to be touched by any of the plagues.

August strolled by sluggishly as the town adjusted to its reconstruction. One day my aunt's husband came rushing into our house. For his past errors, he had spent a week at a concentration camp. Luckily, the government exempted my grandfather from the same hardship because of his disability. The day my uncle was released, he came to warn my mother of the news he had learned in the camp.

All over the city, the Communists had adopted a new strategy to break down capitalism, starting with the rich communities up in Chinatown and spreading to the outlying villages. It was a simple plan. Each day, the community leaders would pick out a target area at random. They ransacked every house in that sector, paying special attention to the once rich and famous. The object was mainly to find hidden treasure or evidence that linked the people to their sinful past. As the government agents probed through the owner's belongings, members of the household were pushed into a corner. Anything with monetary value would either be confiscated or destroyed immediately. If they found proof of the owner's involvement with an unacceptable past, depending on the degree of guilt, the person would either be taken away to a death camp or held for trial. Even the children did not escape the military's search, since many cunning parents had learned to hide their treasure in or on their offspring.

With my cousins' aid, my mother went through her belongings and separated the memorabilia that was related to her past life, particularly items linked to my father or Jimmy's father. She put them all in a shoebox, together with half of her jewelry. The other half of the jewelry still remained hidden inside my trousers. As night fell, my mother went out alone to the front lawn and buried the box.

Next door, Duy's family was not as fortunate. The Communists ripped his home apart. They left with his father handcuffed in the back of a military truck. Duy's mother ran after her husband, wailing like a wounded animal as the vehicle drove off along the dusty road spitting a dark fume of smoke at her face.

My cousin Moonlight came up behind me as I was standing next to my grandmother on the front lawn, watching the chaos next door.

"Listen, Kien," she whispered in my ear, pointing at Ty Tong. "Please, will you give him this note for me?" She stuffed a small piece of paper into my hand.

"Now? During all this?" I asked, unsure whether I had understood her correctly.

"Yes, now," she repeated. Before her parents could notice anything, Moonlight straightened up and stepped away from me.

I walked next door, searching for Ty among his family. He stood tall next to his mother, with his arm wrapped around her waist to keep her from fainting. Mrs. Tong cried on her son's shoulder, ignoring the bystanders' curious stares. Duy's brother appeared proud and mature, considering the devastation of the situation. He did not notice me as I crept closer to him. Duy, on the other hand, stopped crying to look at me with surprise.

"Sorry, Duy," I muttered to him.

Duy did not answer me. I stood among his distraught brothers, feeling out of place as they gathered themselves up to go back inside their house. When Ty went past me, I nudged Moonlight's note into his hand. Before he had a chance to walk away from me, I said in his ear, "This is from Moonlight."

He thanked me and I ran back home. In the front yard, Moonlight smiled and winked at me.

After waiting for the Communists a few weeks, my mother realized that since the loss of her mansion, the new government no longer considered us a serious threat. Relieved, she went to retrieve her hidden possessions from the ground. To her dismay, the entire box had disappeared. After five hours of turning the lawn upside down, she concluded that the box must have drifted to sea due to the water current below the ground. Such occurrences were common when people buried things too deep in the soil.

In the last few months of my mother's pregnancy, the stress was heavy for all of us. With nobody in my family working, she was forced to live off her jewelry. Her term also did not go as smoothly as she had hoped. More than twice in the last month, she experienced complications. The last bout of bleeding came with severe cramping, which led her to believe that the baby was coming prematurely. In her panic, she rushed to the hospital, where the incident proved to be a false alarm. She particularly regretted the waste of money, which she could ill afford.

At about this time, the town leader summoned Lam for fifteen days of community service, which would entail hard labor in a jungle fifty kilometers from town. Lam refused to go. To keep us from getting into trouble, my mother hired one of my cousins to replace him. The whole matter might have passed without anyone's notice. However, that unlucky day, the town leader accidentally discovered the crafty substitution when he was looking to nominate Lam as the group's guide. He found my cousin Le instead of Lam.

Even though Lam survived the incident with no significant trouble, the conflict between my family and Mr. Qui Ba, the town leader, took a new turn. To the commander, my mother's ability to hire a stand-in raised the possibility that my family was still withholding some fortune from the government. The situation pushed my mother and Lam further apart, so that now they hardly spoke a word to each other. Someone in town observed to her that they no longer appeared to be a couple at all.

With every new day, my mother grew more restless and disturbed. The incessant rain and the tension of her advancing pregnancy erased any tolerance she had for petty irritations.

One evening at dinnertime, we sat together on the floor eating some salty fish with rice, prepared by my grandmother. Since Loan left, my grandmother had taken over the household chores of cooking, cleaning, and doing the laundry. If her arthritis had allowed, my grandmother could have been a good cook. But mostly, like that night, we were stuck with white rice and dried fish for dinner.

Lam spoke up to my mother, who sat on the opposite side of him and was eating calmly. "Look at me," he said.

My mother continued to eat her food as if nothing happened. Jimmy, on the other hand, jumped up with fear, looking at both of them. I held on to my brother's hands, knowing that he was on the verge of tears.

My mother's silence enraged Lam even more, and he yelled louder, "Why don't you look at me?" He slammed his fist to the floor. "I am not going to take this abuse any longer." Again, my mother's only response was an exaggerated detachment.

"Don't toy with me, dirty whore." In his vehemence, the insult came out as a hoarse cry. He threw his half-eaten bowl of rice at my mother and marched outside to light a cigarette. Specks of rice spilled onto my mother's long hair and on her face, but she made no attempt to brush them off. Next to me, Jimmy began to cry.

Sometime that night, Lam crept into my bed. Lying asleep on my stomach, I was not fully aware of his presence until my body was crushed by his weight. His hands covered my mouth, preventing me from making a sound. I woke up groggily, not understanding what was happening.

His voice whispered next to my ear, "Scream, and I will break your neck."

At first, I was sure I was having a bad dream, and I struggled to wake up. Lam brought me back to reality by tightening his grip on my face. I struggled for air, but I was not strong enough to break away from his grasp, and I felt myself suffocating. Surely, I was going to die.

"Please," I screamed in my head. I felt my brain swell like a balloon that was ready to explode. I wondered if Lulu had felt a terror of this sort before she died. Weakened, I stopped fighting. As soon as I ceased to move, Lam released his fingers to allow some air to rush back into my lungs. Eagerly, I sucked in life, choking on my own phlegm.

"Listen to me and listen good, little muck," he said in a hushed tone. "Someday when you grow up, if you ever have to blame this on anyone, blame it on your mother. She started this war first, the moment she destroyed my unborn child." His voice was nearby, but it sounded far away. Nevertheless, I understood what he said, as it seeped into my soul like ink.

Outside, the night had deepened, with the moon beaming through the window. Its light drenched everything in the room, including the thick, clawlike fingers around my neck. Lam peeled the bottom of my pajama off, taking off his own clothes with one hand, while continuing to hold me with the other. I was scared and humiliated yet did not understand what Lam was about to do. In my confusion and panic, I felt paralyzed. Suddenly, a deep pain soared through my body in waves, while Lam grunted and rocked on top of me. I wanted to scream but could not. My will to cry was gone and all that was left in me was an emptiness that grew bigger and colder with every minute.

Before he climbed off my body, Lam waved his fist in my face. "Keep this between you and me, boy, and maybe I will be more gentle next time. And if you are stupid enough to tell your mother about this, I will go after your brother next."

He did not need to warn me about keeping my mouth shut. The shame and isolation I felt were not feelings I wanted to share with anyone. I lay with my head buried in the pillows, listening to his footsteps as he left, and trying hard to block out the humiliation that was eroding my soul.

Long after he left, I remained naked and motionless on my bed. My mind was empty. I retreated into a white cocoon, just like death, cold and vacant, and at that moment it was the only comfort I could find.

THE NEXT DAY I stayed in bed late with the sheet over my head. When it was time for breakfast, my mother came in to look for me. She found me shaking silently under the bedspread. Worried, she pulled the covers off to examine me. I stared past her face into the space beyond the ceiling.

Grasping me in one of her hands, she slapped me with the other and screamed, "Kien, get up." When I remained unresponsive, her panic increased. "What is going on? Talk to me. What is happening to you? Oh, God, where is the blood coming from?"

Her hysteria pulled me back into the room, where everybody was staring at me with curiosity. Sprawled across his bed, Lam watched me. His dark look jerked me out of my stupor.

"I'm — I'm fine, Mommy," I stammered. "I am just a little tired."

"Where does this blood come from? Where are you bleeding, Kien?" she asked, touching the dried stain on my bedspread.

"He is fine," Lam interrupted. "Just leave him alone." His eyes never left my face as he spoke to her. "Early this morning, his nose bled a little bit. I helped him take care of it already. Right, Kien?"

I nodded. My mother, however, was not convinced. She frowned with skepticism.

"Nosebleed?" she asked. "Impossible, he never had a nosebleed before. Are you sure?"

"Of course I am sure," he assured her. "Leave the boy alone to rest. If his condition doesn't get better, we'll take him to the hospital, okay?"

His words seemed to calm my mother, and she laid me back down on my pillows. He took her by her shoulder and led her outside.

Soon after, Lam returned, pulling the sheet off me. "Get up, and out of bed," he said. "You have to convince your mother that you are not sick. Otherwise, she'll find out what a little tramp you were last night, and then I won't be about to cover for you anymore." He pushed me out of my bedroom and into the front lawn.

For several minutes, I sat on the front steps, holding on to my belly. The pain inside me was excruciating. I could also feel the blood oozing into my underwear, and its odor nauseated me. From the other side of the wall, Duy waved, beckoning me to come over. Gathering myself, I played with him and Goofy for the rest of the day and did not return home until dinner.

That night, my mother came to tuck me in. Her soft hand rested on my forehead, checking my temperature. In his bed, Lam watched us through his half-shut eyes. His presence made me anxious.

"How are you feeling, Kien?" she asked me.

"Fine," I answered her.

"Are you sure? You don't look fine to me." There was a moment of silence before she went on in a voice filled with worry. "Tell me what's wrong. It has been several weeks, you can't possibly still be upset about Lulu."

Instead of answering her, I closed my eyes, pretending to fall asleep.

"Listen," she said, "this is very hard for me to do, but I promise to get you another dog tomorrow if you promise to get well."

I opened my eyes. Under the dim light, my mother's face sagged with new creases. There were tears in her eyes. I shook my head at her suggestion.

"You don't want another dog?" she asked.

"No."

"Tell me what you want then. The butcher's dog just had a litter. I already told him to reserve a puppy for you. What am I going to do with the puppy if you don't want it?"

"Give it to Jimmy," I suggested to her, and added, "Mommy, I don't want another dog."

"Okay, if you are sure. But please be well. I need you."

My mother kissed me good night and turned off the lantern on her way out. Once she left the room, I became paralyzed with fear. In the dark, I anticipated Lam's approach with every fiber in my body. At last, his snoring sawed into the silent room, and then I heard him mumble something unintelligible in his dream.

I crawled out of bed, holding a pillow in my hands. Quietly, I tip-toed out of the room and into the garden.

Outside, dark clouds hung low above the trees, warning of the coming rain. Trees transformed into monsters, chanting in eerie rhapsody. Again, to my active imagination, everything in the garden materialized into weird forms around me. Even so, it was a much less threatening place than my bedroom.

I lay down on my back near the house. About ten feet above me, a corrugated scaffold concealed most of my view of the sky. A short distance away, Lulu's grave lay hidden in the ground. Her presence somewhat softened my anxiety, and I began to relax. Sleep came quickly, but not for long. From the depth of my subconscious, I recalled Lam's threats: "Hey, Kien," his voice echoed, "I will go after your brother next. I will go after your brother next. I will go after…"

I jolted from the cold ground and ran back inside. Drawing a deep breath, I sneaked past Lam's bed in my bare feet. Deep in his own dream, my brother was not aware of my presence until I was next to him. I shook him awake, keeping him from making any noises with the palm of my hand. Jimmy opened his big eyes to stare at me.

"Get up, and come with me," I whispered in his ear.

"Kien?" his eyes blinked, but he did not yell. Matching my whisper, he asked me, "Where are we going?"

"Don't ask any questions. Just take your pillow and follow me."

I helped him out of bed and guided him outside to the front porch. Jimmy did not ask any more questions, only looked at me with his trusting eyes. I told him to lie down on the pavement, and I lay next to him, holding him in my arms to shield him from the cold air as much as I could. We fell asleep holding on to each other as the rain began to fall. The scaffold kept the raindrops from reaching us through most of the night.

The next morning, my mother was furious to discover that we were not in our beds. She yelled into our faces, jolting us from our sleep.

"Wake up. Why are you sleeping in the rain?"

We jumped up, not knowing what to say.

"Oh, kids," she moaned. "Why are you such a problem for me? Tell me what I have done to deserve this? And you," she turned to me, "don't you remember anything I told you last night?"

Behind her were my grandparents, holding on to the door and looking at us with worry. On the floor, Jimmy sneezed. His face was covered in sweat and reddened with fever.

"Look what you have done," my mother cried. "Your brother is getting sick." She picked him up in her arms and snarled to me, "Get inside. I am going to kill both of you."

She put Jimmy in bed and shifted her attention to me. "Was it your idea taking your brother outside last night?" she asked.

Fearfully, I nodded.

"I knew it," she shrieked. "Are you crazy, or are you rebelling against me?" She grabbed my shoulders. Her fingernails found their familiar way into my flesh.

"I am sorry," I cried out in pain. "I got scared last night."

"Why? What are you afraid of?"

"I don't know, Mommy."

"Stop! He is just a child, for God's sake," my grandfather broke in. "Haven't your children gone through enough already? Give them some time to adjust to the new situation, please. The child must have a reason why he got so scared. Why don't you find out from him instead of beating him up like he was your enemy?"

"He is spoiled, Daddy," she barked. "He is making the other one sick, and I can't even imagine what other stunts he is going to pull next. What am I supposed to do?"

"Stop yelling," my grandfather said. "Something must be terribly wrong for my grandchildren to leave their warm beds in the middle of the night and sleep on the cold dirt outside. Let me ask him." Turning to me, he lowered his voice to almost inaudible. "Kien, tell Grandpa why you didn't stay in your bed last night. Why did you sleep outside like the homeless people? What are you running away from?"

I did not answer him. Strength ebbed from my body, leaving my face hot with dizziness. I leaned against the wall for support.

My grandfather sighed with frustration. Turning to my mother, he spoke with unusual vigor.

"This is a new plan," he said. "From now on, Kien is going to sleep with me, and Jimmy is staying with Grandma for a while. Would this make you feel better, my boy?"

I nodded. Satisfied, my grandfather retreated back into his bedroom. From his bed, Lam sucked his teeth noisily and stepped outside. My mother muttered with annoyance, "I hope you are not spoiling them, Father." She then also went out, pounding her feet on the ground with frustration.

At the front door, the butcher appeared with a small puppy, resting peacefully in the palms of his hands. No one paid any attention to him, except for my brother. He got up from his bed, reaching out to receive the dog from the butcher's hands with a small cry of happiness.

My grandfather kept his promise. Night after night, he rocked me to sleep in his arms, trying his best to keep my nightmares away. At the same time, in the next room, Jimmy shared his bed with my grandmother.

MY MOTHER WENT INTO LABOR in September, two weeks early. In a dirty room of the hospital, next to the venereal disease section, she gave birth to my sister. The moment that she was pushed into the world, she began crying nonstop, as if she were constantly in pain. My mother called her BeTi, meaning "little girl" — a name that reflected my mother's indifference to her.

A few days later, Lam came in for a visit. BeTi was feeding at my mother's breast. Without touching either of them, he leaned over to stare at his daughter. My mother avoided looking at him. In her tired voice, she asked, "What is on your mind, Lam?"

He whispered to her, "I don't want to be here anymore. I am getting myself out of this mess." Then, without waiting for her answer, he continued, "Let's face it, we are making each other sick by staying together. To make it easy for you, I came up with a plan to help you get rid of me."

"What can you possibly be thinking?" she asked.

"I have a connection." The tip of his nose almost touched my mother's face, and he said, "I need some money. Help me escape."

1978

CHAPTER EIGHTEEN
Nhatrang, 1978

For the next three years my family continued to live in the house next to my aunt and her family. My mother was busy caring for our baby sister, BeTi, and our only income came from selling her jewelry. We wore the same clothing that we had brought with us from the Nguyen mansion. For many years, Jimmy and I never outgrew these outfits because my mother kept adding length to the hems and width to the waistbands in order to accommodate us. We had two meals a day; the mainstay of our diet was rice, which my mother bought from the market at eight dong per bushel. Rain or shine, we concentrated on surviving from day to day.

As I grew older, my hair got darker. I do not know if it happened because of my mother's wish when she poured liquid dye all over my head or simply because of my own urgent desire to fit in with the other children in our community. By the time I was eleven, my blond hair had become a rich brown. Even on the hottest day of summer, the sun could not bleach it back to its original silvery hue.

Jimmy and I attended the local elementary school, where our studies focused on math, literature, history, and science. All were taught from the Communist point of view. Miss San, who continued to teach my class, decided to hold a free tutorial session at her home every Sunday afternoon. Those were the only lectures in my experience that were not delivered with any political overtone.

Miss San lived in a two-story dwelling several blocks away from my street. She used her first floor as a fish-sauce factory, and three enormous earthenware jars were constantly at work there. Each container could hold two to three hundred pounds of fish, marinating in an equal amount of salt. She explained to us that making fish sauce was her main source of income. Teaching was just a recreational activity. The rancid smell of rotten fish was deadly, like the stench of tooth decay, only stronger. The odor permanently clung to her clothes, seeped into her hair, and like a miasma, spread to her surroundings. The adults, especially men, avoided her. They feared her eccentric nature. Children, however, were drawn to her warm personality, and no one found her more magnetic than I did.

As each Sunday afternoon approached, we eagerly wondered what surprise she had in store for us this week. Sitting on the floor in her rumpled bedroom among her scattered clothes, we waited for her appearance like the audience of a performing artist. One of Miss San's favorite subjects was English. "The only way for us to grow as a nation is to learn from other countries' technologies," she often told us. "How can you learn their technologies? You can start by learning the universal language — English."

She winked at us with a mischievous smile. "Today, let's not learn from the textbook. Instead, let's test our vocabularies, shall we? For the next hour, all of us must speak in English. I know this is a very difficult game, but we can try. Let's have some fun together."

We were trembling with excitement. Abandoning our language in a large group discussion such as this one was a forbidden act, yet it seemed so natural and harmless to us in that moment. As if she sensed our uncertainty, Miss San continued, "Let's keep this our own little secret, children."

She switched to English and the lesson began. "Duy went out last night," she said, and I saw my friend sit up a little straighter. Pointing at a small girl in a ponytail, Miss San ordered, "Chi, please finish that thought."

Chi pondered a few seconds and then said carefully, "Duy went out with a girl last night."

There were some giggles among the students. The image of Duy with a girl was funny in any language. Miss San turned to me. "Kien, please?" she asked.

"Who was that girl?" I formed a sentence quickly.

"Yes, that is a good question," she said. "Tell us who that girl was, Duy."

Duy stood up. Scratching his ears, he stuttered, searching the room for help. Someone whispered an answer, and he seized it as though he were drowning. "That girl was — was — was — my — mother," he shouted. His voice cracked from the excitement. We fell into each other's arms with laughter. Leaning against the wall, Miss San, too, was smiling. In the shadow of the room, I thought she was quite a beautiful lady, almost like a vision.

That day, after dismissing the class, Miss San asked me to stay behind. "Do you think these curls would be gone completely if you, let's say, cut your hair really short?" She ran her fingers over my head thoughtfully. Something about the way she posed her question made me sit up with apprehension.

"I don't know," I replied. "Why do you ask?"

"The school is planning to celebrate the unification of Vietnam. The dean has chosen our class to lead the parade because of our academic achievement. You are my best student, and I have decided that you will be the front-runner of the march, holding the national flag in your arms." She paused. "There is one small problem, though. I fear that your appearance may cause some distraction among the spectators."

"I can get a haircut tomorrow if you think it would help."

She nodded. "Yes, love, I think it's a wise decision. Do it and the honor will be yours." A cloud darkened her face. "Kien, please do a good job. We won't be together for much longer. School will be closed for summer the day after the parade. You will be in junior high next semester and I won't see you much anymore."

"I'll visit you often."

"We'll see. It's difficult to plan for the future. I may or may not still be here," she said sadly.

"Of course you will be here, helping other students," I said. "Where else could you go? You belong in a classroom, Miss San."

She bit her lower lip and turned away. Outside, my classmates' laughter echoed through the sultry air as they raced each other to the juice stand at the end of the road. Miss San searched her bedroom and located her fake leather bag. She rummaged through it for several seconds and then looked up, brushing a heavy lock of curled hair away from her face.

"I have a few teacher coupons left over from the beginning of the semester that I never used. Why don't you take them and buy some notebooks for yourself? You'll need them for next year." She handed me a couple of red tickets.

The new regime reserved special vouchers solely for schoolteachers so they could purchase books and educational supplies at very low prices. To augment their meager salaries, many professors sold their coupons on the black market instead. Miss San's unexpected and generous gesture surprised me. The thought of showing my mother a couple of new notebooks and observing her happy face prompted me to reach for the tickets. At the same time, an awareness of my destitute condition came over me, burning my cheeks red with shame. I took a step back and shook my head.

"They are expensive gifts. I can't accept them, Miss San."

"Why not?" she asked.

I sighed, searching for my answer. "My mother usually buys enough supplies for us at the market."

"I know," she said. "I saw her there the other day. We talked for over an hour. She was upset because she wanted to buy you and your brother some new clothes, but there wasn't any money left after she bought the books. I thought I could help her with these coupons, since next year you are going to need a lot more than just a few notebooks."

I lowered my voice. "We can manage."

Miss San furrowed her brow. "Are you ashamed of being poor, Kien?" she asked me.

I avoided her stare by concentrating on a dot of sunlight on the ground.

She pushed the coupons into my hand. "You should not be ashamed of your humble condition or of who you are. In fact, you should be proud. Look at it this way: you are no longer a capitalist. In the Communists' eyes you have achieved the lowest and most desired status — the class of the poor. Be pleased, Kien, for you now have nothing to lose but much to gain. Wait, there is more." She searched in her bag a second time. "Take this money, too. I want you to get a haircut, so that no other teacher in this school can criticize my brand-new parade marshal. I want them to be just as full of pride as I am when they watch you lead the march. Now go home. You have a lot of chores to do, and so have I." She stroked my hair and simultaneously pushed me out the door. I muttered an incoherent appreciation to her as I left.

THE NEXT DAY, I visited the local barbershop for the first time. Before then, my mother had always cut my hair. The shop, where most of the male populace went for a haircut and a nose-hair trim, was a small hut built crudely out of four wooden posts and a black poncho. It stood under a large oak tree, a few steps away from my school. The barber gave me a military-type haircut. His instruments seemed to have been around for at least twenty years, and he occasionally sharpened them on a piece of cowhide nailed to the tree trunk. He left about an inch of hair on top of my head, shaving the rest with his gleaming blade.

For the following three weeks, under Miss San's supervision, we practiced marching around the schoolyard like small soldiers. The rest of the school lined up behind my class according to their ranks of achievement.

A week before the parade was to take place, Miss San failed to show up for school. Even the teachers seemed to have no idea what had happened to her. A substitute was assigned to take over my class — a man in his early thirties with greasy hair and teeth that were so dark they made his mouth look purple. He, too, refused to discuss Miss San's absence.

One morning, as usual, before the classes began, the entire school stood at attention in the schoolyard. I stood at the rear of the assembly, paying close attention. The moment the national anthem began to play over a loudspeaker, it would be my cue to march down the long center aisle, past the principal's podium to the flagpole. Hearing the opening strains of "Hey, Vietnam citizens, our country has been liberated . . ." I strode forward with my head high, my eyes forward, and my back straight. In my arms was the country's new flag, with its red background and yellow star in the middle.

After everyone recited the salute to the flag, the dean took the podium. His features, always severe, had turned darker with foul temper. The wrinkles on his face sagged and his mouth, thin as a pencil line, hid beneath a faint mustache. Glaring at his audience, he switched off the radio that was playing the last notes of the national anthem. His abrupt gesture sent a screeching noise through the speakers to pierce our ears. Then, holding the microphone in one hand, he waved us to silence with the other.

"Listen up, people." His voice rose impatiently into the fog that was settling from under the trees. "I know that there have been rumors around the school, especially about Miss San, teacher of class 5C. You all are curious about her absence. My advice to you is: don't be!" He scanned the crowd with his birdlike eyes. "Why not, you might ask? Well, here is my answer: it's none of your business. It is an act of opposition for anyone to continue probing this matter. And if you are caught breaking this rule, don't expect any mercy. You will be expelled immediately. Now, before you all return to your classrooms, I would like to shift my attention to another matter." Looking straight at me, the dean resumed his usual calm manner.

"The school board has decided to vote for a new parade marshal," he said. "To earn the honor of opening the parade, one needs to be more than just an outstanding academic achiever. He also has to develop strong relationships with all of his classmates and teachers. He has to participate in many extracurricular activities and be a positive symbol of our school. Kien Nguyen is a good student but by no means the best candidate to represent our school. There are many other students who have exceeded him in all aspects. Therefore, we will reassign his position to a new parade marshal who will lead the march with much more success." He strode over to where I stood. Abruptly, he snatched the flag from my hands and handed it over to the vice president of my class.

Turning back to the assembly, he said, "This is the end of my speech. You can now return to your first-period classroom." He dropped the microphone on top of the podium with a loud thud and stepped back from the stage, his hands folded together in front of his chest.

As we dispersed from the schoolyard, my face burned with shame. Wordlessly, I slipped away from the crowd and disappeared from sight.

THAT SUMMER OF 1978 marked three years under the Communists' rule. Even though the new government had successfully taken over the south of Vietnam, many of its citizens still hoped for the Americans' return, and they listened in secret to the forbidden BBC news report every Monday night. As life grew increasingly harder, hope became the only luxury that the Communists had not yet snatched away. Sadly, for many, hope became a destructive force that held their lives in a prolonged limbo of futile expectancy. Instead of relishing life, people merely existed. Such was the case with my family.

My mother had accomplished nothing in three years except for waiting. She had waited for the Communists' collapse, from either inflation or the government's weakness. She had waited for a possible revolution or war to overturn the new regime, since tension between the people and the officials was always strong. But the waiting had dragged on for too long; the fire in all of us had been extinguished. Shame was no longer the primary issue in my mother's mind. Piece by piece, the stash of jewelry in my pocket had been sold for the family's survival. Finally, she was flat broke and at a dead end.

Tired of waiting in vain, my mother rented space in the city's largest market, five kilometers from my home. Her shop was a small compartment of one hundred square feet wedged between a sticky-rice vendor and a sandwich store. The market, composed of hundreds of small businesses like my mother's, was divided into sections that specialized in seafood, livestock, vegetables, fabric, electrical appliances, pharmacy items, and, at the farthest border, farm produce. Beyond this was the city dump, supermarket of the homeless.

My mother sold mainly rice, plus a few other agricultural products, such as potatoes and beans. The Communists, however, took a dim view of businesses like my mother's, believing they drove up prices and disrupted the economy. In a sweeping proclamation, the government prohibited the middle class from carrying out their trading activities and sent troops to confiscate their supplies. They promised to help my mother find new employment if she gave up her business, but despite the agreement, her applications for employment were repeatedly denied.

My mother's shop was forced to close after being open for only a few months. In the last minutes before the raid, she managed to distribute some of her goods among her friends. More sophisticated searches by the government soon followed, thorough and without warning.

At the market, most businessmen were less fortunate than my mother. The authorities, through the legions of youth volunteer squads, raided many shops at night, seizing their inventories. The next day, they required the owners to show a bill of sale to prove their right to the impounded goods. Since most of the supplies had been traded through black-market channels, the owners had no receipts. Forfeiting their stocks, the merchants were wiped out.

The day the youth squad closed my mother's shop, their anger and frustration at finding nothing of value left a trail of destruction behind. One of the squad members, a fourteen-year-old girl in a blue uniform, spat in my mother's face. "Don't you dare reopen this counterrevolutionary shop! We'll come back to make sure that you don't."

Long after they had gone, my mother remained sitting on the floor with her head bowed, calm yet unmoving. From outside, a figure ventured into her shop, stopping at the threshold to stare at her. All that my mother could see was the guest's dirty feet, clad in cheap sandals.

She looked up to see the familiar face of Mrs. Dang, who was staring back at her. Three years under the yoke of Communism had turned her boisterous friend into a repressed, aged woman. However, Mrs. Dang's laughter still was contagious, ringing like crystal the moment she recognized my mother's face.

"God and Buddha!" she exclaimed. "Is that you, Khuon? Oh, heaven, what has happened to you, darling?"

My mother gazed vacantly into space past Mrs. Dang's face. Bursting with excitement from the unexpected reunion, Mrs. Dang fell to the floor among the broken pottery containers and pressed her face against my mother's neck. My mother, however, did not return the embrace. Her mind was somewhere beyond the pungent stench of the market, shocked from the loss of her property.

For several days my mother stayed in bed, refusing to eat with the family. She talked to Jimmy and me about abandoning us to go live somewhere else. Sometimes, her elaborate plans to escape life's troubles focused on the mass suicide of our family, excluding my grandparents. Frightened by her depression, Jimmy and I avoided her bedroom as if it were a lepers' colony.

Fortunately, with the help of Mrs. Dang, who became a frequent visitor, my mother decided to pick up the pieces of her life and plunge back into the trading markets. Although she understood business from her experience at the bank, the idea of competing with other traders to purchase a line of goods and then sell them at a higher price was unpleasant to her. Still, she knew she had to find some way to put food on the table.

THAT SAME SUMMER Loan returned from the Young Volunteers. After three years of running through the jungles in a unit of over two hundred young women proving her dedication to the government, her service time was up.

The day the dean dismissed me from the parade, on the way home I spotted Loan on the street among her comrades. Even though she wore the standard oversized blue uniform made of thick khaki that concealed any remotely feminine curves, I saw her lovely face at once. Years of hard work under the direct sun had turned her skin brown. A large military backpack containing all of her possessions weighed like a rock on her slim body. She smiled when she saw me running toward her, screaming her name. We held each other tearfully in a long embrace before we could break apart to examine one another, laughing at the changes we saw.

"Why didn't you write to me? Didn't you get any of my letters?" she asked me.

"No," I replied. "We've never gotten any. And we couldn't write to you because we didn't know where you were. How many letters did you send us?"

"I don't know." She looked confused. "A lot. At first, it was almost one letter a week. I even asked for personal delivery from a friend. It's strange that you didn't receive any." She mused for a moment. "I can't believe that they all got lost. It is too bad, but you know how it is, living in such conditions. But it doesn't matter now because most importantly, we are together at last, right? Let's go home."

We were stopped at the door by Jimmy's dog, wagging its tail happily and licking our faces with its rough tongue. No longer a puppy, it had grown to almost the size of a well-developed German shepherd, and its weight almost knocked Loan over. It barked and Loan hid behind me to watch it in disbelief.

"That can't be Lulu, can it?" she asked, then answered the question herself. "Of course it isn't. This dog doesn't have a crippled paw."

"Lulu is gone," I said, scratching my brother's mutt behind its ears. "This is a boy. And his name is Lou."

CHAPTER NINETEEN

That night, as my family gathered in my grandparents' bedroom after dinner, Loan told us about her recent experiences. Despite the fact that the Young Volunteers' assault squads were not a branch of the military, Loan had learned combat skills, such as how to operate a gun, how to use various fighting tactics, and even how to kill if necessary. However, her job was to purge the country from negative elements, fight capitalism, and discipline anyone who refused to cooperate with the new social order.

After three years of service, Loan had seen enough chaos. When her contract was up for renewal, she declined to reenlist. The time she had spent serving the government was already enough to ensure her a comfortable position.

"Are you going to stay with us?" I asked Loan after she finished telling us her story.

"No, Kien. I came to bid farewell to you all," she said ruefully.

No one seemed surprised at this news. With her improved "revolutionary" status, associating with members of the "reactionary" class like my family would just weigh her down.

"Where are you going from here?" my grandfather asked her.

Loan let out a heavy sigh. "I am getting married, Uncle Oai."

She avoided looking at my grandfather's face. "The wedding is next week."

"I am happy that you can finally settle down," my grandfather exclaimed. "Congratulations. Who is the lucky guy? Was it someone you met in the volunteer corps?"

"No, sir," Loan muttered. Her breast heaved under the faded khaki fabric of her blouse. "He is someone you know, sir. He used to be your gardener."

The smile vanished from my grandfather's face as he blinked his eyes in disbelief. "Mr. Tran?"

"Yes, sir."

My grandfather turned away and buried the lower half of his face in his hands. Loan attempted to finish her news.

"He is forty and has never been married," she said, "but by the standards of today's society, he is quite a good catch. In the last few years, he has been taking good care of me. While I was in the volunteer unit, far from home, he came to visit me often, keeping track of every place I'd been to. He kept me company through my toughest times. And most importantly, he has promised not to trouble any of you anymore. I feel like I owe him my life, sir."

"Please don't do this because of us! He can't hurt us anymore," my grandfather whispered.

"Of course not, Uncle. I chose to marry him for my future. I am just looking out for my security and peace. Your safety was an added bonus. You, of all people, should understand that."

My grandfather nodded. "You're right. I understand, and I think you made a good decision. I am happy for you, Loan. I'll give you my blessing, if that is what you've come here for." He continued, "But if there is nothing more you wish to share with us, I would like to excuse myself, since I am getting a little tired in my old age."

"Actually, Uncle," Loan said with hesitation, "there is something else. This matter concerns Miss Khuon. After the wedding, I will be moving to the Nguyen mansion with Tran. It was his idea to keep the house in his name, and the only way is to get married and build his own family. I hope you someday can understand and forgive me. You now know where I live, and if you ever need anything, anything at all, come look for me. I mean that from the bottom of my heart." She turned to me. "Especially you, Kien. Please come visit me sometime."

My mother finally spoke up. "What happened between you and Mr. Tran is not shocking news. I saw the way he looked at you years ago. I knew that it was just a matter of time before you belonged to him."

Loan got up and let herself out of the house. From the window I could see her blue fatigues as she hoisted the heavy backpack to her shoulders and turned down the street.

A FEW DAYS LATER, my grandmother discovered a small cut on the side of her right heel. She had no idea what had caused it. My mother insisted that the wound was caused by the sharp edge of the flip-flops that my grandmother habitually wore around the house. The cut did not heal; instead, it got worse every day.

One morning, I woke up to the sound of my grandmother's cry. She lay in her bed, surrounded by my grandfather and my mother and some of my cousins. All were examining her foot, which had flared up to the size of a barbecued piglet and looked just as oily. The skin that covered her leg was stretched to its limit, shining with an angry red tint, threatening to burst. My mother punctured it with a knife, hoping to drain out the purulence. Instead of pus, a mixture of dark blood and decayed flesh trickled out of my grandmother's leg and dripped into the metal container below her bed. A putrid smell permeated the air.

We took her to the big hospital in Nhatrang, where the doctors kept her immobile on a gurney while they ran tests. After a few days, because we could not afford the bill and the doctors could not agree on the cause of her condition, she was discharged with a diagnosis of cancer.

At home, my mother sought help from a respected herbalist in town. After a few treatments, my grandmother's fever slowly diminished, even though the swelling in her foot did not go down.

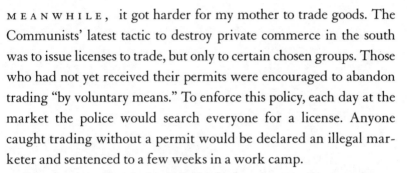

MEANWHILE, it got harder for my mother to trade goods. The Communists' latest tactic to destroy private commerce in the south was to issue licenses to trade, but only to certain chosen groups. Those who had not yet received their permits were encouraged to abandon trading "by voluntary means." To enforce this policy, each day at the market the police would search everyone for a license. Anyone caught trading without a permit would be declared an illegal marketer and sentenced to a few weeks in a work camp.

One day, just after the herbalist had left and my mother was changing the dressing on my grandmother's wound, Mrs. Dang stormed in. Like my mother, she had been subjected to the most stringent restrictions due to her regressive background. Except for a few articles of clothing, a small rented room facing the market, and the memories of her glorious past, Mrs. Dang had nothing. The overwhelming odor of infection didn't seem to affect her as she rushed to my mother's side.

"I want you to listen to this for a second, Khuon," she said. "I have found a way for both of us to make a living."

"I am listening," my mother said.

"Okay, here goes. You know that we can't keep trading goods without a license. Sooner or later, the police will catch us. I know a few people who have licenses. They need someone to bring them fabrics and other merchandise from Saigon."

"Meaning?" My mother stopped in the middle of wrapping the bandage around my grandmother's ankle.

"We are going to Saigon to get the goods."

"You are joking." My mother turned away from her.

"We can do it, Khuon. There is no law that stops us from traveling. We have our own identification. It is no longer required to carry the Proof of Existence everywhere we go." Mrs. Dang paused for her words to sink in, then continued, "So, what do you say? Go to Saigon with me?"

My mother shook her head.

"Please, Khuon. What do you think about my plan?"

"I don't know, it sounds complicated. Besides, I can't leave my mother in this condition, not to mention my children. What if my community leader won't allow me to leave town?"

Mrs. Dang seized my mother's wrist. "What alternative do you have? If we don't do this deal, are you going to risk selling goods without a license in the market? Or would you rather stay home and starve with your family?"

My mother knew she was losing the argument. "How long is the trip?" she asked. "And how much money do we need to start?"

"If my calculations are correct, we need about two thousand dong for a five-day trip. Minus all of the expenses, we each could make at least a few hundred dong."

"A thousand dong per person to start?" My mother let out a small cry. "I don't have that much. Where am I going to get a thousand dong?"

"Sell your furniture," Mrs. Dang said coldly. "That's how I raised my money. We can leave the day after tomorrow. However, I need your word that you are with me in this."

In the other room, my little sister woke up from her nap and started to cry. At the age of two and a half, she was still physically and mentally a one-year-old child, trapped in a frail and wrinkled body that had always been covered with painful ulcers, mostly on her head and neck. She had learned to walk and talk with great difficulty. Mainly, she preferred to crawl on the floor instead of walking; cry instead of asking for food. Her face was like that of an old woman, and her voice was tiny, like the mew of a newborn kitten.

My sister's cry startled my mother, and she stopped tending my grandmother's wound. "Kien, shut her up," she yelled out in frustration. "I am busy with Auntie Dang."

I picked my sister up in my arms and rocked her as she clutched a torn pillow to her chest. Although it was half decomposed and smelled like fish sauce from her drooling, the pillow was her source of security. In my lap, BeTi looked at me dully with her large, bulging brown eyes and favored me with a toothless smile. Her baby teeth had rotted away before her adult teeth could come in to replace them.

In the next room, my mother was asking my grandmother's opinion about Mrs. Dang's proposal. I heard my grandmother's weak voice as she offered her advice.

"I think you should go to Saigon," my grandmother said. "Don't worry about us. I will be fine with your father, and Kien can take care of his brother and sister. Your staying here won't make things any better."

Two days later, with the money she had received from selling her sewing machine, my mother was ready for her trip. She crammed a fifty-dong bill in my hand. Reassuring me that it would be sufficient to keep the five of us comfortable for the next five days, she bid us good-bye.

THAT SAME DAY at my school, the great parade marked the last day of the term. Leading the march were the members of the Ho Chi Minh Communist Youth Union, distinguished from the rest of the students by their red neckerchiefs. My class's vice president led the parade proudly with the national flag fluttering in his arms. They marched through the city, singing the national anthem and chanting Communist propaganda before a zealous crowd.

I stayed inside my classroom to avoid the festivity. Keeping me company was Duy, who sat by the window watching the parade from a distance. It was half past noon; the early summer sun was already merciless with its heat. The faint smell of cow dung mixed with the sweet odor of ripened rice in the nearby fields. All this had a sedative effect, and my lashes hung heavily over my eyes.

"Did you hear what happened to Miss San?" Duy asked me.

"No." I sat up, my drowsiness replaced by curiosity. "What did you hear?"

Duy said with little emotion, "I heard she tried to escape a few days ago, and there was a traitor in her boat. She was shot. No one is supposed to know. The police were talking to the dean. They said she's dead."

"Oh, no!" My ears rang as though a bomb had exploded inside my head.

"Yes, isn't that terrible? And there won't be any funeral either. They won't allow the students to mourn her loss." He stared at me. "If Miss San were still here, she would definitely fight to keep you in that parade."

I shook my head. "The dean said that I don't deserve that honor. I don't think he would believe Miss San deserves a proper mourning, either. It's nothing personal. That's just the way things are."

CHAPTER TWENTY

On the fifth day of my mother's absence, I took my brother and sister to the bus station to welcome her home. To our dismay, the bus arrived with no sign of her or Mrs. Dang. We stood by the entrance, searching for her familiar face among the strangers, until every last person was off the vehicle. At last I found the driver and asked if he had a message from her. He shook his head and walked away.

That was the first night in my eleven years that I did not rest. Lying awake in my bed, I wondered what had happened to my mother. Silently I cried in the dark, not so much to mourn for her disappearance but because of the uncertainty of my future and my sense of responsibility for the rest of my family. Morning came, and I returned to the bus station. At the end of the day I returned home alone once more.

The household was beset by crises. The money my mother had left us was spent. My grandmother's condition took a turn for the worse and she had to be readmitted to the hospital. My grandfather stayed by her side, leaving me in charge of my siblings. My aunt could offer only two explanations for my mother's disappearance: death or abandonment. She considered informing the government about our situation. She felt no responsibility to feed us, telling the neighbors that it was my mother's fault for deserting her own family.

After eight days had passed we ate the last grain of rice in the house. I took my brother and sister to bed hungry, not knowing what to do. In the dark, Jimmy and I lay awake, listening to my sister keening through the night like a tormented ghost. Hearing her cry from hunger was the worst thing I had ever experienced. And just a short distance away we could hear the sound of my cousins dining noisily.

The following morning I went to my aunt's door, carrying my sister on my back and leading Jimmy by my side. In the kitchen my cousin Pink was boiling a pot of sweet potatoes on top of a stove. The food was part of a little business she had after school selling snacks at a local market to earn extra cash. The rich aroma swept up into the air, and instantly, my sister begged to be fed. I pushed her pillow into her hands and ventured up the steps to the main house.

Inside the living room, my aunt was sitting on her divan chewing betel nut. Its juice, when mixed with the saliva, would become a rich, thick vegetable dye. She used this mixture to stain her teeth black, as among women of her generation gleaming black teeth were considered highly desirable. My cousins were scattered around the room, watching us with aggressive glee.

"Auntie, I want to borrow some money," I stammered in my shaky voice. "My mother is missing and we have run out of food."

"Wait till tomorrow," she said.

"I beg your pardon?" I asked her.

"Wait till tomorrow," she repeated through a mouthful of red saliva, triggered by the betel dye. "If your mother doesn't return by then, I will think of something." Next to her, Moonlight lay on a pillow and coughed softly into a handkerchief.

"I don't think I can wait any longer," I told her. "We haven't eaten for two days. I was hoping that you could give me a loan now, please."

In a bed near the window, Tin raised his voice. "She said to wait till tomorrow. Are you deaf or stupid?"

"A loan?" My aunt snickered. "How are you going to repay me?"

"My mother will be home soon. She will pay you back."

My aunt raised her eyebrow. "Are you sure about that?" she asked. "What if she doesn't come back?" She spat into a metal basin next to her, wiping her lips with the tips of her fingers, then added, "Ever."

Jimmy pulled on my arm. "Let's go, Kien."

We walked back to our house, passing the kitchen one more time. The smell coming from the pot tugged at our empty stomachs. The door was open. No one was inside.

Jimmy looked at me, and his stomach growled from within his thin abdomen like a broken whistle. "I am so hungry, Kien. Do something," he said miserably.

"Me, too, very hungry," my sister joined him, hitting the back of my head with her pillow.

I put my sister down and crept into the kitchen. Near the stove, Pink had left a small notebook that she used to keep track of her customers' accounts. Choosing a clean page, I scribbled a brief note to her. *"Dear Pink, I took three botatoes from your pot because we were very hungry. I promise to pay you back when my mother returns. Thank you. Kien."*

I set the note by the stove where it could be easily spotted. With a chopstick I speared out three scalding potatoes into a bowl and ran outside, joining my brother and sister. But before I could reach the back door of my home, I bumped into Pink. She let out a scream, but her shock turned to rage in seconds.

"Mommy," she shouted, "the half-breed stole my potatoes."

"No, no, Pink." I covered her mouth with my free hand, hoping to gain some time for my explanation. "I am going to buy these. See? I put them on your tab. I did not steal them. Please, stop yelling."

But it was too late. From their living room, her family rushed down to the kitchen. Tin stormed like a wildcat in front of me, snatching the food from my hands. The potatoes fell onto the dirty cement and broke into small pieces, which made him madder.

He clenched his hand into a fist and punched my jaw with all his strength. The impact crashed my head into the wall a few feet away. I registered the metallic taste of blood from my cut tongue, the sound of my sister's cry, and the barking of Jimmy's dog before my consciousness drifted away. Tin rushed forward to pull me to my feet. I slowly regained my senses, but couldn't see clearly. Tin punched my face again, holding me upright by the front of my shirt. In desperation, I grabbed his arm and bit down hard on the flesh. He let out a surprised growl and shook me off him. I fell back on the ground, while his family watched in silence.

Tin ran back inside his house, only to reappear a moment later. His hand was curled into a fist, and the handle of a hammer stuck out from between his fingers. My aunt spoke warningly to him.

"Be careful, Tin, don't hit him in the face."

From their living room, Moonlight called out weakly. "Stop it, please. What are you doing? They are your cousins —" Her cough drowned down her last few words.

"Shut up," Tin spat to Moonlight. "Whose side are you on?" To his mother, he continued, "Don't worry, Mother. I am going to teach this half-breed a lesson today about stealing from my sister."

I saw him lunge at me, the weapon aimed at my face. All I could do was wrap my head in between my arms before he got too close. Jimmy jumped in to grab Tin's legs, pulling him away. I was aware of my brother's dog above me as it leaped out to bite Tin on the side of his abdomen. Tin let out another frustrated scream, but only for a second. He shook the dog off and kicked my brother in the groin. Jimmy fell down, gasping and holding his privates in agony. However, the dog did not give up. It bared its fangs and launched itself again at my cousin. Fully prepared this time, Tin swung the hammer and whacked it across Lou's face. His strength sent the dog into the air to land a few feet away, howling wildly. He then dove on top of me, pounding on my exposed back with his fist, which was still wrapped around the head of the hammer. Lying on the ground, I lost count of his punches and passed out.

Sometime later I was dimly aware of someone poking my side. The sunlight blinded me as I opened my eyes. My cousins' faces were looming above me, with my aunt's head poking in between them.

As one of my cousins kicked me, she asked, "Is he dead? Can someone check? Tin, you are in trouble, child. You've hit him too hard."

I turned away from them. From somewhere behind his brothers, Tin's voice exploded mockingly. "That dumb half-breed misspelled *potatoes*. If he is too stupid to spell, maybe he shouldn't write any note at all."

"Why didn't you tell us that you left Pink a note?" my aunt asked me.

I stood up, and pain shot up my spine like an electric current. My knees wobbled and I fell back to the ground. Ignoring their stares, I pushed myself up again. Clutching the wall, I took baby steps back to my house. An eerie numbness began to spread from my waist downward.

Pink caught up with me. With a solemn look, she shoved a bowl of potatoes in my hand.

"Take these. Go ahead," she said. "They are on me."

I pushed my way past her. All I wanted to do was get away.

My aunt's sour voice chased after me. "You caused this to happen to yourself. Didn't I tell you earlier that you should wait for your mother to get home? Why must you be so stubborn all the time? You've provoked my son, knowing his short temper —"

Tin interrupted her. "Why bother to explain, Mother? He is lucky that I didn't kill him. Didn't you see him and that damned dog bite me?" He called after me, "You animals. I hope you all go to hell."

I limped inside the house with Jimmy's help. "Are you all right?" I asked him. "Does it still hurt where he kicked you?"

"Just a little bit," Jimmy answered me. Next to him, Lou tried to lick away the blood around his neck with little success. With his hind leg he scratched the injury in frustration. Blood dripped from his coarse fur to the floor, drying instantly in the heat.

I sank to a chair with difficulty and said to my brother, "Let's wait a few minutes until I feel better, then we will get out of here."

"Where are we going, Kien?"

"We are going to see Loan."

CHAPTER TWENTY-ONE

L oan?" Jimmy looked at me with surprise. "But she lives so far away, and we have no money to take the bus."

"We are going to walk to her house," I told him.

Jimmy looked at me in disbelief. "Are you sure you can walk at all?"

"Yes," I said, nodding. "We have no choice. I don't want to die here. Give me a minute to rest, and if you can carry BeTi, then I will be able to go with you."

"No problem, I will carry her, Kien."

It was about ten o'clock in the morning when we left the house through the main gates. Some of my aunt's family watched us from their windows. The numbness in my lower body had slowly dissipated, giving way to a sharper pain that dug like long fingernails into my back with each step I took. Jimmy trudged a few feet ahead of me, carrying my sister on his back, and Lou was by his side. Occasionally, my brother and his dog would turn back to examine me with their intense dark eyes.

As we approached the first turn from our street, Jimmy stopped. His face was full of anxiety. "Do you know how to get there?" he asked.

"I remember the route, " I reassured him. "It is not very difficult.

Once we get on the highway, if we keep on walking, we will come to a market. Do you remember it? Loan's house isn't far from there."

"It used to be our house, didn't it?" he asked.

"It is her house now," I corrected him. "Don't ever say that in front of Loan. It will upset her."

As the day got older, the temperature got hotter. By the time we set foot on the highway, the tar was melting in colorless fumes; it stuck to our sandals like glue. The heated air made the scenery before us tremble into a haze. Ahead, we saw the boundless fields on either side of the road. The highway faded into a blurry dot at the end of the horizon. The stillness of summer draped over the land like an invisible blanket that smelled like burned rubber.

Jimmy whispered to me, "Are you sure we have to do this? How far is it, Kien?"

"I don't know, maybe five or six kilometers. If we want to eat, we have to find Loan. Unless you have a better idea." I pushed myself onward, knowing he would follow.

I lost track of how far or how long we walked. I only knew that we had gone too far to turn back. There was no indication that the journey would ever end. I kept on moving, for fear that if we stopped to rest, we would not have the strength to start again.

I became acutely aware of my dried, scratchy tongue, which flopped around like a fish inside my mouth. Next to me, Jimmy dragged himself on the hard pavement with my sister on his back, trailing her dirty pillow carelessly along the dusty road. Their lips began to blister. Finally, Jimmy stopped in the middle of the road. I looked around, dimly aware that we were utterly alone on the deserted road. There was not a car, not a pedestrian in sight, just the three of us amid the endless rice paddies. A few steps ahead of us, Jimmy's dog turned to regard us, his red tongue hanging from one side of his mouth, dripping with white foam. Jimmy dropped my sister onto the ground. She looked at us and began to cry. The odor of her body was like the smell of a rotten fish.

My brother shook his head. "I can't go anymore, Kien. I have to find something to drink."

"Keep walking," I yelled at him. "We'll drink when we get there. You can't stop now."

He ignored me, looking around for a cool place under a tree to rest. My sister screamed louder, kicking her feet.

"Shut up!" I shrieked, grabbing her diminutive body. "Why don't you shut up? Leave me alone. I am not responsible for you or your problems. I don't have to feed you. I don't have to take care of you. I don't have to do anything. Do you hear me? You want to die? Is that what you want?" I could not stop screaming. My face was inches from hers, and I reached for her neck. "Let me give you a hand. Let me put you out of your misery."

I hit her repeatedly, slapping her face, pulling her hair, dragging her around the pavement, and, finally, throwing her facedown in the middle of the road.

"What are you saying now? I can't hear you. Do you want to die?" My voice cracked as I wrapped my hands around her thin neck. BeTi blinked at me.

"No, no," she said, choking, and tried to peel my firm grip off her neck. The pillow was still clutched in her hand.

"Are you going to walk now? Or should I let you stay here and get run over by a truck?"

Her eyes continued to fix on me with the same bleak expression. I let go and staggered a few steps back. BeTi remained in the middle of the road. The hatred for my sister was so strong in me that I could taste it. Secretly, I prayed for a truck to run her over. With her death, I could be free again.

From the empty road, my sister crawled back to me on her bony limbs. Her face smudged with dirt and tears, she begged me to hold her. Exhausted, I sat down next to my brother and gasped for air. Finally, Jimmy suggested that we should continue with our journey. We got up with great difficulty, reluctant to leave the comfortable shade. Together we moved forward on the road, and my sister struggled a few steps behind.

A thought flashed through my mind. "Let's go down to the rice field," I said to Jimmy. "If the people are planting rice, they must have watered the fields, right? Let's find the water supply together."

Jimmy ignored my suggestion. He tilted his head, concentrating. Then he turned to me and asked, "Did you hear that?"

"Hear what?" I asked.

He put a finger to his lips, motioning for me to be quiet. "Listen," he said.

Suddenly, I could hear it too. From beyond a hill came a buzzing sound reverberating through the empty sky — the kind of sound made by a crowd of people. We looked at each other without uttering a word. The image of a bazaar appeared in our heads, and we ran screaming up the hill. The long-anticipated market opened before our eyes like a page out of a fairy-tale book, spreading itself beyond the foot of the hill. Behind it, the city glittered under the orange sun like Utopia.

CHAPTER TWENTY-TWO

It did not take us long to get from the market to Loan's house. I did not forget the route, even though it had been three years since my last visit. The city was much the same as before, but the mansion had changed a great deal. Remnants of a wedding were evident in the festive decorations on the white railings and the red debris of firecrackers on the ground. The house, no longer my mother's favored eggshell color, had been painted blue. New windows and doors replaced old, broken ones. On the top floor overlooking the street, where my family name once appeared, hung a national flag.

The garden was again lush, with a variety of hybrid plants in expensive antique pots. Flowers bloomed under the encouraging sun as though to mock us with the illusion that behind the tall gate, life was still carefree. The pool, however, was empty, standing in the middle of the garden like an unsightly blemish. I found myself playing the role of an outsider, looking in like one of the dirty children my mother had trained me to despise in the old days. With a heavy heart, I rang the doorbell.

Within moments, Loan appeared at the front door with an apron around her waist and a pair of chopsticks in her hand. Upon seeing us, she grasped her face in disbelief and the chopsticks fell to the floor. Jimmy and I cried her name with joy. However, our enthusiasm died as soon as we recognized Mr. Tran's silhouette from behind the screen door. He walked out and stood beside Loan, frowning at us.

Irritably, he asked her, "Why are they here?"

"I don't know." She ran down the steps toward the gate. "I think something happened, and they are coming for help."

"Come back in the house this instant. I need to have a word with you. Inside." He disappeared behind the front door.

Loan pressed her face between the railings of the gate to look at us. "How did you get here?" she whispered. "Where is your mother? Wait, tell me later." Her eyebrows lifted. "Listen, children. Remember the back door? I'll meet you there in about five minutes, okay? Mr. Tran doesn't want the neighbors to see what's going on from this side of the house. Do you understand?"

We nodded and she hurried back inside.

Half an hour later, we sat on the wet dirt under the thick canopy of a clump of wild lilacs. There was no sign of Loan. Down the alley, a woman turned on the motor of her juice stand and began making fruit drink from long stalks of sugar cane. The sudden noise and the sweet smell churned our empty stomachs with painful waves. My sister hid her head in her moldy pillow and sniffed quietly.

A rustle of leaves behind us brought Jimmy and me to our feet. Loan appeared outside her kitchen and held the door open. "Leave the dog outside," she said to Jimmy.

When we were inside, she noticed the bruises on my lower face. "What happened to all of you?" she asked. "Where is your mother? Is she all right?"

I didn't know where to begin. Instead, I began to cry. In fact, we all sobbed in Loan's arms. She got up from the embrace a moment later.

"I was in the middle of cooking when the doorbell rang. Let me make lunch for all of you," she said. "Look at you. Poor kids, you must be starving."

I sat down on the floor near the hot stove, feeling exhausted yet content. Before Loan could open the food cabinet, Mr. Tran stormed into the kitchen. His hands hung in tight fists beneath his long-sleeved denim shirt. Ignoring us, he marched toward his wife, who froze the moment she saw him. He grabbed her arm and dragged her outside.

Over his shoulder he ordered us, "Stay where you are. Don't move!"

Soon Loan returned to the kitchen. She stood in the doorway and bit her nails for several minutes. I raised myself up from the floor.

"Loan, is everything all right?" I asked.

Loan's eyes were red and wet with tears.

"Are you okay? What is wrong, Loan?" I asked her again.

She touched my hair the same way she used to when I was younger. "Kien, do you remember when I said to you that I want you to come and visit me?"

"Yes."

"I am sorry, darling," she said between her sobs. "I shouldn't have said that to you even though I meant every word. Neither you nor your siblings can stay here. I don't know what kind of trouble you are in, or what caused you to come here. I can't help you. I am not allowed to get involved."

"Why? What do you mean you are not allowed to?" I searched her face. "He wants us to leave, doesn't he?"

"Remember all the letters from me that you've never gotten?" she asked me.

I nodded. "What are you trying to tell me?"

"Mr. Tran was supposed to deliver them to you."

Suddenly I understood. "But he didn't."

Loan was shaking visibly. "I can't have anything to do with your family as long as I am staying here in his house."

Each word she said cut a new wound into me. "I understand," I said coldly. "Don't worry! We are leaving right now."

"I'll walk you out. I am sorry, children. I wish I could be of more help to all of you."

"It's quite all right. Let me get my brother and sister ready."

"Where are you going?" she asked.

"Home."

I lifted BeTi to her feet. Jimmy walked outside to untie his dog from the fence. Loan turned to me and asked. "Is there anything I can do?"

The scent of sugar-cane juice still lingered in the air. "We could use a cold drink from that stand over there," I suggested. "If it is not too much trouble."

WE WALKED on the familiar yet empty streets to the market once again. Each of us held a heavy plastic bag of sugar water mixed with crushed ice. The soothing taste replenished my body with new burst of energy. Without turning back, I could sense Loan standing alone in the middle of the road, watching us.

At a trash bin near the fish section, two flaxen-haired boys were busily digging in the trash. They looked up just to glare aggressively at Jimmy and me, as though preparing to defend their territory. One of the boys had lost an eye. He blinked his single blue eye and bared his tiny rat teeth while searching for a weapon among the rocks nearby. His partner quickly ate something that he had found in the garbage. Purple slime smeared his face.

"What do we do now, Kien?" Jimmy asked.

"We could beg for food," I suggested.

"No," Jimmy moaned weakly.

"Do you have any other plan?"

We continued to walk through the bazaar. It was overcrowded with aggressive shoppers. We hung on to each other against the surge of traffic.

"Then get ready to beg for food," I screamed so that my voice could rise above the shrill noises around us.

"Please, Kien. I don't want to beg. We can go home and sell something."

"What can we sell, Jimmy? Besides, who would want to buy anything from us?"

Jimmy's eyes filled with water. "We could sell Lou to the butcher."

"You are crazy. He'll kill your dog."

"Not if we get him to promise and hold the dog for two days. Once Mom gets home, we can buy Lou back from him with interest."

"What if she never comes back?"

Tears rolled down his face. "Don't be evil. She will be back."

I lifted my sister up and ushered the dog forward. "So, let's assume that you were right. Even if Mom came back, what makes you think that the butcher would keep your dog for two days?"

He ran to catch up with me. "He will. Listen to me, Kien. The man owes me a favor. If you reminded him, he would have to agree." The enthusiasm had returned to his voice.

"Me?" I stopped in the middle of the muddy path, holding on to BeTi. "Why do I have to remind him? Are you suggesting that I have to negotiate instead of you?"

"You know I can't sell my own dog. How could I?"

"So you really want me to do this?"

Jimmy looked at my sister, who sagged in my hands like a dirty puppet. Her skin was the color of a lemon, hot to the touch. He nodded sadly.

I sighed. "Fine. Tell me what act of kindness you granted this man, so that I can remind him."

"Okay, it happened this way. A while back, one evening," he began uneasily, "I was playing hide-and-seek with the Tong brothers on the street when Mrs. Butcher approached us. She asked us for help. Her husband had gone out drinking with our uncle early that afternoon. In the middle of our game, we saw Uncle come back drunk and pass out on the front lawn without Mr. Butcher. Of course, his wife got real scared."

The hill that led to the highway opened before us as the market fell behind. Beyond it, the landscape was immense, wild, and desolate. We moved slowly down the road while Jimmy continued with his story.

"So, I told her that I would find her husband. It wasn't easy, but I remembered the way. And the three of us — me, Duy, and little Roi — went across the rice fields to the next town. That night, there was a blackout and the whole city went dark. We didn't see much of the road, and we all kept falling into the potholes. Also, we were telling ghost stories and spooking each other."

"Get to the point, Jimmy."

"Well, you remember the stream that runs through Mr. Qui Ba's lands? It waters his rice fields even during the drought, while everyone else prays for rain —"

"Get to the point."

"All right, I will. When we got close to the stream, we heard a moaning sound. It was weak, shaky as if it belonged to a ghost. Roi wanted to run, so did I. But Duy stopped us. We crept closer, and we found Mr. Butcher leaning against a tree, looking down at the stream. He was crying bitterly. 'Please, God and Buddha,' he said, staring at his crotch, 'what have I done to deserve this? If it doesn't stop, I am going to die for sure.' We approached him from behind. 'Hello,' I said to him. 'What's troubling you, sir?' He looked up. Under the pale moonlight, his face was smeared with tears. 'I am dying,' he said. 'No, you are not. You are just very drunk,' I said, to which he replied, 'For the last three hours, I've been doing nothing but pissing myself away. It won't stop. I think I am going to piss to death.' I told him, 'It's okay. You are not pissing. It is just the sound of running water in the stream. You need to go home with us.' So we zipped him up and got him home safely."

Despite everything, I broke out laughing.

"On the way home, he was so relieved that we'd saved him, he promised to return the favor one day."

Jimmy stopped to finish his sugar-cane drink. "Please," he continued, "mention the story to him and his wife. Make them agree to our condition before you sell them my Lou. Otherwise, don't do it!"

"I will, I promise."

"Okay," he said, sighing.

He lifted my sister to his back. She flattened her greasy pillow against the nape of his neck and rested her head. As usual, the dog strutted a few feet ahead of us, sniffing the ground as we went.

Jimmy turned to me. "Kien," he said tensely.

"Yes?"

"If Mom doesn't come back —"

"I thought you didn't want to talk about that."

"I don't. But just in case, what are we going to do?"

"I don't have any idea."

"You are not going to abandon us, are you?" he asked.

I looked at my brother. Just nine years old, he looked like an old man, depleted and out of breath. Beads of perspiration hung at the tips of his hair. Shaking my head, I answered, "I would never leave you. I promise we'll stay together."

CHAPTER TWENTY-THREE

A t the entrance to our village, Jimmy stopped, sighed, and readjusted BeTi on his back. "I am taking her home. You take care of Lou; make sure that they understand the agreement."

I lifted my sister off Jimmy's back. "Let's forget the whole thing. I can't do what you are asking me. We'll manage somehow."

It was dark. The streets were empty, flickering with fireflies in the bushes. The alley that led to our compound seemed endless, but the longer we walked, the stronger the smell of my uncle's ripe guavas became. My brother's dog whined softly as we approached our front door, and Jimmy patted it between the ears to keep it silent. Both houses were lit up. There were many shadows in my grandparents' bedroom. From a window, someone spotted us and let out a blood-curdling scream.

The town commander, Mr. Qui Ba, ran out the front door, followed by my mother. Behind them were Mrs. Dang and a few policemen. My mother burst into tears upon seeing us. Flooded with emotion, we held on to each other. I could feel my sister struggle to get air. My mother's body trembled.

She picked up my sister, noticed the ugly bruises on my face, and demanded an explanation. Under the pale streetlights, I showed her the bumps and contusions Tin had left on my back while Jimmy relived the potato story. Her face registered pain and anger, making her skin redden like blazing coal.

Turning to Mr. Qui Ba, my mother wiped her eyes with the back of her hand. The community leader seemed lost in thought with his eyebrows knitted together. She cleared her throat. "You saw what has happened. Please do something to help us. I demand satisfaction."

He started. "What are you asking, Khuon? You were gone for nine days, leaving your children behind. We all thought you had abandoned them. Report to the community center tomorrow — maybe we can deal with this issue then. However, now is not a good time; it is getting dark, and your children are safe. Please go to bed."

Ignoring his advice, my mother marched straight to my aunt's house and pushed the front door open. With her hands on her hips, she faced their living room and yelled out Tin's name. Her voice penetrated the dark, without the slightest trace of fear.

In her room, Moonlight woke up and began to cough. My aunt's voice yelled back at my mother, "What are you doing, screaming like that? Can't you wait till tomorrow to settle things with him?" She appeared from her bedroom, where she had shared a bed with her youngest four daughters for the past several years.

"I want to settle things now," my mother screamed.

"All right, then," my aunt screamed back. "Tin, come out here, now."

"Listen, ladies," Mr. Qui Ba interrupted. "Stop making a scene. I don't want to arrest any of you."

A light switch clicked, and light flooded the living room. Tin walked nervously out to face my mother. She glared at him, then at his parents.

"You almost killed my son today," she said, "over three small pieces of potato. Were my children's lives that cheap to you? Look around you, what do you see?"

Tin shifted on his feet uneasily.

"What do you see?" she asked Tin once more, but decided to answer the question herself. "All of this, the house, the furniture, even the food that is still stuck between your teeth, all came from me. That's right. Just ask your incompetent parents if you want to know. You may not have any respect for me, or any feeling for my children, but you cannot deny the fact that your existences are made possible because of this lowly prostitute. Don't you dare ever touch any of my children again! The next time I see you lay a finger on them, I will torch this entire place. Compared to you, I have nothing to lose, so don't back me into a corner."

"And you —" she pointed a finger at my aunt, who was pale with embarrassment — "each time you told me that I am your only sister, in my heart, I truly wanted to believe you, but I won't anymore. It always ends up hurting too much. Today, your son beat mine to within an inch of death. I am terminating this relationship, sister. From this point on, we are just two unfortunate families sharing a well and a shit house." She stamped her foot for emphasis. "Take a close look at your life if you dare. Do you understand why you allow your children to harass mine? Jealousy, that's why. You are jealous of the fact that all of your fourteen children could never measure up in Daddy's eyes as much as one half-breed of mine. It hurts, doesn't it? Knowing that your children can never be good enough. But how could they? Just look at them, and the parents that gave life to them. I sincerely hope that I never have to see your face again."

My mother took us back to our house, slamming the door behind her. Mrs. Dang followed us. The community leader and his men stood in my aunt's garden. He quickly regained his composure and shouted after my mother, "Khuon, report to my office tomorrow morning."

Turning to us, my mother noticed my sister's sickly face for the first time. "How are you feeling, sweetheart?" she asked.

"Food," BeTi moaned.

"Of course, what am I thinking?" she exclaimed. "We are going to the noodle shop. Dang, would you like to accompany us?"

CHAPTER TWENTY-FOUR

T he noodle shop was fifteen minutes from our home, next to an old buffalo farm. Behind it, gleaming under the pale streetlight, were railroad tracks. The stench of animal dung mixed with the smell of grilled pork in the air. The shop was an annex of somebody's kitchen, extended into the garden with a couple of large tables and a few benches. The owner was a middle-aged woman with an overwhelming smell of curry and burned fat in her clothes. She sat on a small wooden stool cleaning a pig carcass by the well. Her salt-and-pepper hair was pulled back in a tight bun and held on top of her head by a single porcupine quill. At her feet lay an aluminum pan filled with cooked sausages, some of which spilled over the side and floated above the muddy ground. The pig's belly bore a longitudinal cut that extended from throat to tail, gaping between her expert hands to reveal a bloody darkness within. In the dimly lit kitchen, two pots of broth boiled fervently over the stoves, sending the odors of spices, fish, and meat into the night.

We sat on a bench. The shop lady stopped, washed her hands in a basin, and took my mother's order with a bored look. "Would you like some snacks?" she asked.

"No, thank you. Just three bowls of Peking duck soup for the kids, the largest portions that you have."

177

"You two ladies are not eating?" She looked at my mother and Mrs. Dang.

They shook their heads in unison.

At a table next to us sat a half-naked local prostitute and her customer. They clung together with legs crisscrossed and arms locked like a pair of Siamese twins, slurping their noodles loudly. My mother sat at the edge of the bench, playing with my short hair.

"Where did you go this afternoon?" she asked.

"I took Jimmy and BeTi to see Loan."

"You are very smart for an eleven-year-old boy, Kien," she remarked. "What made you think of going to see her?"

"I didn't know where else to go, but I knew we had to get away from the house."

"What happened at Loan's?"

The lady returned with a tray full of food. The bowls she set in front of us had faded flowers painted on them. Steam rose from the rich, tawny broth, burning my face with its vapors. My stomach gave a violent twist, and my mouth ached from salivating too quickly. I collected myself by giving my soup a twist of lemon.

At the next table, the prostitute suddenly sat up, screaming into the dark yard with a harsh voice. "Get out of here, you whores." On her naked shoulders and arms, tiny sores bloomed like red carnations in spring. "Stop following me everywhere."

The soup lady shrugged. "Her children," she explained to us matter-of-factly. "They come here every night to watch their mother eat. And every night she kicks them away."

"I don't see anyone," Jimmy said.

"Of course you don't," the woman answered. "They are too black to be seen, but they are out there."

I looked out into the thick night. There was not a star in the sky, not a streetlight in the alley. Yet, I could see two pairs of eyes burning at us like hungry wolves.

"American mixed?" Mrs. Dang asked.

She nodded. "The 'burnt-rice' kind."

"That's too cruel," my mother remarked. "Why didn't the mother just give them away if she doesn't want them?"

"Well, folks, don't think she hasn't tried." The soup lady mused. "That wretched woman sold most of her kids as soon as they sprouted their first baby teeth. Those two she couldn't sell. They are black girls. Who wants them?" My mother didn't answer. "I'll tell you something even sadder than this," the woman continued. "A few months ago, she lost a child, an older sister of those two, about ten, eleven years old. The girl used to come around here begging for food. They grabbed her one day. It happened right here down this street. Three men. They had some sort of agreement with the mother, buying the kid's virginity. Well, they took her to that deserted farm next door. One of them put his you-know-what in her mouth while the other two pinned her down. The poor child didn't know, so instead of pleasing him, she bit down on it."

My mother interrupted her, looking at us. "Eat your soup, kids. Don't listen to the adult conversation!"

Mrs. Dang spoke up. "I've heard about that story. They killed her with a rock."

"That's right," the woman agreed. "Smashed her head like a bug. Nobody heard her screaming. The train was too loud when that happened. Then they paid the mother to keep her mouth shut. The police couldn't find the killers, and the girl died in vain. No one cared."

"I remember that little girl," Mrs. Dang said thoughtfully. "Her hair was so bushy, it looked like a beehive from afar."

"It got shaved the day before she died," the soup lady said. "It was so kinky, anything that fell into it disappeared. They got all kinds of stuff out of her head; you name it, toothbrushes, combs, paperclips, rubber bands, and God knows what else. I tell you, your children are lucky that they are white. At least they have a chance to live. The burnt-rice have only bad luck."

I finished the soup and laid the empty bowl back on the table. My sister lapped at her soup slowly like a kitten. My mother looked at me in astonishment. "You ate so fast. Would you like to have another bowl?"

I hesitated. "Why don't you eat, Mom?"

"I am not hungry," she said.

"What happened to you, mother? Why did it take you so long to come home?"

She avoided my stare. "You don't want to know."

"Of course I do. You were all we could think about. You went to Saigon, right?"

"We got arrested in Saigon for trading without a license." Her eyes fixed on her nails. "The real let-down wasn't the jail time we had to serve, but we lost all of the money."

"What happened?"

"How in hell should I know? We were having breakfast at the market when I noticed this Chinese guy sitting across my table. I thought I recognized him as a merchant. Dang and I went over, making small talk."

"Small talk?"

"Business talk. The next thing I know was, he pulled out a gun and handcuffs and arrested us in the middle of the crowd. We were thrown in jail."

I pushed the empty bowl away. "Maybe I shouldn't eat anymore, Mom. You don't have much money."

"Don't worry," Mrs. Dang interjected. "I have a couple of red Chairman Ho's left in my pocket. You kids go ahead and enjoy yourselves."

LATER THAT NIGHT, after she had put BeTi and Jimmy to bed in my grandparents' room, my mother came to say good night to me. She sat on the edge of my bed, looking at me through eyes filled with pain. The once highly maintained beauty had long abandoned my mother's face, leaving behind a mask of naked desperation. For a moment, I couldn't recognize who she was, and the confusion stirred up panic in me.

"What would you have done if I had never come back?" she asked.

"I don't know, Mother," I told her. "I'd have waited for your return."

"What if I didn't come back?"

"Why wouldn't you? You have responsibilities."

"I couldn't be responsible for you if I were dead. That could happen sometime. If it did, what would you do, Kien?"

"I don't know. Please stop asking me these questions. Just tell me what to do," I cried out in fear. "We were going to beg for food if you didn't come back. Jimmy wanted to sell Lou, but we couldn't."

My mother burst into tears. "Would you abandon your brother and sister?"

"No."

"My poor boy." She reached out to hug me, and I could taste her tears mixed with mine. "I want you to know that if the thought of walking out on them did cross your mind, you don't have to be ashamed of it. I understand." She lifted the sleeve of her blouse to wipe her eyes. "It's all right now. I am here, and you are safe. So go to sleep."

As she left, I called out to her.

"Yes, darling." She turned to face me. "What is it?"

"Please don't leave us."

CHAPTER TWENTY-FIVE

I woke up the next morning, doubled over from a stabbing pain in my lower back. Even breathing was painful. I crawled out of bed and walked slowly toward the bathroom, passing by Moonlight's room on the way. She sat in front of a mirror, staring dully at her reflection. The path that led to the outhouse seemed endless. With each step a thousand specks of glittering black light exploded in my eyes. I didn't bother to lock the door behind me.

It was not until I was in the middle of relieving myself that I realized instead of urine, I was passing blood. Thick globs of scarlet liquid gushed out of me. I was so frightened, I pulled my shorts back on, letting the rest of the blood stain the front of my shorts as I staggered out to search for my mother. She was in my grandparents' bedroom with Mrs. Dang. When she pulled my shorts down to examine the problem, nothing looked out of the ordinary except for the red streams I released.

"What is wrong with him?" my mother cried out in distress. "Help me, Dang."

Mrs. Dang shook her head. "The beating has broken something inside him. We've got to take him to the doctor."

"I can't afford a doctor," my mother said. "Besides, what good can a bunch of college graduates do? They never know what they are doing."

"Then take him to your mother's herbalist. See what he says," Mrs. Dang suggested.

I had taken a sharp blow to one of my kidneys, the herbalist pronounced. Since I was young and strong, it would not leave any permanent damage. The bleeding stopped after a few doses of the bitter herbs he prescribed.

A WEEK LATER, my grandparents returned from the hospital. My grandmother's foot was still swollen and throbbing, filled with pus. From afar, it looked like a giant, overripe eggplant. Sitting in her favorite chair in the garden under the shade of a jackfruit tree, my grandmother listened as Moonlight read the Buddha's scripture to her. Gusts of afternoon heat tumbled down on top of them, creeping through the branches like dozens of snakes. Their tan skins reflected the sun, and their naked feet buried into the hot sand. They lost themselves in the chapters of the sacred book.

In the past few months, Moonlight's health had noticeably declined. Every morning she woke up coughing. Then, by the well, she sat for hours with her shoulders drooped in between her knees, trying to expel mucus out of her lungs. A couple of times she threw up blood. Her cheeks had lost their rich shade of oolong tea and taken on the gray of a rotting lemon. Moonlight carefully tried to conceal her sickly appearance with makeup. The thick powder made her look like an opera singer before a performance.

She greeted me the moment I walked into the garden. "Hi, Kien. How are you?"

"Fine, thanks," I replied.

"How is your back?"

"It is much better. The herbs helped."

"I want to go to the temple and get some blessed medicine for my cough. Do you want to accompany me? Maybe the monks can give you something for your back. Or we can pray to the Buddha for Grandma's health."

"Okay."

I accepted Moonlight's invitation, simply because I adored her company. She had not seen Ty Tong for several weeks due to her illness. I missed keeping guard for them under the magnolia bushes down the street at night, as they stole eager kisses in each other's arms.

The temple was located on a side of a mountain, twenty kilometers from the house. Local people knew it as Spirited Mountain Temple. Its door was open for the sick everywhere. The trip took us twenty minutes by bus, another twenty minutes to climb the mountain. From the ground, a total of one hundred and forty-two steps cut into the rock led to the main lobby. Moonlight had to stop several times on the stairs, but in due time we found ourselves walking into an open ground filled with visitors.

The lobby overlooked the entire city and the nearby towns. Its floor was covered in dark blue tiles, which were constantly being swept by the faithful worshipers until their surface had become like a dark ocean, reflecting the sun. A giant lotus with each of its petals carved from marble sat in the middle of the ground. Its base, a cylindrical octagon, depicted hell in a series of eight pictures. Sitting inside the petals was a statue of Buddha, four stories high, of white marble. His hands folded neatly on his lap, he sat with closed eyes as he pondered his own tranquillity. Rumors said that his third eye had originally been made out of a large emerald, which got either lost or stolen through time. A green light bulb had since replaced the stone to cover the hole in the Buddha's forehead. Its light illuminated his serene face, keeping the sacred place in order, regardless of the vast number of visitors each day.

The red pointed roofs and golden columns of the temple stood behind the Buddha, as beautiful and ancient as the mountain it rested on. Each worshiper was allowed to pray for one wish inside a large room filled with incense clouds. The altar was set at the far end of the room, decorated with more Buddha statues in various shapes and sizes. Most of them were covered with gold leaf, or made out of bronze. A large copper urn in the center of the room held the incense. In rows from either side of the room, monks dressed in yellow robes sat in meditation.

Along the mountain, a sheet of water flowed against the rocks, entering the temple from the roof. Once inside, it wound its way behind the altar and escaped through a drain in the floor to join the river below. The mist it left behind rose like fragrant steam, keeping the temple cool all year round.

On a side of the temple, a small brown brick road led to an area where the monks dispensed herbs. A small cottage behind a dense bamboo forest at the end of the road served as a hospital. Moonlight took a number from a nun standing by the entrance and we walked inside the waiting room.

After she had received three little bags of herbs, we strolled out to the lobby. The city seemed minuscule below our feet.

"Tell me, when we were inside the temple, what exactly did you pray for?" she asked.

"I was praying for Grandma. Hoping she would get better soon. Then I asked the Buddha about my father."

"Which Buddha did you ask? By the way, that is more than one wish, Kien."

I sighed. "I know. But I prayed to the biggest one in the center, the statue that has lots of hands coming out of his body. I was hoping he could give me another wish."

"Of course, the famous one-hundred-hands-and-thousand-eyes Buddha." She cleared her throat. "He is very powerful. He could grant you any wish that you may have. What did you ask him about your father?"

"I asked him who my father is, whether he is thinking of me, or if he knows about my existence at all."

Moonlight raised her eyebrows. "Difficult questions! What if you don't get the answers?"

"Then I will continue to ask him every time I come here until I do get the answers."

"Why do you want to know about your father, Kien?"

"I hate living here," I said without thinking. "I want my dad to take me to America someday."

Moonlight began to sing. In the muggy afternoon, her voice sounded like a mournful cry.

"How are you and Ty Tong?" I asked, trying to stop the sad song. "When are you going to see him again?"

"I don't know," she said. "In a few years if I am lucky. He was drafted by the military last week to fight in Cambodia. He will be leaving by the end of this month."

"Really?" I sat up and looked at her. The thought of Ty Tong in the military service was incomprehensible to me. "But today is the last day of the month."

"That's true," she said. "He is leaving this afternoon."

I stared at her in disbelief. "Then why didn't you stay home to say good-bye to him?"

She didn't answer.

Suddenly, I understood. "You didn't come here for the herbs. You came here to ask the Buddha to protect him, didn't you?"

She nodded. "Yes, but there is a catch. He is not going to Cambodia."

"How come?"

"He is going to escape. And I am praying for him to get away safely. That was my wish."

"No!"

"Yes. It's getting late. He probably has left already. Let's go home." She got up from the bench.

I offered my arm, which she held tightly. "Don't worry," I reassured her. "I'll pray for your health next time, Moonlight."

She smiled and leaned over to peck my cheek with her cold lips. "Thanks, sweetie. But if you are going to pray for me, who will ask the Buddha about your father for you?"

I shrugged. "That can wait. You are my only friend in that house. I want you to get better."

I LEARNED LATER from Duy that Ty Tong had left for Singapore while we were sitting at the temple that afternoon. His mother had bribed many officers in town to enable him to escape. Moonlight received a letter from him a month later, stamped with the Singapore postmark. It was the only letter she would ever receive from Ty Tong.

1980

The herbal treatments did not cure the infection in my grandmother's foot. For two years we watched her waste away until she could no longer leave her bed. Each morning, we drained the wound into a basin. At night, her monotonous praying would keep us up, and the clicking of her fingernails on the Bo De beads echoed in our ears. The herbalist suggested that my grandmother's foot be amputated at the city hospital. But medications were scarce and when available, expensive, and the hospital offered minimal care, so my grandmother remained at home and anticipated death.

One afternoon, my mother and I traveled deep into a forest on the other side of the mountain. For hours we followed an overgrown path until we came to a large soursop tree. Tentacles that grew from its thick branches reached down to the ground like locks of hair. The soil was covered with the black, velvety shells of soursop fruits, which sprang softly under our footsteps like a satin bed. My mother pointed upward. Following her gaze, I saw a bamboo cottage that hung like a bird's nest from the top of the tree. This was the home of Dr. Ang, a wizard who had built a reputation among the poor for the bizarre miracles he had performed.

It got dark early in the woods. Since the wizard did not invite us into his home, we spent the evening sleeping on the ground next to the ancient tree's powerful roots. In the eerie blackness of the jungle, flickering lantern light made his cottage glow like a tinderbox and kept the wild animals from venturing near.

The next morning, we took the guru home with us and led him to my grandmother's bedroom. The old man squinted his eyes with curiosity at my grandmother. Politely, he asked my mother to tie my grandmother's hands to the bedposts as he prepared for the surgery. When he punctured my grandmother's foot with a sharp knife made out of a human femur bone, a jet of pus and blood squirted out, spraying his face. Pouring wine into his mouth, he then blew it out in a vapor mist all over her foot. Like a vampire feasting on its prey, he sucked out the pus and spat it into the basin below. The wizard cleaned the wound in that fashion for almost two hours. Finally he laid her foot back down on the bed with a look of satisfaction and sat down on the ground.

"All done," he said to my mother. "Your mother will heal. But she won't walk again."

The old wizard's words were true. The nasty wound healed a few weeks later, but her foot shrank down to the size of a twig, black and lifeless. The cancer, however, had spread to her internal organs. For the remainder of her days, my grandmother lay in bed, staring past the window into space. It was as if a part of her mind had died before her body had time to give up.

I EARNED MONEY by delivering fish from the seaport to the market after school. Jimmy's job was to gather firewood in the forest. In order to work and look after my sister at the same time, every afternoon I tied her to a post near the shore, despite her crying and pleading. At five years old, BeTi was slow-witted and skinny. Leaving her alone in the sand, I joined the crowd of children at the harbor, waiting for the fishing boats to return.

After a captain hired me for his boat, I ran down to its stern, where the fish were piled up on the deck. A seaman shoveled the fish into a large black lacquered basket then lifted it and balanced it on my head. Fish blood and salty seawater would gush from the holes in the basket, running down my back, and dripping out through the hem of my shorts. Staggering away from the boat, I pushed the other kids aside to get to the street, watching my sister from out of the corner of my eye. A good day or a bad day depended on how large the catch was, and how many other children I had to compete with for the job. The market was just about two blocks away. Sometimes if I was lucky, I could deliver up to four loads of fish. At the end of the day, I went back to the head fisherman for my pay, and rushed home to prepare dinner for my family.

One afternoon, as I balanced a large fish basket on my head, I saw a girl leaning over my sister, unhooking the rope that bound BeTi's hands to the wooden pole. She must have been fourteen or fifteen, and she wore a sleeveless blouse as red as blood. I walked over to them, and I couldn't help noticing that the skin on the girl's neck was smooth and white like lotus blooms.

"What do you think you are doing?" I barked at her, as ferociously as I could.

The girl looked up. Her eyes were bright and huge in her delicate face. Her long, jet-black hair fell over her face. She closed her eyes to think before responding, and the ocean, the blue sky, and the bustle of the docks faded in my mind. As I watched her pink lips, like rose petals, the heavy basket and its foul odor no longer seemed to exist.

"You can't tie her hands like that," she said to me. "It's so cruel." Her voice was harsh with the thick, nasal Hanoi accent. Everyone in the south despised the inflection of the North Vietnamese, as it represented all the repressions of Communism. But to my ears, a songbird could not have sounded sweeter.

I stammered, "But if I don't, she would wander away and get lost."

"In that case, I'll stay around and watch her for you."

"You can't do that! You don't know us," I said.

She laughed, showing me her white, straight teeth. "Actually, I do know you. I've seen you and your sister on the beach every day. Would you trust me more if I buy a tuna from you?"

"I can't sell you these fish. They are not mine."

From his boat, a fishmonger called to me, "Hey, Curly. Get back to work!"

"Go on," the girl urged. "Don't worry about us! Your sister will be fine."

BeTi stared at me fearfully, her face swollen from crying. I turned away, embarrassed. As I walked down the street and headed to the market, I could hear them giggling together.

When I returned to collect my sister, the girl in the red blouse was gone. The sun had set, and its pale purple rays shimmered over the waves. BeTi sat on the sand, eating a spring roll. She beamed at me with her toothless smile.

"Where is your friend?" I asked BeTi.

"Kim's gone," my sister said. She raised her hand and opened her fingers, revealing an oily wrapper with another spring roll inside. "This is for you."

Kim. My mind echoed her name. I reached for my sister and lifted her up off the sandy beach. "Did she talk about me?" I asked BeTi.

"Yes," my sister said with excitement, "a lot."

1981

CHAPTER TWENTY-SEVEN

My grandmother stopped talking. The only sounds she made were moans. She barely recognized any members of her family. She stopped eating, except for a few drops of soup my grandfather forced down her throat. As she got sicker, her bladder and digestive tract stopped working. In bed, she passed her bodily wastes continuously. Nobody in my aunt's family helped us to take care of her. The stench of her illness became part of our existence.

Even my mother's patience was challenged on numerous occasions. After being cleaned up, my grandmother would soil herself on her cheap tatami mat again. Sometimes I could hear my mother's frustrated scream from the front of the house, cursing my aunt's family for not helping her, and cursing my grandmother's cruelty for being alive in such a pitiful condition.

My grandmother lay motionless for days, looking without recognition at my grandfather through her crusty eyelids. As she drifted away, an incessant stream of gibberish came out of her mouth. She grasped wildly at invisible objects. Jimmy and I sat on the floor a few meters away, watching her delirium, and wishing for death to take her quickly.

One afternoon I came home from the seaport drenched in fish blood. As I walked through the thick, wild grass of my aunt's garden, I heard my grandmother calling for me. Her lucid voice surprised me, and I paused at her window to look inside.

She was lying on her back and staring at the ceiling. Her hair was mostly gone, revealing her whitish, wrinkled scalp. She was naked. Her hands froze in midair, catching an invisible butterfly. She defecated, and her feces mixed with her urine to drip from her mat to the cement floor below. She lifted her head to meet my gaze, and her lips trembled as she called out my name.

I wanted to rush to her side, but somehow my feet were buried deep in the ground. I wanted to call out for help, but the words were trapped inside my parched throat. I saw two lines of red ants along her legs, feeding on her flesh. Eerily, I wondered how long they had been there. Her eyes never left my face. Her voice weakened as she begged for my help. Her hands dropped down on top of her sagging breasts. Then, with one last, rasping breath, she was gone.

I started to scream. At first, the cry that escaped my throat sounded like a broken duck whistle. I sucked in air and tried again. The next sound that came from my lungs was so foreign to my ears, I wondered if it belonged to someone else. Nevertheless, I couldn't stop.

From her room, Moonlight ran outside. Seeing me at my grandmother's window with my finger pointing into her bedroom, she understood immediately. She, too, began to scream.

The news of my grandmother's death spread through the village. My grandfather had gone out for his usual walk, and my mother was at the market. By the time they came back, a crowd had gathered in front of the compound. The news did not seem to surprise my grandfather. Without a word, he closed himself behind the bedroom door to be alone with the corpse. The rest of us stood outside and waited in silence. Nobody in either family shed a tear.

Night was falling, and the sun melted over the red tile roofs. More and more people were coming to my house. The town commander came up behind my mother. His face was inches away from her hair.

"I am so sorry about your loss," he said to her. "We are here to help you with the funeral arrangements."

My mother didn't look up. "Thank you," she muttered, "but we can manage. We wouldn't want to trouble you."

"No trouble at all. It is the town's responsibility to take care of its citizens. Your mother is a part of the community," he said.

"It's okay, sir." My mother looked up. "You may be our community leader, but you have also worked so hard to relocate your wife and daughter from Hanoi. They are finally here after fifteen years. It's only right that you should be home celebrating with them. We can take care of our own misfortune."

My aunt interrupted, "Shut up, sister. Let the honorable comrade do his job."

"Your sister's right." The community leader looked hurt. "But if you don't want me here, I'll leave. It's been our country's tradition to pay respect to the dead. I've ordered the town to prepare for the ceremony. Tonight, I give everyone permission to help your family. You have my deepest sympathy and best wishes." He turned and exited through the front gates.

An hour later, a group of men from the funeral home arrived. With my grandfather's help, they cleaned my grandmother's body and marinated it in rice alcohol. When the wine had straightened her limbs, which had stiffened from rigor mortis, they dressed her in new clothes. Using a thick red thread, they tied her two big toes together to prevent her spirit from wandering.

A cheap red lacquered coffin was brought into my grandparents' bedroom. A layer of sand was spread at the bottom to cushion the body. Rich families would use tea leaves instead of sand. The more expensive the tea, the richer and higher in status the dead were. We covered the sand with coarse, loosely woven cotton gauze. After my grandmother's body was laid inside the coffin, a small dish filled with burning oil was placed on the ground beneath it to keep her spirit warm. Incense in a large urn perfumed the air. It was time for friends and relatives to pay their respects.

That night, my family slept by the coffin to keep my grandmother company. On the cold cement, Mrs. Dang and my mother were discussing the details of my grandmother's burial. Lying next to them, Jimmy and I slowly drifted to sleep. Mrs. Dang leaned over to my mother and whispered in her ear. Drowsily, I heard her every word.

"Are your sons asleep, Khuon?"

"I think so, why?" my mother answered.

"I don't want them to hear this, but I am leaving soon."

"What do you mean? Leaving my house, or planning to escape?"

"Planning," she whispered. "I found a connection. The owner of the boat will allow me to take one more person with me. My parents are too old and live in Saigon. Since I have no one else, I can take one of your sons. You have to decide which of the boys you want to let go."

I lay quiet, but inside I screamed out to my mother, begging her to pick me over my brother. Her silence drove me wild with anticipation; I could barely keep still.

Then, I heard my mother murmur, "How much will it cost?"

"Not a dime. We are good friends, aren't we? It's my way to say thank you, darling."

"How long do I have before I must give you the answer?"

"A month. You can decide after the funeral."

"Let's talk about something else," my mother said.

CHAPTER TWENTY-EIGHT

We buried my grandmother on a rainy February afternoon, three days after her death. The funeral bus dropped us at the entrance to the cemetery, which lay fifty kilometers outside the city, draped alongside a mountain. A few hundred feet below crept a wrinkled sea.

We trudged in silence along the steep, rock-strewn trail that led to the gravesite. The wind wailed over the white salt banks, rippling the red-and-black funeral flags above us. Drops of acid rain stung my eyes as we moved numbly across the desolate landscape.

Flashes of lightning cut through the sky, turning the clouds an electric blue. Thunder followed, roaring through the air like bombs. Jimmy and I walked next to our mother. Our white tunics and headbands were soaked in the salty rain, filthy with mud. My grandfather leaned heavily on his wooden cane as he limped beside my grandmother's glossy red coffin, which was hoisted on the shoulders of my aunt's sons. His eyelids, puffy as if stung by a bee, blinked away the tears. A few steps behind, Loan walked alone. Her wail rose sharply over the sound of trumpets and flutes.

Loan had showed up at our house on the second day of mourning. She wore a well-tailored black suit, which she quickly exchanged for the white tunic of mourning. Sitting on the floor next to my grandmother's coffin, she faced us with a red and embarrassed face. Her hair, tied into a large bun beneath a cotton headband, carried the sweet smell of jasmine. My mother had reached out and patted Loan's shoulder.

"How are you, Loan?" my mother asked. "It is good to see you again."

"I am doing fine, thank you."

"How is Mr. Tran?"

"Problems." Loan smiled sadly. "We are being investigated. It's part of the Sixth Plenum's rectification campaign against the negative aspects within the Communist Party. The government has reason to believe that Mr. Tran is no longer a purist or a socialist in his thinking. It started as far back as the day he confiscated your mansion and made it his own. It is very tense in the house with him." Her delicate fingers clenched together on her lap. Each nail had a purple rim of dried blood, a result of her biting habit.

"Maybe it would help if you have a baby with him," my mother suggested. "Good fortunes always come with a new life."

Loan turned away. Her voice lowered to a whisper; we had to strain in order to hear her. "I can't have children. The lining of my uterus has too many scars from the abortion. The doctors said it wouldn't hold the egg anymore." She got up and walked outside.

Now her voice rose from behind my grandmother's coffin. She threw herself on the ground, crying, "Oh, Auntie, why did you abandon us? Who will help me when I need guidance?" She wiped her face with muddy hands. Dirt matted her long hair and stained her clothes in large blotches. My aunt drew Loan along until we reached the gravesite. The cemetery stretched into the gray distance, while the wind-whipped funeral flags flapped noisily.

A rectangular grave had been dug prior to our arrival. My aunt's sons, following the funeral director's instructions, lowered the coffin into the grave with two thick ropes that were held parallel at each end. Loan and my aunt wailed, reaching out for the coffin lid. My cousins dragged them away as the men threw dirt into the hole. The downpour intensified. Its salt tasted bitter at the tip of my tongue. My mother's grip tightened around my fingers. Tears mixed with rain flooded her face.

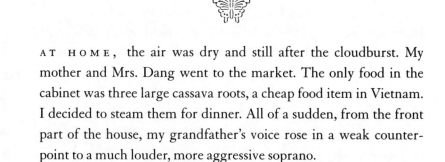

AT HOME, the air was dry and still after the cloudburst. My mother and Mrs. Dang went to the market. The only food in the cabinet was three large cassava roots, a cheap food item in Vietnam. I decided to steam them for dinner. All of a sudden, from the front part of the house, my grandfather's voice rose in a weak counterpoint to a much louder, more aggressive soprano.

I ran out and saw a strange, middle-aged woman arguing with my grandfather. There were bruises on her eyes and around her cheeks. Her face was red with indignation. She pointed a finger at my grandfather and spoke in a heavy northern dialect. The girl in the red blouse, whom I had continued to encounter at the seaport, huddled next to her. Kim looked at me with her sad eyes.

"What is going on?" I asked.

My grandfather spoke up with irritation. "These people are looking for your mother. I told them that she isn't home, but they wouldn't leave."

The woman was tall and thin, and her voice was harsh with anger. "I won't leave this place until I see that whore's face, if she dares to show it to me."

"Let's go, Mother. Please!" Kim tugged at her mother's arm.

"My mother is not a whore," I protested.

The stranger stepped up until her face was a few inches from my nose. I could smell the faint stench of farm animals from her clothes. She pulled up her sleeves to show me more bruises on her arms, and others around her neck. "My husband did this to me," she said. "He beat me near death because of your mother. Don't tell me she isn't a whore."

"Who are you, and who is your husband?" I stammered.

The woman proudly pushed her chest forward. "I am Mrs. Qui Ba, the wife of the community leader. Your mother has no idea what kind of hell is waiting for her when she messes with me."

"Mr. Qui Ba?" My mind conjured up the image of the community leader, his silver hair, and his catchy smile. "Impossible. They hardly know each other. You must have gotten the wrong person, lady."

"Please, Mother. Let's go home. You are making a scene," Kim begged.

"I don't care if the whole world is watching. I am not leaving," Mrs. Qui Ba said.

From the other side of the street, Pink's voice called out in gleeful anticipation, "Kien, your mother is coming home."

Mrs. Qui Ba ran out into the street and shouted. "Where is the slut? Show your face."

Her daughter looked at me, her eyes filled with pain. I remembered the sandy beach, the distant ocean covered with silver waves, and the way her lips had reminded me of rose petals. She turned and ran after her mother. I followed them.

My mother and Mrs. Dang stopped at the far end of the street. Someone from the crowd outside had warned them about the crazed woman, who now charged at them with a howl of rage. The crowd kept pace with her, eager to watch a fight.

"Which one is the whore?" the woman demanded.

Mrs. Dang stepped forward. "Can we help you?" she asked calmly.

"I want to meet a whore named Khuon."

"You want to talk to her, talk to me first," Mrs. Dang said.

The woman looked at my mother. "So, you must be the whore then. My damnable husband called out your name while on top of me. Then he beat me up to hide his shame. Fifteen years I waited for my husband while he served his country. I never expected to be treated this way. You have corrupted him, you dirty imperialist slut."

She lunged at Mrs. Dang, pushing past her to get to my mother. Mrs. Dang fell to the ground as the woman attacked my mother's face with her sharp nails. Her daughter and I jumped behind her to pull her back, but it was too late. She grabbed a handful of my mother's long hair and yanked at it with all her might, shaking my mother's head the same way she would have smoothed out a wrinkled bedspread. At the same time, she kicked furiously at my mother's abdomen.

Mrs. Dang got up. She grasped the woman's arm, peeling her fingers from my mother's hair. Mrs. Qui Ba struggled to get free, but ran out of strength and finally collapsed. I held on to her waist, watching her gasp for air. Next to us, Kim cried quietly.

My mother leaned against Mrs. Dang. Her hair spilled over her face, and red scratches streaked her cheeks. She screamed at Mrs. Qui Ba, "I did not have anything to do with your husband."

"Don't lie! He told me all about you. This is not over yet. I will not rest until your bloody corpse is rotting in a jail somewhere."

"Get out of here. Go home. You want to teach somebody a lesson, start with your husband. Teach him not to stray if you can. I am not afraid of your empty threats," my mother said coldly.

The woman straightened up. "We'll see about that," she said, reaching out for her daughter's hand.

Kim turned to me. Her eyes widened. "Why does it have to be your mother?" she moaned.

Her mother pulled her along as she pushed through the crowd. I closed my eyes. Somewhere beyond the curious onlookers, my mother called out for me.

CHAPTER TWENTY-NINE

I helped my mother inside. Silence fell upon us as we walked side by side through the garden. In front of their house, my aunt stood next to her husband, holding a bucket of water. Her lips puckered to suck the smoke out of her wet cigarette, making a repugnant kissing sound. Without warning, she lunged forward and emptied the bucket on top of my mother's head. Dirty water flooded her face. My mother howled in shock.

My aunt shouted, "How dare you make a scene in front of my house? Have you no shame? Now the whole town knows you are sleeping with the town leader."

My mother turned to my aunt, who took a few steps back to hide behind her children. "Go to hell, all of you," she spat at them.

Then she adjusted her wet clothes and walked past my aunt to get to our house, ignoring the stares of her relatives.

My aunt cursed under her breath. "A wild horse never forgets its old track. I wish someone would feed that slut to the elephants."

As soon as Mrs. Dang and my mother withdrew into her bedroom, the house returned to its usual serenity. I prepared dinner, watching a spider scuttle along the kitchen wall. A fly was trapped in its web, struggling frantically to get free. The spider brandished its tiny feet in defiance. Its venom paralyzed the fly. My head felt as empty as the inside of the lucky Buddha's belly. I searched the food cabinet for any additional course I could make to accompany the cooked cassava. There was only a small saucer of salt and pepper in lime juice. I set everything on the floor and invited my grandfather, Jimmy, and BeTi to come in for dinner.

Then I knocked on my mother's bedroom door. Mrs. Dang opened it. Sleep clustered around her eyes like tiny flakes of dandruff. I entered, and the close confines of my mother's room encompassed me like a shut coffin. I searched my mother's face for some sense of grief. Instead, I found nothing. My mother sat on the edge of the bed, combing her hair under the light of lantern.

"Dinner's served," I said curtly.

"Kien, is there a problem?" she asked.

"No."

"Then please don't give me any trouble. I don't need that from you."

"See you outside," I said and walked out.

"Listen," she called out after me. "Tomorrow I'll take you to the market. I want to buy you some notebooks and clothes."

"It's midsemester. I don't need any more notebooks. Why don't you take Jimmy?"

She shook her head. "No."

"Why not?"

My mother tapped her comb impatiently on her desk. "I don't want to take him," she said. "It's very important for you to do well in school. Jimmy never was much of a student, not like you. But if you don't want to go, then don't."

"I don't want to go."

"Fine, suit yourself, but you will go to school. Don't ever blame me for not trying to do my best for your future."

The sadness that I had nursed for the last few days suddenly went off in an explosion of anger. "My future?" I shouted. "What about Jimmy? Do you have plans for his future? Would it be better than mine?"

My mother turned to Mrs. Dang, raising her eyebrows in shock. "What is wrong with him?" She shifted her eyes at me. "Where are your manners? Why don't you invite Auntie Dang for dinner?"

CHAPTER THIRTY
Nhatrang, March 1981

The beach in late afternoon appeared darker under a thick and gray sky. With the absence of the wind, tiny waves lapped the sandy shore with a constant, sleepy stroke. The busy pier, where all the boats had docked earlier, suddenly was empty again after the fish had been unloaded and transferred to the market. A flock of seagulls circled the wet sand that was still soaked in fish blood and seawater, searching for dinner. Their loud squabbling screeched through the murky sky, like the ending of a dirge. That day, I went to work without my sister. It was Jimmy's turn to watch over her.

Without BeTi, I decided not to hurry home. Instead, I strolled along the beach, watching the sunset. Somewhere on the horizon, a small strip of island, reaching itself out as far as my eyes could see, separated the ocean and the sky into two discernible entities. Above my head, the sun was out of sight, but fragments of bright orange light still peeked through the sky as if someone had hidden red coals in the clouds. As I walked closer to the water, my bare feet touched its cool surface, and the intense weariness in my muscles slowly dissipated. I took a deep breath, lifting my arms outward. Salty air rushed into my lungs. With no one in sight, I pretended to fly like an airplane — a game I had not played in years.

"Kien, wait for me."

From behind a clump of young coconut trees, I heard Kim's voice. Her inflection pierced my ears, as sharp as the seagulls' chortle. My cheeks felt hot. The embarrassment of being caught in the middle of a childish game made me blush from head to toe. This was our first encounter since the dispute between Mrs. Qui Ba and my mother. I was glad to see her, but equally glad that no one else was on the beach.

"Hello." I turned to face Kim, scratching my ear.

She ran across the sand to catch up with me. "Where is your sister?"

"I work alone today. BeTi is at home with my brother."

"I see, I was waiting —" she stopped in the middle of her sentence, looking at me.

The awkwardness returned between us. I avoided her eyes, feeling very much like an insect before a glorious but deadly Venus's-flytrap. We stood facing each other, and the ocean watched us with its inquisitive waves.

Finally, I broke the silence. "How are you?"

"I am fine, thank you." She touched my hair with her hand. I could smell a mixture of lemongrass and talcum powder from her skin — the scent of freshness. All of the sudden, I was keenly aware of my own stench, resulting from fish waste, and I recoiled from her touch.

As if she read my mind, Kim asked, "Do you want to go for a swim with me?"

I pondered the invitation while she took off the outer layers of her clothes and stood before me in her two-piece bathing suit. The red fabric pressed against her golden skin, outlining her female anatomy as if she were nude. Or was it my imagination? I could not make the distinction. Again, I fought the urge to stare at her.

Kim ran into the sea. Her hair flew wildly in the wind. Her smooth, long legs disappeared in the water. She turned to face me. Under the silver light, the ocean, the sky, and she seemed to liquefy together, as if they were all made out of mercury. She waved, beckoning me to follow. I took off my shirt and dove in after her. Before long, I, too, felt myself slowly melting away in the extraordinary twilight.

I swam away from Kim. I didn't want her to see me scrubbing myself. She stood in one place, yet her eyes never left my face. Through the thin mist that was evaporating above the water surface, I watched the surf crash against her firm belly. Her forearms pressed together in front of her chest as if she had suddenly become aware of how tiny her bikini top was. I washed myself quickly and swam under the water toward her, only to come up for air when my nose was inches away from her thighs.

"You swim very well," she observed.

I nodded proudly. "I grew up on this beach. I spent most of my free time here."

"I wish I knew how to swim."

I extended my hands out. "Want me to teach you? I am a very good teacher."

She shook her head and took a step back.

"Trust me, it is easy to learn," I insisted. Her fear ignited an unexpected urge in me to watch her cry. The thought of Mr. Qui Ba, her father, and how his dirty, uneducated, Communist hands had fondled my mother enraged me. I reached for her hands, and when I found her cold fingers, I grabbed them tightly.

"Not today, please." She pulled away from me.

"Yes, now. You better run, Kim. Because I am going to catch you, and I'll drag you out to the deep part of the water." A bantering tone concealed my seriousness.

Taking my threat as a joke, she ran back to the sand, screaming and laughing. I leaped after her. My arms, like the hungry waves, encircled her thin waist, lifting her off the ground. My cheek pressed against the side of her breast. I smelled her moist, babylike skin. Yet my thought was still about her father, and how much I wanted to hurt him. Kim kicked her feet in the air, begging me to stop.

"Ah-hah, the half-breed has a Commie girlfriend."

On the boardwalk, a group of boys stood in a half circle, waving and yelling profanities at us. These were my co-workers, who had just unloaded their last baskets of fish and were on their way home. Their heckling stopped me instantly. I let go of my fingers and Kim slid off my chest.

"The half-breed fucks a Commie whore. Her nasty hole has teeth, and that was how the half-breed got sore —" The wind carried their mocking through the empty atmosphere. Each word rubbed more salt in my already gaping wound.

"Let's go, Kien. Don't pay any attention to them." Kim pulled my hand and gathered her clothes on the sand. I wanted to push her away, but I had no strength.

In the sallow afternoon, I watched her get dressed. When she was done, she handed me my shirt, which I hooked in the pocket of my khaki shorts.

"Does it hurt you, their teasing?" she asked me.

My answer came so fast that it felt like a defense mechanism. "No, I am used to it."

"Let me ask you then, does it bother you that I am from the north?" Her eyes stared directly at me.

Instead of answering Kim, I attacked her with a series of questions. "I don't know, does it bother you that I am below the poverty level? Or that I am a half-breed? And let's not forget that your father is wooing my mother?"

"No." She shook her head. "None of that bothers me. I like you. And I think you are the sweetest boy on this beach. Not to mention the cutest."

"Besides those jerks," I joked, feeling a little better, "I am the only boy on this beach."

Kim laughed. She held my hand. "Let's walk home together."

"People might see us."

"So? I thought you don't care about that."

"I don't. But I can't afford to make your father mad."

Kim nudged against me. Her hair tickled my neck. "Okay, I'll leave as soon as we reach the highway, but I want to see you tonight."

"How? Where?"

"You know where I live. You can meet me at the back gate behind the kitchen around eight."

"I will be there," I said. "Tonight, tomorrow night, and any other night that you might want to see me. All I ask from you is please keep what we have a secret. I don't want my mother or your father to find out."

Before we separated, Kim nodded in agreement.

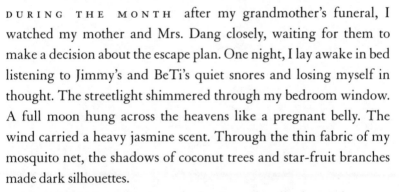

DURING THE MONTH after my grandmother's funeral, I watched my mother and Mrs. Dang closely, waiting for them to make a decision about the escape plan. One night, I lay awake in bed listening to Jimmy's and BeTi's quiet snores and losing myself in thought. The streetlight shimmered through my bedroom window. A full moon hung across the heavens like a pregnant belly. The wind carried a heavy jasmine scent. Through the thin fabric of my mosquito net, the shadows of coconut trees and star-fruit branches made dark silhouettes.

My mother tiptoed into my bedroom and walked straight to my brother's side. I watched her with the eyes of a hungry leopard. She tapped on Jimmy's shoulder.

"Get up, Jimmy," she whispered as she shook him.

Jimmy hoisted himself up on his elbows and a look of confusion formed on his face.

"Get up," she murmured. "Get yourself ready, Jimmy. And keep quiet."

"Where are we going, Mother?" His voice was slurred with drowsiness.

"Come with me, I'll explain outside."

Jimmy hopped out of bed to follow my mother's lead. When they walked past my bed, I sat up and glared at both of them. My mouth could form just one word. "Why?" I cried.

"Go back to bed, Kien. It's one in the morning," she said to me.

"Why him?" I jumped out of bed, blocking their path and sobbing feverishly. "I know what you are plotting. I overheard your conversation with Auntie Dang last month after Grandma's funeral. You are not leaving unless you give me an explanation: Why him?"

My mother placed her hand on my shoulder. "I need you here with me. You are the man of this family. You have responsibilities to take care of us. Besides, Jimmy is much younger. If he got into trouble, the police wouldn't keep him in jail. You would fare much worse, and I just can't take that chance. Please let him go. He needs to be on the boat in an hour."

"I am not the man of your family, Mother." My voice shook as though it were ten degrees below zero in the room. "I am not even fourteen. They can't lock me and throw away the key. But, even if they do, I don't care. I can't live like this anymore. I want to go, please."

She dug her nails into my skin, the familiar punishment for misbehavior. "Listen to me," she enunciated. "You don't like to live this way? Who does? Since you both were kids, I've always favored you over your brother. You always got better toys, a bigger slice of cake, more love, and more attention than he did. For once in your life, let him get preferential treatment. I need you here with me. Go back to bed."

From behind my mother, Jimmy spoke up. "Is it true that I am going to escape, Mother?"

"Yes, Jimmy. She's letting you escape with Aunt Dang. Tonight is your lucky night," I answered him bitterly.

"No," he shook his head with apprehension. "I want to switch places with Kien. Let him go. He needs to get out of here more than I do."

Hope returned to me. I turned to my mother. "I can help you much better if I am in America. Please, if I stay here, I will kill myself."

My mother's eyes shifted between my brother and me. Seizing the opportunity, I pressed my case.

"I mean it, Mother. If you keep me here, I will die. You might risk losing both of us. Ask Aunt Dang how she felt when she lost her children. Besides, Jimmy doesn't want to go. Why force him?"

My mother uttered a small cry. "Go." She waved her hand to dismiss me. "Aunt Dang is waiting outside by the gates."

I ran out the door, fearing that she might change her mind.

"Hold on a second!" my mother called. Her voice froze me on my track. "Please, wait. I'll take you outside." Turning to my brother, she looked into his face intensely. "You understand that you are taking over his responsibilities, taking care of your sister, and helping me with everything? From now on, you are my eldest son. Do you understand me?"

Jimmy nodded.

"Good, go to bed. I'll be back in about fifteen minutes to tuck you in."

Jimmy ran to me. He put his arms around my waist to hug me with all his might. "Good luck, Kien. I love you."

I turned away from his touch. My cheeks were hot with shame.

We left the house together. Across the street, Mrs. Dang was waiting behind a coconut tree. Her expression changed from excitement to surprise once she saw me.

"You decided to send Kien instead?" she asked.

My mother nodded. "The other kid didn't want to go. Take care of him for me, Dang. Make sure he doesn't get hurt. I trust you with his life." She touched my head as she spoke.

"Of course," her friend answered. "I will adopt him the moment we get to America. I'll make sure he has a good education, and I will remind him every day about you, so that he won't forget his roots."

My mother broke into tears. Under the pale streetlight, I noticed the crow's feet at the corner of her eyes, the strands of gray hair around her temples. Still, the passion in her eyes was bewitching.

"Look how much you've grown," she whispered to me. "You are already taller than I am. From now on, you belong to Auntie Dang. She is going to take care of you. So listen to her, and pay her all the respect that you've given me. I love you, Kien. Take care of yourself."

She pushed me into the bosom of Mrs. Dang, who was crying.

"Tell Grandpa good-bye for me," I said. "Tell him I love him."

"Go, may the gods bless you," my mother murmured.

CHAPTER THIRTY-ONE

By two o'clock in the morning, we reached the beach. The docks where I worked during the day delivering fish to the market were now vacant. At the end of a narrow and secluded wharf, a small wooden rowboat waited for us. We ran across the shore. With every step I took, the sand became wetter and softer, until salty water seeped into my flip-flops. A dark figure of a man jumped from the boat and waved to Mrs. Dang. She waved back.

"Good evening, you are on time." His bare chest, where the light hit, was contoured with oily sweat and rippling muscles. His thin lips didn't quite cover his large buck teeth, which glowed in the dark like a fluorescent light.

Mrs. Dang and I huddled together on a bench near the aft of the boat. The man rowed skillfully, checking his compass now and again for the direction. His ferry headed east past a clump of dark islands, which were almost invisible in the mist.

Above us, the sky flickered with a million stars. The round moon reflected the ocean's waves into silver coins, spilling over the water's surface. The salty air's soft touch caressed my skin. Like a tiny leaf in a pond, the boat skimmed the surface in silent rhythm.

"Where are we going, Auntie? Where are other people?" I asked Mrs. Dang.

"Quiet," the man answered. "Kid, the less you know, the better off you are. So, shut up."

"We are going to Turtle Island," Mrs. Dang said to me. "There, we'll wait for another, bigger boat."

The ocean seemed to expand around us. On the side of the boat, the waves made a steady murmur.

"Here we are," the man finally said. Facing the stern, I was unaware we had reached the island until the bottom of our boat came into contact with the rocky ground.

"Listen to me," the man said as he searched for a place to dock. "This is Turtle Island. Like the name, it is shaped like a turtle. The island is off-limits to civilians. The turtle's body is the mountain. The beaches are its legs. The mountain has three layers. We are going to the middle part. If we go too high up, terrorists and leftover guerrillas of the old government will kill us. If we get too close to the beach, we'll be in the hands of the Communists. They like to shoot first and ask questions later. Be extremely careful. Sometimes we run into illegal lumberjacks. Avoid them, too, if possible. The big boat will come tomorrow night. Now, let's get out of here before the brown dogs smell us." He was referring to the Communist police, who wore dark brown uniforms.

Turtle Island was a lush jungle filled with tropical trees and thick clumps of wild berries. Bushes grew past the shore and reached out into the water, making it an ideal place to hide out. We walked deeper into the forest on a narrow path across the swampy ground. Each time we moved, clouds of flies and mosquitoes swirled up, breaking the quiet with their buzzing.

The man handed us each a knapsack. "Take this," he said. "It contains your portions and some blankets for tonight. Watch out for the quicksand. Keep your feet steady on the rocks. And don't forget to keep an eye out for snakes."

We ran in single file through the wet and tortuous road leading to the middle part of the turtle's hump. Under our feet, the muddy ground was covered with dead leaves that sloshed as we marched further uphill.

The rest of the escapees were waiting for us in a large open area not far from the trail. There must have been about thirty people, all women and children; not one was younger than ten years old. Their plastic mats were scattered on the ground, held down by rocks. Some of the women huddled under the blankets against the cold wind. The only men in the group were the two leaders. The young man who brought us to the camp was Can Junior. The older man was his father, Can Senior. He had just been released from a death camp a few months earlier. As I learned later, the old man had been an army sergeant under the old government. He, too, was bare-chested and barefoot. A pair of faded, cutoff khaki shorts covered the lower half of his body, and in his thin waistband I could see the steel handle of a pistol. A large, ugly scar on his left cheek sprang to life like an animated lizard every time he spoke. His black eyes glared as he introduced us to everybody else.

We were told to share a space under a wild tamarind tree with two other people — a teenage girl and her younger brother.

Mrs. Dang sat on a rock, worn out from the long hike. She beckoned to me, wiping the perspiration off her forehead. "Come here, Kien. You can rest next to me."

"Welcome to Turtle Island," the boy said to me. He was about fifteen years old, his face covered with freckles and his eyes slanted like those of a puppet character from a Chinese opera. He and I were the oldest boys among the children.

His sister, who was a few years older, had beautiful hands and feet. I helped her clear the dead leaves from our rest area. She looked up to smile at me. Her face, with its high cheekbones, appeared pale in contrast to her red lips. She, too, reminded me of a character in the opera playhouse — a marionette princess.

Far beyond the trees, the sun peeked its carroty face over the dark blue water, sweeping away the silvery darkness. Some of the children ate breakfast out of their knapsacks. Soon, the shells of hardboiled eggs and banana skins littered the ground. The women watched their children and daydreamed about their new lives in America.

"Come here, darling," Mrs. Dang said from behind me. "Let me comb your hair for you."

I sat down in front of her, feeling the soft touch of her fingers on my scalp.

She said softly above me, "Isn't this exciting? Tonight, we'll be boarding the boat. Who knows, in a short week we might get to Hong Kong, or the Philippines, or Malaysia, and then to America. I definitely would like to settle in California and look for my children. Together you and me, we'll get a small house by the sea, like Nhatrang almost. And when my kids come to join us, you'll be their big brother. You'll go to school and study anything you like. Then you can sponsor your family to America. Is this a nice dream?"

Instead of answering, I snuggled closer to her body.

That evening, we ate the caramel chicken that had been packed in our knapsacks, while Can Junior left the camp to wait for the boat signal by the shore. We huddled in the dark, covered with the thin blankets, cold but full of hope. Some of the children fell asleep, while others stirred restlessly. An old woman squatted down on the ground to urinate. Somebody tried to muffle a cough. Around us, the jungle hid inside a dense fog. Curled up against the tree, I slipped into a deep sleep in Mrs. Dang's warm embrace.

When I awoke, the morning sky was as white as milk. The fog had lifted from the tall trees, except for a few tendrils that lingered in the blue shadow of the forest. In front of me, Mrs. Dang and a few other women were talking with Can Junior. I clutched the blanket around my shoulders and walked over to join them. An air of sadness hung over everyone.

"I am sorry, I don't know anything else. We just have to wait," Can Junior said to the women.

"Wait for what, and for how long?" someone asked him.

He walked away. "I don't know, but we may be here for a couple more days."

"What is happening?" I asked Mrs. Dang.

She noticed me for the first time. Her eyes wore the frightened look of a trapped animal. "Someone stole the boat last night," she said.

"Oh, God. The big boat that takes us to America?" I uttered in shock.

"No." She shook her head. "The small ferry. About the ship, we couldn't get any signal from them, so we are stranded here, with no way out."

"What do we do?"

"We wait," she said mechanically, echoing Can Junior's answer.

THE SECOND DAY went by uneventfully. We huddled next to each other to keep warm. Mrs. Dang watched me eat the cold food without touching her own. Above us, dark clouds started to form.

On the third day, it rained. I ran out on the soggy ground, joining the other children to take a shower, while at the same time, storing rain water in the empty bottles for future use. The adults hid under the surrounding trees to keep from getting wet. Hope had dwindled along with our food supplies. Below us, the ocean moved like a giant dish of blue Jell-O under the sweeping winds.

ON THE FIFTH DAY, the women scattered into the jungle in groups to search for wild mushrooms, berries, and greens, while the two men fished at a nearby stream. The island offered little in the way of food. Sea spinach and wild berries were among the meager vegetables we harvested near the swamp. Despite the elders' warning, we ate the cooked vegetables and became violently ill that night. The next morning, when the cold rain revisited the island, we washed the vomit off our clothes. As hungry as we were, the incident instilled a fear in all of us, and everyone gave up the food search. The children sucked on the last of the rock candies while the adults slept their starvation away.

On the afternoon of the sixth day, Mrs. Dang pulled me deep into the woods, away from the other escapees. Not until we were at least thirty feet away from the camp did she unwrap her shawl and show me the contents. Three hard-boiled eggs appeared like props in a magic trick.

"Here, darling," she whispered to me. "Eat them quickly before someone sees us."

Unable to tear my eyes away from the food in her hands, I asked her, "Where did you get these?"

"I saved them for you," she answered.

I swallowed loudly. "What about you, Auntie? Aren't you hungry?"

"No, darling." She smiled and shook her head. "They are yours. Go ahead, eat them."

BACK AT THE CAMP, Can Senior was holding an emergency meeting. Mrs. Dang and I joined the rest of the runaways on the dirty ground. He stood on a rock in front of us, licking his lips nervously. Like everyone else, he had lost a lot of weight in the last six days. His chest caved inward, and his rib cage stuck out from his torso.

"Let's talk about our alternatives." He asked the crowd, "Who among us want to surrender to the brown dogs?"

A wave of dissent swept the group. People cursed the boat that never came, blamed their own bad luck and each other, jumped up and down, and shouted at one another. Can Senior waved his hands to quiet them down.

"Be quiet," he yelled. "There is still hope."

The group froze.

"There is a way out," he continued. "We have a gun. We can steal a motorboat from the illegal lumberjacks and escape. Who wants to take this risk? Let me see a show of hands."

"Don't those woodsmen have weapons with them?" a woman asked. "What if we lose?"

Can Senior shrugged. "We don't have much choice, madam. If we lose, we'll die, but if we surrender or do nothing, we'll also die."

I searched Mrs. Dang's face for guidance, but she turned away. I stood up. All eyes were on me as I spoke. "I don't want to surrender. Just like all of you, I got stuck here because I was searching for freedom. Let freedom guide us out of here."

Someone cried out from behind me, "Well put, child. Let's fight for a ride home."

There were whimpers of disagreement among the women, but most of them finally agreed that we should seize control of a boat. Can Senior looked at me and asked, "What is your name, son?"

"Kien."

"And you?" He turned toward the boy with slanted eyes, who stood next to his sister under a tree.

"Van," the boy answered.

The old man then said, "My son and I will attack the loggers from behind. Can you two back us up?"

"No," Mrs. Dang and the boy's sister cried simultaneously.

"Sorry, ladies," he said. "I need them to balance the fight."

"What do we have to do?" I asked him.

"Take me instead," Mrs. Dang said, holding on to my arm tightly. "I can fight if I have to. Leave my boy out of this."

"Not a possibility," he told her. "In the old days, whenever I tangoed with Death, I needed my men. Death is here right now, and your son will do just fine."

CHAPTER THIRTY-TWO

In a single line, Can Senior, his son, Van, and I moved deeper into the jungle, leaving the women and children behind. Far away, a thunderstorm growled like a hungry stomach. Lightning flashed against the reeds, turning the purple branches of the trees around us into monsters out of a horror story. Can Senior held the gun in a tight grip. We hung on to each other and crawled on the slippery ground like a giant earthworm in the eerie blue light of an early afternoon.

Can Senior suddenly stopped. He signaled for us to duck further down on the sloppy ground. "Don't anybody move! Stay where you are," he whispered.

From my position, I could see a shadow chopping at a tree thirty meters away. The logger was not alone. I could hear other voices blending with the rumble of the thunderstorm and the scream of the winds. Can Senior gestured for us to crawl closer to him.

"Here is the plan," he whispered. "There are four of them. Two men are having lunch. You can't see them, but they are behind that tree. You see the other two, don't you? Kien and Van," he said, pointing at the two loggers, who were within a few meters of each other, "can you two take care of them? My son and I will stand guard right here to cover you. Take a rock like this one and sneak behind them. Make sure you knock them unconscious. Do not worry if they see you. If it happens, just try to distract them as long as possible. We'll come out and rescue you. Easy enough?"

He handed me a rock that was slightly bigger than my fist. Van chose his own weapon, another rock that had a similar size and shape.

"How can we sneak up to them while they are facing us?" I asked the old man. The thought of wounding someone made me sick with fear.

"I have a way to do it," Van said.

"Tell us," Can Senior ordered.

"We can attack the targets from above the ground." He pointed at the branches that shot out like dark spears over the two men. "Kien and I can pussyfoot from branch to branch and get close to them. Then when the time is right, *sssssfurt*" — he made a dropping sound — "right on the skulls."

"Excellent idea, son," Can Senior said. "Now, go, both of you."

Van got up and shoved the tail of his shirt inside his pants. Like a kangaroo protecting its young, he stashed the rock inside his shirt and tightened the belt around his waist. With his hands free, he climbed up a tree. I copied his every move and followed. From the branch of one tree, he hopped to another like a squirrel, making little sound. I trailed after him shakily, finding it hard to keep myself steady on the slippery bark. The strong winds screeched between the lush green leaves. Gravity pulled heavily at the rock in my shirt. Far ahead, Van reached his destination. He perched in the tree above his enemy, waiting impatiently for me.

As I moved closer to my target, the branches grew smaller and farther apart. I prayed silently, looking deep inside myself for new strength. Finally, through a thick curtain of leaves, I saw the lumberjack's dark hair and a section of his red flannel shirt. Another branch and I would be directly above him.

Across from me, Van held the rock in his hands. I followed his lead, reaching out to steady myself with one hand so I could pull out my weapon with the other. But instead of the hard surface of the branch, my hand brushed across a soft, cold, slippery, and moist foreign object. I looked down at a python, larger than my leg. Its body was twisted around the branch right underneath me. It cocked its diamond-shaped head to stare at my face.

I shrieked and jumped backward. The branch under me snapped in half. I fell onto a bed of dead leaves below, a few steps away from where the logger stood. At that moment, Van dropped the rock on top of his victim, knocking him to his knees like a chopped tree. He fell facedown on the muddy soil.

The ground had enough of a leafy cushion to break my fall; however, my blood-curdling scream and my unexpected appearance alarmed the other loggers. They dropped their lunches and ran out from behind a bush, their axes gleaming in their hands. The enemy closest to me also lifted his ax. His face was dark and deadly. I pushed myself away from him, but fear paralyzed my limbs. I froze and blinked at him, waiting for doom.

"Stop, or I'll shoot." From the hidden path, Can Senior and his son stormed out. His gun pointed at the lumberjacks.

The logger in the red-striped flannel shirt screamed at us, "You damned spirits, you killed my brother."

"He didn't die. Just passed out," Van answered matter-of-factly. He had gotten down from the tree and was examining the body on the ground.

"Who are you people? What do you want from us?" one of the woodsmen asked. His face was dotted with chickenpox scars, which kept his expression somewhat emotionless. It was difficult to tell whether he was surprised or angry.

"We need to borrow your boat to go back to Nhatrang," Can replied.

CHAPTER THIRTY-THREE

The scar-faced man glared at the gun in Can Senior's hand. "You wouldn't dare. The police will be here as soon as you fire that gun."

Can Senior spat on the ground. "I wouldn't bet on it if I were you. In this rain, who could hear anything? Do you want me to prove it?"

"No," the logger said. "Please, trust us! We'd like to take you to shore, since we are the only ones who know how to make that cranky motorboat of ours run."

"Why should I trust you?" Can Senior asked.

"You've got a gun. Just tell us what to do, and don't hurt me or my men."

Can Senior nodded. "In that case, I'll take two of your men with me. The other two can stay on this island. Once we get to Nhatrang safely, the ones who take us can rejoin their friends."

The scar-faced man pointed at himself and the man in the red flannel shirt. "Take us then. We know the route."

Can Senior turned to Van and me and ordered, "Look in their stuff for ropes, and tie those two up against each other. Make sure you gag them."

With Can Junior's help, we positioned the two prisoners on the ground with their backs to each other. One man was still unconscious as we moved them closer together. Blood from the man's head wound left a trail of red dots on the jungle floor. We made tight knots around their ankles and wrists. Some of the blood dripped on my fingers, and I fearfully wiped it away.

With his hands high above his head, the scar-faced man said, "Just tell me, how many of you are there?"

Can Senior ignored him.

BY THE TIME we got down to the sandy beach, it was early evening. The sky was dark with heavy clouds, and the rain fell harder. Thunder again boomed through the trees, which flashed with lightning. Along the coast and concealed under stacks of coconut leaves was the boat. Thirty feet in length, it was made out of plywood and tin plates and painted a rusty orange, though most of the paint had peeled off. The engine, composed of a generator and a jumper wire, sat between the bilges in the stern. An iron shaft connected the engine to the propeller through a hole in the aft bulkhead. Along each side of the deck was a row of benches that could accommodate six to ten people. The boat had been loaded with about a dozen freshly cut logs, all the same length. Can Senior ordered us to toss the stolen lumber back on the beach to make more room for the passengers.

We pushed the boat out to sea. The loggers' axes lay together on deck under a sheet of plastic. We huddled in each other's arms on the benches, while the smaller children lay on the floor. Can Junior and Can Senior settled themselves at the bow. Their gun aimed at the boat owners, who sat at the far end.

With Can Senior's permission, the man in the red shirt pulled the jumper cord to start the engine. His partner held the control bar connected to the generator and steered a steady course. The boat shrieked loudly. Its sharp keel rode the water like a sea horse. Soon, the island was left behind. Before us, the sea opened up its immense embrace, rocking the vessel in all directions. The rain was falling hard, making visibility impossible. Soon we were all drenched. Seeing that I was shivering, Mrs. Dang held me closer.

At the stern of the boat, the scar-faced man pulled another plastic sheet from under his seat and handed it to Van's sister, urging her to cover herself against the rain. She took it from him shyly.

In the tense atmosphere we rode for almost an hour. Finally the clouds parted and the moon, once again, showed its sallow face over the turbulent sea.

The scar-faced man shouted to Can Senior, "Listen to me and don't shoot! I need to feed the engine some fuel. She is getting empty. The gas can is over there." He pointed to a large tin-coated iron container lying next to the axes.

"No," Can Senior replied.

"Please, listen to the engine's sound. She will stop in a few minutes if we don't feed her."

Can Senior warned him, "Fine, but do it slowly so I can see you. Stay away from the hatchets. If you do anything suspicious, I will not hesitate to shoot."

The prisoner nodded and reached for the container. The tank seemed heavy; he had to use both arms to lift it up and drag it across the desk. He turned his back to Can Senior as he moved slowly toward his seat. Suddenly, he tripped on a piece of wood on the floor and fell forward. Still holding the container, he swung his arms a hundred and eighty degrees, whirling to face Can Senior. The tank of fuel in his hands flew through the air like a flash of lightning.

"Be careful!" Can Senior screamed out.

To our shock, the scar-faced man burst out laughing and looked at us triumphantly. The fuel container was locked in his fingers and dangling over the edge of the plywood gunwale above the dark sea. He winked at Can Senior, waving the tank back and forth. "Shoot me, if you dare. This can will end up in the bottom of the ocean, and so will you when the boat's out of gas."

"What in hell are you doing? I thought we had a deal," Can Junior blurted, standing up with clenched fists.

"What deal? You wounded one of my men, abandoned two of them in the jungle, and then kidnapped us. What kind of deal is this?" He ordered the man in the red shirt, "Stop the engine."

"No," Can Senior yelled.

His partner pulled a switch. The boat shrieked one last time before it came to a halt. Alone in the ocean, it rocked from side to side.

Can Senior raised his pistol. "I guess I have no choice but to shoot you and take control of the boat."

"Proceed if you will. I am not lying about the gasoline."

"We'll take our chances."

The scar-faced man pointed his finger upward. Somewhere beyond the clouds, the sky glittered faintly with stars. "Follow that star," he said. "Do you know its name? The fishermen call it the North Star. We were supposed to go west to reach Nhatrang."

He waited for the effect of his words to sink in, then continued. "But we didn't. We have been traveling north all along. You asked us for a ride, Mr. Leader. So we are taking you on one. And now, we are running out of gas. So either you drop the gun or pull the trigger. Just do us all a favor and make up your mind, before I make up mine."

Some of the women moaned with fear. The children began to cry. Can Senior stood up. The tip of the gun shook slightly in his hands. "Shut up!" he screamed at them.

"Drop the gun, please," a woman urged him.

Ignoring her, Can Senior said to the scar-faced man, "Surely we could agree to settle this in peace. I have a proposal."

"My ears are open," came the reply.

"Let's drop all of the weapons in the ocean, the gun and the axes. You take us to Nhatrang, and we'll pay you."

"Pay us? With what?"

"Jewelry."

The scar-faced man cocked his head. "Interesting proposition. Show me what you've got."

Can Senior looked straight ahead, one hand clutching the gun while the other unhooked the watch from his wrist. "This is an Omega. It's worth a lot of money. I'll trade it for my son's life."

"Father," Can Junior whispered. "You can't give that away. It's mother's gift."

"Shut up," he snapped. Turning to us, he ordered, "Take out your possessions. Show the men that we want to make peace."

The runaways fumbled in their clothes and pulled out their hidden treasures. A pile of watches, diamond rings, gold necklaces, and bars of gold and silver collected at the feet of the logger. His partner scooped them up and shoved them into his pockets.

The scar-faced man said to Can Senior, "I am not yet agreeing to this deal. Without the weapons, you still outnumber us. We won't stand a chance."

"What do you want us to do?"

"Send that buck-toothed guy over here." He indicated Can Junior. "We'll hold him hostage. If you don't behave, we'll kill him."

Can Senior swallowed. "Take me as your prisoner instead. Leave my son out of this."

"It doesn't matter which one. Just drop the gun and come over here."

Can Senior laid down the gun and said to his shaking son, "Make sure you throw away the axes first, then the gun."

With his hands above his head, Can Senior walked across the deck. The man in the flannel shirt grasped his wrist and twisted it against his back, forcing him to his knees. Silently, the women threw the weapons into the ocean, and Can Junior did the same with his father's gun. In front of our frightened eyes, the scar-faced man lifted the gas tank and slowly opened the cap. An evil smile appeared on his face. He threw the cap on the floor and turned the container upside down. A few drops of dark liquid trickled out.

In the pale moonlight, Can Senior's face twisted with rage. Without much success, he tried to spit in the direction of his enemy.

Reaching into a toolbox under his seat, the scar-faced man pulled out a hatchet that we had not seen before. He bared his teeth at Can Senior. "You foolish man, do you know how many boat people like you we encounter each year? Do you think you can outsmart me? I'll kill you, you stupid son of an ox."

His hatchet rose over his head, making a silver line across the dark night before it struck Can Senior's chest. The blade cut through his bony torso with a dull sound. The old man's body shook as though he were being electrocuted. The refugees screamed, pushing each other down toward the stern, away from the hellish scene. In the confusion, one woman fell overboard. Her daughter cried out and frantically stretched her arm to take hold of her. Mrs. Dang gripped my wrist, wailing in horror.

The man in the red flannel shirt released Can Senior's wrist and the old man dropped on the floor. The logger pulled at the jumper cord to start up the engine. The boat jerked backward, sending more screaming people into the ocean. The scar-faced man stepped on his prey and yanked the ax from his chest. Blood spurted onto the deck. With a couple of kicks, he propelled the dying man off the boat.

Pointing at Van's sister, who was cowering among a group of terrified women and children, he ordered, "Get that girl." His partner grabbed her long hair and pulled her forward. She fell to the floor and cried out for her brother, who was caught in the arms of the runaways, helplessly watching her.

The scar-faced man walked toward us and swung his weapon over his head, shouting from the tops of his lungs, "Get off my boat."

"Let's jump, Auntie," I yelled to Mrs. Dang.

She looked at me with a strange calm. "I can't. I don't know how to swim."

All around me, people were leaping off the boat in groups, screaming their way into the darkness below. I held her hand. The madman was approaching. "Let's go, Auntie."

"No," she whispered.

"Please, follow me."

Still she held back.

"Please," I screamed. "I'll help you. Just hold on to me, okay?"

She nodded. Together, we jumped into the sea.

CHAPTER THIRTY-FOUR

Deep water pulled Mrs. Dang and me into its violent embrace. Years of growing up near the beach had taught me how to stay afloat in the turbulent waves. I kicked myself upward, and her hand slipped off me.

I surfaced, and all I could see was the vastness of the ocean surrounding me. A few heads bobbed in the darkness, but none of them belonged to Mrs. Dang. The boat was still close by; I could hear the loggers' laughter. Van's sister's cry seemed to come from a million miles away.

"Auntie, where are you?" I called out. "Please, Auntie Dang, answer me!"

A flopping noise startled me. I turned around and saw Mrs. Dang fighting desperately to keep her head above water. She saw me and struggled harder. I swam to her and grabbed the small of her back, lifting her upward. She coughed and took in several deep breaths. I kept her on her back, floating atop the water. The rocking motion of the waves seemed to quiet her.

"Relax, Auntie. It's all right now," I whispered to her. My teeth were chattering in the initial cold.

"Thank you, love," she said softly. Her eyes closed tightly.

We floated for about half an hour, until the rain came back. The drops that fell from the heavens were much warmer than the water we were submerged in. Unfortunately, the wind also picked up, propelling the waves higher. Mrs. Dang let out a nervous cry each time they splashed in her face.

"We are going to ride the waves. Do you understand me?" I told her. "Push your body up and let the water flow underneath you. Can you do that?"

"Yes, darling."

But it was too late. In her fearful eyes, I could see the reflection of a powerful wave, towering above the sea's surface. It crashed down on us like a ton of bricks. I held on to her as we were pushed downward. She grabbed my face, trying to climb on top of me. At last our natural buoyancy carried us back to the surface. Mrs. Dang vomited out the liquid she had swallowed. Her face paled and I could see the whites of her eyes glisten in the dark.

Pushing me away, she said in desperation, "Leave me."

"No," I said. "Listen to me, calm down."

"No, leave me." She fought to get away, but I held her.

"Please, Auntie," I cried. "You are hurting me."

She flapped the water and touched my face with her cold hand. "No, love. Leave me!" Her voice was determined. "I can't do it anymore. And I don't want you to die with me. Tell your mother goodbye when you see her." Tears spilled down her face. "Let me go see my children."

She shifted her gaze past my shoulder, "Over there, Mr. Dang is waiting for me."

With a mighty shove, she escaped my grip and sank into the water. I reached for her, but she again pushed me away. From below the surface, her white face smiled at me with tenderness before the darkness swallowed her. I looked up to the soggy heavens, realizing that I was alone. "No," I sobbed. "Please, come back, Auntie Dang." I hit the water in frustration.

"Don't leave me, please! I am scared." My voice ran helplessly across the ocean. Around me, the rain made a low, hissing noise.

The thought of thousands of meters of water, filled with lurking sea monsters, made me dizzy with fear. I began to swim, heading west from the faintly lit North Star and crying inconsolably with each stroke.

I do not know how long I swam. All that I remember is gliding across the water as if I were running a marathon. The will to live powered me with a single thought: swimming forward. Then, my thoughts shifted to my warm home, freshly cooked food, and a steaming cup of hot tea. My heart beat wildly in my chest. With a new surge of endorphins, I strained my eyes for a sight of dry land.

Suddenly, the muscles in my lower back jerked into an enormous knot. Pain shot up my spine and paralyzed my right arm. My fall from the tree earlier that afternoon had left me bruised, and now my tissues were locked in a spasm. To ease the discomfort, I swam sideways like a fish with a broken fin. Sometime later, I turned on my back and floated. The turbulent water massaged my muscles, bringing temporary relief. The urge to live stirred in me, and I again swam toward the west.

Time crawled. My skin blistered from the salt. I tried to drink the rain, not realizing that each time I opened my mouth I couldn't help swallowing seawater, which was causing dehydration.

Finally, the rain stopped. The sky draped like a large, starry blanket over the world. The moonlight painted the tiny waves around me the color of my grandfather's hair. I lifted my hands and laughed hysterically. My fingers dripped lustrous, metallic water like mercury. Specks of light danced on the ocean surface, beckoning me to join them. Time melted into space, letting me flow with it into oblivion.

"Fall with me," the sea murmured in my ears, promising the happy incantation of a new freedom. Fear had no meaning, and neither did pain. All I felt was an absolute calmness, spreading into every fiber of my being. It told me to give up fighting. Like an obedient child, I stopped swimming.

I let myself sink, and the water closed over my head. It pulled me down to the center of the earth. But, to my surprise, my descent stopped abruptly. My feet touched the roughness of sand. Realization lit up my numb mind: land! The shore couldn't be far away.

I shot up like a bullet, gathering my strength to swim forward. The indifferent sea spat me out onto a sandy beach. I embraced the wet sand, kissing it happily.

CHAPTER THIRTY-FIVE

I crawled out of the water with no sense of time or place. I had no idea how far I had swum. Before me lay a foreign shore, submerged in darkness. Beyond the sandy beach, thick pine shrubs shaped like beach umbrellas grew along a deserted street. The only sound was the ocean's rhythmic murmur.

I doubled over and vomited seawater onto the sand. My muscles trembled uncontrollably, and I struggled to remain conscious. My wet clothes smelled like seaweed. Pushing to my feet, I staggered toward the walkway in search of a safe place to rest. A pine shrub with broad branches reaching over the ground created a sanctuary that looked like a small shack. On my hands and knees, I ducked into the darkness, only to encounter two pairs of naked feet, entangled next to a pile of clothing.

A man's voice called, "Get out! Find your own bush. Can't you see we are in the middle of something?"

I jerked back outside, too shocked to make a sound. Luckily, it was not difficult for me to find an unoccupied shrub nearby. Under its wide branches, which encircled my body like a canopy, I curled into a fetal position, massaging my shoulders to warm myself, then surrendered to a deep and dreamless sleep.

I awoke to the sound of a dog barking and hasty footsteps. Through the dense greenery, shimmering rays of sunlight dappled the ground with tiny yellow dots. I kept still, praying that my piney shelter would conceal me. Under the curtain of arching branches, which ended about a foot shy of the sand, I saw the distinctive, metal tips of police shoes as they strode back and forth. The recognition paralyzed me with fear. Then the steel toes stopped right in front of me.

"Get out of there!" a rough voice commanded.

I knew I had no choice but to obey. But before I could, I heard rustling from the bush next to mine. The same voice that had yelled at me earlier shakily replied, "We are coming, please don't shoot!"

I peeped through the sheer veil of pine needles. A naked couple, with their backs toward me, stood with their heads bowed in front of three policemen. A German shepherd sniffed at their clothes, which hung at the tip of a rifle, held in the hand of a policeman. The same policeman pulled at the animal's leash to keep it still.

"Show me your IDs," he said to the couple.

The man groped through his clothes and pulled out a wallet. Distracted, the dog cocked its head my way and bared its fangs. Unable to help myself, I jumped back fearfully. The dog howled.

"Ah-hah," a policeman said. "More trash for us to clean up."

I fell back into the cradle of pine branches. The black tip of the rifle poked through and aimed at my chest. "Get out," the owner of the gun said.

I wriggled outside, raising my arms up high. One of the policemen pulled me up by the neck of my shirt. He seemed surprised to see me.

"What in hell are you doing in there, kid?" he said.

His cold rifle nudged against the skin of my belly, threatening to spit fire. I stammered for an answer. "I — I was sleeping."

"At the beach, next to prostitutes and hustlers?" His eyebrows rose. "Are you homeless?"

"No, sir."

"Got any ID on you?"

"No, sir."

"Where do you live?"

"Nhatrang, Cluster Six."

He turned to his partners. "Comrades, what do you make of this?"

One of them pushed past the naked couple. His gaunt face, with high cheekbones and a long jaw, tightened upon seeing me. Behind a sparse moustache, his thin lips parted in a smile. "Do you know where you are, kid?"

I shook my head. Afraid to look straight at him or the dog, I focused my eyes on my bare feet. Green lines of sea scum colored the folds of my skin.

The policeman surveyed my crumpled clothing. He reached out to pick a strand of seaweed from my hair. "When did you go swimming, kid?"

"Last night," I answered.

"What are you doing at a beach seventy kilometers from your home, swimming at night and sleeping under a tree?" His eyes devoured my face like a hungry wolf. "Do you think I am an idiot? Where are the rest of the escapees?"

"I am not an escapee," I said. "I don't even know what that word means, sir." Through my mind flashed a lie that I seized as if it were a life preserver. "I ran away, because it was bad at home. I don't know how I ended up here."

Turning to his colleagues, the policeman said, "I don't believe this kid. He stinks so bad, give him a fin and a tail and he would be a fish. I'll take him back to the station and make him talk. You two parade the whore and that miserable devil a few laps around the beach to teach them a lesson. And search the coastline for more boat people."

He grabbed my shoulder and dragged me down the street. Through a purple horizon, the sun, enormous and glorious, erased the last shadow of night. The sleepy town beyond the lines of coconut trees roused lazily. I could hear the clanging sounds of utensils against clay bowls, and a cock crowed expansively. Up the hill, we headed toward a parked jeep. The policeman cuffed my hands behind my back, shoved me in the backseat, and drove off, honking the horn to signal his partners. On the hard pavement, two naked people jogged slowly with their hands behind their necks. Strutting a few feet behind, the policemen stabbed the tips of their guns into one bush after the next as their search for the runaways continued.

CHAPTER THIRTY-SIX

The jeep drove through busy streets and stopped at a police station. Its front room was an ornate salon with a fake leather sofa, framed Chinese calligraphy on the walls, and a low chandelier. Rare orchids in terra-cotta vases sat on the windowsills.

From behind the bar, which was opposite the entrance, a clerk took my snapshot and fingerprints, as well as a short report of my background. When she released my hands, my fingers added more smudges to the glass of the bar top. Soon, a couple of policemen escorted me down a long hallway and shoved me into a small cell. They slammed the metal door shut. I heard a click as they inserted the key to lock it, then their footsteps as they walked away.

The cell reeked with a mixture of rotten meat, urine, and cigarette fumes. Its stucco walls were streaked with what appeared to be blood and feces. It was cold. From the center of the ceiling hung a corroded hook with its sharp edge pointing upward. Underneath sat a crooked, wooden table with an enormous steel mallet and a few rusty bent nails on it. At the far end of the room, against a wall, I saw a large iron tank the size of a library desk filled with dirty water, its surface vibrating with chunks of feces. Desperate to hide, I squeezed into the only secluded spot in the room, a corner next to the tank. I drew my knees up against my chin and made myself as small as possible.

I heard footsteps approach and once again, the clicking sound of the key. I withdrew further into the corner and tried not to breathe. I didn't want my captors to see that I was crying, for fear that they would interpret tears as a sign of admitted guilt. Two policemen entered the room. The iron door squealed on the hinges and clanged shut.

One of them walked in, unhooking his belt. He laid the items attached to it, including a gun in a leather case and an array of bronze bullets, on the table. He looked like an ordinary middle-aged man, with coarse black hair and a flat nose. The younger policeman leaned against the wall and watched his partner in silence. In his hand, he held a cache of roasted pumpkin seeds, which he popped into his mouth one by one as he tapped his grubby shoe on the floor. The noises he made stirred my anxiety until it built inside me like a volcano, ready to erupt.

He spat a husk in his partner's direction. "Did you sleep well last night?"

The other man took the gun out of the casing and unloaded its contents on the table. "No, I spent the night in bed with this juicy girl downtown. Who needs sleep?"

"Good for you," the young man agreed. "I didn't have much sleep either, for a different reason. I was on watch."

"I heard you guys caught a couple of hookers down in Cam Ranh Bay and paraded them along the beach. Must have been quite a sight to watch."

"Yes, it was fun —" He stopped, looking around the room. "Hey, where in hell is that kid?"

I shrank deeper into the dark corner.

The older man replied, "He's behind the tank. Hey, you, get out of there." He banged the tank with his gun, and I sprang from my refuge.

The younger policeman threw away the rest of his snack and approached me. His hands seemed enormous, and his forefingers and thumbs shared the same brown, nicotine stain as his teeth. He seized my neck and pushed me against the tank, pinning my throat and cutting my air supply. I struggled to breathe. Like an angry water buffalo, he flared his nostrils and hissed in my face, "Tell me, you little rat, who is in charge of your boat?"

My voice came out as a whisper, "I don't know what you mean, sir. I ran away from home."

"That is a good answer, but how long can you hold up that lie?"

"Mr. Comrade, I am not lying."

He enunciated, "Understand this: I am not your comrade." A look of hatred contorted his face.

Suddenly, from behind the young policeman, the older man struck a sharp blow across my face. A thousand stars exploded in front of me. The two men lifted me up and threw me into the iron pool, splashing water onto the cement floor. I hoisted myself up to the surface, but a strong hand pushed me back into the filthy water. Trapped inside the tank, I felt my lungs burning. One of the policemen banged on the outer shell of the tank with the mallet. The shrill noise vibrated into my ears with a thousand excruciating pins. I lost control of my bodily functions, but still my captors would not let me surface. At last, they pulled me out of the water like a dirty dishrag.

The older policeman shook me and laughed, "Are you ready to talk now?"

Their voices faded as the ringing in my ears grew louder. I vomited, coughing helplessly in an attempt to expel the liquid from my lungs. They pushed me under the water again. The world faded to black as the tank swallowed me up, and I felt myself go limp in their hands.

I WOKE UP in a dark space, with my wrists tied together in front of my chest. My left cheek was pressed against a cold, moldy tarpaulin-covered floor. I seemed to be in a cell that swayed in a tedious, rocking motion. Then, the sound of an engine and the smell of a dusty road entered my awareness. I was inside a large vehicle. Each time a wheel crashed against a rock, my gut wrenched painfully; however, I had vomited all that was in me. The aftertaste was bitter and dry on my throat and tongue. Curiosity overtook me, and I propped myself up to peek through a tiny hole on the sheet-metal wall.

It was daytime. The truck was climbing a barren and desolate mountain. Jungles of dead trees clinging to hard, clay soil disappeared into the horizon. At the end of a long and tortuous road, I spotted a rusty gate, standing next to a series of gas tanks. Above it was a sign scribbled in black paint: REEDUCATION CAMP No. PK 34. And underneath in lowercase were these words: "Reserved solely for boat criminals."

The prison was surrounded by barbed-wire fences and, I later learned, land mines. From either side of the gate, narrow trenches encircled the compound like the outline of a maze. Inside a small, corrugated-tin watchtower, three guards in green security-police uniforms stood at attention with rifles on their shoulders. When the truck came to a stop, one of them stepped down to open the gate. Suddenly, the vehicle's covering tent was ripped open. Bright light poured in, bringing with it the blazing temperature from outside.

More guards appeared. Two of them pulled at the rope around my wrists to get me off the truck. The courtyard was littered with flotsam of heavy weapons and deteriorated U.S. bombs and shell casings, plus the skeleton of a large howitzer. The prison quarters were composed of clusters of long, single-story barracks, joined together as if they were holding hands. The prisoners were segregated according to their age and sex and separated from one another by high fences, and in some places, minefields.

The guards left me alone under the hot sun. Here and there, I saw groups of prisoners marching in single file between the barracks. All were women and children. Their naked scalps baked under the scorching sun, and their shoulders sagged, while their vacant eyes stared dumbly at the ground. Their zombielike lethargy made me turn away with fright.

From inside one of the barracks, a prison officer strode over toward me. He was over forty, short and skinny. His eyes, hidden behind oversized sunglasses, showed no emotion as he grabbed the rope and led me across the square.

We came to a small opening in the ground. A hundred feet ahead was the barbed wire fence separating this prison from the men's penitentiary. Some of the male prisoners stole a curious look at the two of us from afar as they, too, shuffled along in lines.

The warden unhooked a trap door to reveal a large dungeon below. "Get down," he said.

I looked into a dark chamber, about eight-by-nine feet and thirty feet deep. The glossy floor reflected the light and reeked of sewage. Somebody let out a hollow whimper, which traveled upward as if from the bowels of Hell. Horrified, I took several steps backward.

"Use the ladder, half-breed. Or would you like me to kick you down?" the warden asked as he unroped my hands.

I made my way slowly down a wooden ladder, which ended about five feet from the ground. The oubliette was built of red brick, offering no ventilation except for the trap door. As the cold air gripped my skin like dead claws, I realized that my head was completely bald, just like the rest of the prisoners in camp PK 34. During the period that I had passed out, the policemen at Cam Ranh Bay must have shaved my head.

CHAPTER THIRTY-SEVEN

Inside the moldy cell, two feet of stagnant water seeped out of the ground to form a shallow well. The earth was incredibly cold, despite the hot temperature outside. The dark outlines of prisoners, covered in mud, sloshed around in slow motion to make room for me. Once I was inside, the warden withdrew the ladder and closed the trap door. Somewhere in the dark, a child's voice cried out. A woman begged in sorrow. Her voice echoed against the brick walls and died away. As my eyes adjusted to the dark, I made out the shapes of over two dozen inmates huddled in each other's arms. Never had I beheld such despair.

Suddenly, the panel on the ceiling opened again, and I heard the rumbling of motors. People got to their feet and moaned with fear. Although I didn't know what the noise meant, I, too, began to panic.

Two thick hoses appeared through the door and aimed down at us. Before I could prepare myself, jets of bitterly cold water blasted everyone inside. Children cried, clutching at their mothers for protection. The adults leaned against the walls, bracing themselves against the onslaught. Despite the shock, I found the water revitalizing, since it wiped away the bitter dryness in my mouth and replenished my dried-up body.

The hoses continued to spray water for the next few hours. Inside the oubliette, the water level rose to my waist. We sank into the soft, slippery ground. Finally, the motors were shut down, and the hoses withdrawn. Darkness once again filled the doomed space.

I lost all sense of time. Where darkness ruled, day and night were obsolete. I pressed my face against the wall, preferring to inhale its dampness instead of the odor of thirty desperate people. Insects crawled all over me. Some stood at the entrance of my nostril, but I made no effort to push them away. Strangely, my awareness of their presence seemed to keep me from losing my mind.

A few steps in front of me, a woman stood with her shirt open. She clutched a child of about six or seven years old against her naked chest. The child's head rested against her bony shoulder. Her lips, trembling from the cold, formed an inaudible whisper.

I moved closer to her. "I am sorry, lady. What did you say?"

The woman wiped a strand of wet hair away from her face. Then, with the same hand, she caught the child's head. She blinked several times. The words that escaped from her mouth were incoherent to my ears.

I shook my head. "I don't understand what you are saying to me."

She shoved her child in front of me. In the dark, I could feel its still body wrapped in a wool blanket. "Hold her, please," the mother said, clearer this time.

I accepted the heavy child from her mother. In my arms, her head fell backward like that of a broken toy. The wet blanket dropped from her face and my fingers came into contact with her clammy skin, as wrinkled and rough as a piece of leather. I could feel her lips, which were swollen to the size of two filled leeches on her small, lifeless face.

I threw the corpse back into the mother's arms and screamed, feeling my sanity slip away. The woman received her child back against her naked breasts. Her face remained neutral; I pushed away from them and continued screaming until I lost balance and fell back into the dirty cesspool.

AFTER THE MOANING and crying had subsided, the endless desperation, the gnawing hunger, and the ceaseless chill ushered in the next phase of torture. I stopped thinking; instead, I withdrew into myself and allowed my mind to harden like a piece of rock. In that hazy state I lay until the trap door opened. How long had I been buried in that underground cell? I couldn't tell.

Light poured in, blinding us. The warden's voice roared from above, announcing the ending of the hard punishment. The same ladder was suspended from the ceiling.

We crept up like refugees from the grave. My numb feet, black and blue and festering with open sores, could barely follow the commands of my brain. We fell into a line under the sun, gripping each other's arms for support. The generator bellowed, and the guards again turned the familiar hoses on us, washing the filth from our bodies. After the shower, we received our new prison uniforms — a pair of faded black, secondhand, "one-size-fits-all" khaki pants and a black T-shirt.

In front of us, the warden addressed us. His mat of coarse hair, almost blue under the hot sun, seemed enormous over his undersized head. He tried to read through his dark sunglasses from a crumbled piece of paper. After a few unsuccessful attempts, he tossed it aside.

"You just came out of the Lady Death's cavern," he said. "Some of you might be sick, and some of you might even be dead. But I am sure that none of you are deaf, so listen carefully. This is camp PK thirty-four, the home of boat criminals from the three provinces Nhatrang, Cam Ranh, and Tuy Hoa. Once you are here, you must follow certain rules. This specific camp is for women and children. You and the rest of your team will live, sleep, and function as a single unit. You will be fed three times a day, and you must not take the ration back to the shelter with you. No one is allowed free run of the camp, which means you will be traveling in single file, except for the children and the sick, since they will be working on base. The women will work from six-thirty in the morning until four in the afternoon in the sweet-potato fields at the other side of the mountain. You are allowed to write one letter a month to your family. I don't guarantee that it will get delivered, but feel free to write if you like. At this moment, your families should already have been informed of your whereabouts, so you may expect to have visitors sometime next month. Any attempt to break the rules or to escape will send you back to the death cave. Any questions?"

No one spoke. The warden shrugged. "Fine, follow the guards to your cell."

We marched together past the courtyard, heading toward the barracks. I was the last one in line. The lady with her dead child moved a few paces ahead of me. She whispered a lullaby and rocked the corpse in her arms.

Suddenly, from behind me, separated by two layers of barbed-wire fences, a familiar yet haunting voice uttered my name. It was as if an electric current had jolted through my spine. I turned around. A man leaned on the fence from the other side of the prison. His hands clutched the barbed wire like claws. I didn't recognize his face, but the voice was the same.

"Hey, Kien. Is that you?" He grinned, waving at me. "This is Uncle Lam. Remember me?" A guard seized his arm, pulling him away from the fences. The cunning smile, however, remained on his face.

I wanted to run, but my knees wobbled. I wanted to speak, but the words were trapped in my throat. Everything threatened to turn black around me. As I struggled for consciousness, I wondered how Lam had recognized me after six long years.

CHAPTER THIRTY-EIGHT

I woke up sometime that evening inside a new prison cell, shaking like the severed tail of a lizard. The tatami mat underneath me was soaked with my perspiration, yet I could not stop trembling from a chill that came from somewhere deep inside my bones. Pain shot up and down my spine, radiating through me to the joints of my hands and feet.

There was no electricity inside the camp, and the barracks had no window for ventilation. As a result, the inner space of these prisons was always submerged in an eerie, bluish darkness — a perfect environment for starving rats. They emerged at night from the gutter in the back, reeking of feces. Their eyes were tiny red dots, burning like fire as they chased each other and jumped on the inmates to look for food. A pair of them attacked my feet, making a *tic-tic* sound with their teeth. I was too weak to shoo them away. All I could do was to wiggle my toes in misery and hope they would get tired of the game soon. But I had no such luck.

The night was silent. The other children who shared my cell slept on, making little noises as the rats pricked their hair and scratched their skin. Huddled in a fetal position, I struggled against the urge to throw up the ration of cassava roots I had received earlier at the mess hall. As the fever heightened, the churning in my stomach became more violent, and I disgorged the contents on the floor. The puddle of vomit was instantly covered with rats. I dragged myself away, and the chills finally stopped.

Morning's arrival was greeted around five o'clock with the national anthem from a transistor radio. The music screeched through the loudspeakers, followed by the ringing of a bell, long and insistent, pulling people from their mats. Outside, the sun still hid behind the mountains. The compound was encased in a dull, sallow fog so thick it gave the illusion that we were all swimming among clouds. In the courtyard, shivering against the mountain's chilly dawn, we exercised to the radio music. Breakfast came next — a small portion of a thin rice paste mixed with a few strands of spinach. Dead roaches floated in my bowl, and the dirt at the root of the unwashed greens tasted as bitter as my own bile.

Soon, the adults lined up outside their barracks. The other children and I were locked inside the mess hall until eight o'clock in the morning. We watched the grown-ups' activities outside through small windows covered with iron bars and wire mesh. Each woman inmate was assigned a double-wheeled cart heaped with freshly cut potato vines wrapped in bundles and ready to plant. The women pushed their barrows down the path past the junkyard of weapons, through the prison's entrance, and toward the other side of the mountain. The guards trailed behind the prisoners in horse-drawn carriages, their machine guns held ready in their arms.

When it was time for the children's assignment, a guard marched into the kitchen hall. He sat on a chair, opened a thick folder, and called a few names. Another guard stuck his head through the door and signaled for me and two other children to follow him.

We followed the officer to an open field not far from the underground dungeon. He stopped in front of a mountain of rocks the size of a two-story building, about thirty feet away from the double fence.

"Hey, kids." Without lifting his bald head to look at us, he commanded, "Pick up these rocks and stack them against the barbed wire. Continue where it was left off, starting with the black mark over there. Like you are building a base for the fence, understand? This is your assignment for the next three weeks, so do it well, or I will find a way to punish you."

We nodded.

The guard walked away. I lifted the first stone and moved it along the road. At first, it didn't seem like much of a task, and I was thankful to be busy. However, as the sun traveled up, and the temperature increased, my back began to throb under the heavy load. The fever returned, eating through my body like acid. Beside me, the other two boys were sharing the same torment. Their shirts hung around the waistband of their pants, revealing their sparrow chests. Their shoulders were shrunken, and their backs were bent parallel to the ground. Staggering with the weight of the stones, we advanced slowly.

On the other side of the double fence, Lam was on his knees, pulling weeds from the dried soil with his bare hands. His eyes were glued to my face so intensely that I had to look away. His appearance had changed a great deal from what I remembered. His cheeks were now swollen, covered with old and new bruises. His nose, which may have been broken a few times, was flattened and crooked. He looked overweight, but sickly, as if underneath his jaundiced skin, he was bloated with water instead of fat.

"Come over here," he whispered each time I approached the fence.

Finally, I stopped. "What do you want? How did you recognize me?"

Lam threw a weed into a basket that hung on his side. He grinned the same old devilish grin. "It's funny that you ask. At first, I wasn't sure that it was you, but when I called your name, you turned around, so I knew my suspicion was right. Anyway, it isn't difficult to guess. You stick out from the rest like a dog among a herd of sheep." He licked his lips. "Besides, what else could I do in this place for the past six years if I didn't think about your family? What happened to you, boy? Miss the boat to Heaven, so you stop by to visit Hell instead? How is your mother doing?"

253

"She's fine. Thank you for asking." I walked away from him to pick up another rock.

When I returned, I chose to work on a new spot away from him. Nevertheless, Lam crept closer to me.

"No, your mother isn't fine," he said under his breath. "Where is she? She must be here somewhere, doing her time, the evil whore."

"Don't bother looking for her," I snapped. "She isn't here."

His eyebrows rose triumphantly. The whites of his eyes were yellow, like the rest of his skin. "Well, even better than I thought, you are in here alone, and that must have killed her. Thank heavens I've lived to see this day. Now I can die a happy man."

He paused, blinking at the sun. Suddenly, the smile vanished from his face. "Unless this is the monster's plan to get rid of you, just like she did to me six years ago."

I stood up, forgetting the pain in my back. "You are crazy. My mother would never do such a thing. Don't blame her for your misfortune."

Rage washed over his face. He shot up and grabbed the fence as if he wanted to strike me. From behind Lam, a guard walked over to his side. To get his attention, the guard kicked a clump of red soil in his direction. Some sand hit the back of Lam's head. He froze, bit his lip, and turned around to face the officer.

Glancing at the prison number printed across Lam's right breast, the guard asked, "Do you have a problem, x-o-six-seven-five-eight?"

"No problem, sir," he answered quickly. "There was a bug crawling up my pants, sir. But I got rid of it. Squashed it dead!"

"Keep away from the fence. Don't make me come back here again. Whether you are sick or not, I am not hesitant to send a bullet in your head."

"Yes, sir," Lam replied. He resumed pulling wild grass from the desiccated field.

The moment the officer disappeared from view, Lam whispered to me, "Things sometimes aren't what they seem. Your mother is a witch, Kien. She might have had a motive to send you to death camp, just like she did me. After all, you are becoming a member of the species that she loathes most — a man. It is understandable why she destroyed you."

Angrily, I spat in his face and turned away.

Lam burst out laughing. "Take a look at me. Learn my face well, Kien, because I am the image of your future, boy. This is Hell, and it is your new home, where boat people come in but no one leaves."

CHAPTER THIRTY-NINE
May 15, 1981

For two months I wasted away behind the barbed wires. The world ceased to exist. Each night before I drifted to sleep on my tatami mat, I used a piece of charcoal to scribble a line on the wall. As my calendar grew, my hope withered. Slowly but surely, I acquired the look of an inmate. In a single file with the others, my head bowed, my shoulders sagged, and something began to rot inside my body.

On the morning on the fifteenth of May, three days after my fourteenth birthday, the children were locked inside the dining hall after breakfast as usual. Out in the open field, the warden stood on top of a chair, scanning a thin folder. The prisoners stood in lines, tired, sluggish, and impassive. However, deep underneath their vacant looks, an undeniable anticipation mounted.

The officer took his time reading the names of visitors off his list. Standing at a small window, crushed by the other children, I heard my mother's name. I could sense her presence. She was somewhere behind the rusty gate, among the stirring crowd who had come to see their loved ones. The smells of dried meat, sweet rice, and curry powder filled the air. I could hear the clinking sounds of their pots and pans next to a roaring fire they had set for themselves against the cold morning air.

In an unusually sympathetic voice, the warden addressed the inmates. "For those whose relatives' names were mentioned, you have visitors. Stay in your barracks until we come for you. The rest of you, have a nice day in the potato fields."

After the announcement, the children remained inside the mess hall and the adults went back to their shelters. At ten o'clock, the front gate opened and the visitors poured in, laden with heavy sacks and baskets. Under the guards' watchful eyes, the guests' movements were disciplined as they moved into the visitors' barrack. I could not catch a sight of my mother from the window, which faced the gate at an odd angle. Surely she was somewhere in the dense crowd. I wondered whether I could survive the disappointment if she didn't show up that day.

At twelve-thirty, the bell in the warden's office rang in long and continuous tones, pushing us to our feet. We ran out of the barracks and lined up in single file, impatiently waiting for our turn to move.

Fifty feet behind the watchtower and facing the junkyard, the visitors' quarter was built from red bricks and cement pillars, covered with red tiles. People pressed and pushed each other inside a small area, searching for familiar faces. All the noise and confusion faded the moment I saw my mother's face. She sat on the end of a wooden bench in the second to last row, next to a crowd of people. For the first time in many years, I saw her face with full makeup. Her salt-and-pepper hair was pulled back into a big and simple knot. Her lips, always full and well defined, were painted with a humble, natural shade of lipstick. Her pale and aging skin was concealed under a layer of powder. The makeup, however, did not create a distance between me and my mother as it had done in the past. Now it softened her features and drew me closer into her space. Seeing me, she remained seated on her bench and stared. Her eyes, highlighted with black pencil, brimmed with tears.

I fell onto the ground before her. My mother held my head in her hands; my knees pressed against her feet. I could feel my tears leak between her fingers and fall on her lap, but I didn't care. I had not been able to cry openly for so long, and my anguish felt enormous. My mother rocked me in her embrace as she had when I was small. And her soft voice murmured next to my ear, singing "Happy Birthday" to me.

She kissed my cheek. Some of her tears trickled down my neck, but I felt much better, revived.

"I am so sorry, Mother," I told her. "Auntie Dang passed away."

My mother nodded. "I know, son. I learned about what happened to her a few months ago. Three days after your arrest, the fishermen found her body washed ashore in Cam Ranh Bay. Her parents came from Saigon for the funeral."

She paused, reaching for her purse. "Let's talk about something else," she said. "I don't want to get depressed anymore. Let's talk about your birthday present."

"Please, Mom. I don't want any present. I can't keep anything in here, except some food."

Her eyes brightened. "You will want this, son."

She pulled out a piece of laminated paper and handed it to me. "Here is your present. You are free, son. I've come to take you home. As soon as you are ready, we'll leave."

I voiced a cry of happiness, but my excitement evaporated when I saw the green-uniformed police standing guard at the entrance. "What about them?" I asked my mother.

"Don't worry," she assured me. "I've already informed the warden. The deputy commander in chief of Nhatrang personally signed this release. No one would dare to stop you from leaving."

She opened one of the sacks and arranged a few food items on her lap, beckoning for me to eat. Through the sealed containers, I detected the rich, sweet smell of sticky rice wrapped inside banana leaves, the familiar, succulent scent of roasted chicken with ginseng, and most of all, my favorite, the pungent, garlicky aroma of grilled beef paste in grape leaves. I devoured the food quickly, then looked up at her face. My lips were slippery from chicken fat. "Mother, there is something you should know," I said.

258

She studied my face, her eyes questioning. I got up from the floor and gazed out the window. Past the open courtyard, I saw a dark figure, gripping at the wires and staring at me. The raging sunlight beat down on him; however, he remained at the same spot unmoved.

Pointing at him, I told her, "That is Lam over there. He has been here for the last six years."

She nodded matter-of-factly, as if the news was not shocking to her. "Have you been talking to him?"

"A bit. He has this idea — He thinks that you are responsible for putting him here behind bars."

"I see." She bit her lower lip. "I guess that man and I are long overdue for a talk."

Her eyes searched my face, and worry clouded her features. "Listen to me," she said. "Whether you know it or not, you are now a grown-up. I trust you to be part of the conversation I am about to have with him. I want you to go with me and listen, but don't say anything, okay? The next ten minutes aren't going to be easy, but I am here with you. Let's go meet Lam."

She grabbed another sack and pulled out a bottle of cognac. Leaving the rest of her belongings on the floor, my mother walked toward the warden. She greeted him with a smile. "Please sir, I would like to ask you a small favor. This bottle can't measure up to my appreciation, especially for what you are about to do, but do accept the gift. I would like to meet that man over there. I know his relatives, and they had a message for him."

The warden smiled, showing teeth blackened from cigarette smoke. His thick eyebrows rose behind his dark sunglasses. "What message?" he asked.

My mother's fingers picked at the seal on the bottle. "Nothing much, really. Just to see how he's doing, that's all. His family would like to know that."

He reached for the cognac. "Five minutes are all you get. Start right now."

She grasped my hand and pulled me out of the room.

"Hey," the officer spoke up.

"Yes, sir."

"You are a very classy lady —"

"Thank you, sir," she said.

The warden nodded. "I mean it. If I didn't see you together with your half-breed son, I would never have guessed that you were once a hooker for the dirty foreigners. Very classy, indeed."

My mother swallowed and ran outside past the courtyard. Lam stood frozen, his eyes fixed on us. His hands on the barbed wire were white at the knuckles. We stopped about five feet in front of him.

My mother broke the silence. "Hello, Lam. How are you?"

"Fuck you, evil whore."

My mother burst out laughing. Her hand tightened around mine. "Is that all you are going to say? Five, six years away from me, don't you have any questions? Speak up, because if you don't, we'll be leaving."

He sucked in a deep breath, glaring at my mother. "Why did you put me in here?"

"Oh, there were so many reasons: you were a bad father, you dirtied my family name, you spent my money —"

"What was it really, Khuon?" Lam demanded, grabbing his crotch. "Was it because I got a penis and you didn't?"

My mother leaned over and breathed in his face. "Bastard, I sent you away because you hurt my son. I am a mother. I had no choice but to seek vengeance."

"What — ?" He pulled away from her, looking at me. "How did you know? Did he tell you?"

"Yes," she nodded, stroking my head with her hand. Sadness hung over her face as she said, "In a way, my son did tell me. Mostly from the way he behaved. I saw how his personality changed from being so happy to extreme terror at the sight of you. It was the same behavior I had noticed in Loan. You have a gift, Lam. When it comes to destroying people I love most, you truly are a master at work."

"Nonsense," he murmured.

"Of course there were more clues," my mother continued. "I have always been a reasonable woman. I couldn't get revenge if I didn't have concrete facts. There came nights when he just fell apart with nightmares." Tears mixed with her mascara and trickled down her cheeks. "I sat on the edge of his bed and I watched him suffer while I was pregnant with your daughter. Your name was at the tip of his tongue time and again. Then I just came right out and asked him. Still in his sleep, he told me the perverted thing that you did. What am I supposed to do? I couldn't wait for the gods to take revenge for us. And I had to end his nightmares somehow."

She turned away, wiping her tears with the back of her hand. "Good-bye, Lam. Rot in Hell."

"Wait," he called after her.

She paused.

"How did you do it?" he asked. "How did you get them to arrest me?"

My mother sighed and turned to face him. "I informed Mr. Tran about you and Loan, how you raped her, and the abortion. I was so good, by the time I finished the story, he wanted you dead. Personally, I believe death would be too easy a way out for you. Prison, to me, was a much better choice, so I found myself a second trump card to support my scheme. Mr. Qui Ba came to my rescue. With my brain and two community leaders against you, you never stood a chance."

"You whore," he screamed. Droplets of saliva spattered in the air as he spoke. "You killed my child. I only did what I had to do to get even. You have no right to put me here."

"You keep talking about Loan's child, yet you have never made any effort to care for your daughter, BeTi. Do you really expect me to believe you have any concern for anyone besides yourself?"

Lam made no reply.

My mother went on, "I am taking my son home, Lam. In a few hours, we will breathe the air of freedom again. Whatever wounds you inflicted on us, they will heal with time. But you, you will remain here until the day you die, like a stray dog. And I promise you no one will ever remember that you exist."

My mother turned to me. Her eyes were the color of the chestnut, and for the first time, they concealed no trace of mystery. "You now know the story," she said. "You understand why I became friends with Mr. Qui Ba, don't you? It is called revenge. And revenge has a price. I turned to Mr. Qui Ba every time I needed a favor. He thought he was using me, but actually I was using him. I did it so that I could put Lam behind bars, and, most recently, in exchange for your freedom. You can judge me if you want for what I did, but please understand why I did it. It wasn't right, and I would be the first one to admit it. But for your safety, and for all of my children's safety, I would not hesitate to do it again if I had to. Someday, you have to help me explain that to your sister."

"Did Mr. Qui Ba arrest him, Mother?" I asked.

"Yes, son."

"How did you get him to do it?"

She stroked my head, and said. "The secret is in the smile, son."

Taking my hand, my mother led me toward the visitors' hall to gather her belongings. Together we marched outside the gate, where the bus was waiting under the glaring sun. Two hours later, we departed from camp PK 34.

CHAPTER FORTY

We spent the night at Cam Ranh Bay. The next morning, the bus arrived in Nhatrang in the middle of a warm and sporadic shower. These were the days in May when the sun and sky hid above the mud-colored clouds, and a wild wind swept the heavy precipitation across town. Rain crashed into my face as my mother and I walked through our compound's front gate. Large beads of water splashed on the wet surface of the garden, threatening to flood the already drenched ground. Under the guava trees, my aunt's ducks stood motionless and hid their bills under their wings, observing the weather through their half-shut eyes. Beneath the shutters of my bedroom window, a trail of busy termites found a dry and comfortable refuge.

We entered our house through the back door. Dropping her sacks in the kitchen, my mother pulled a reed mat from her room and laid it in front of my dirty feet. From the doorway, my room seemed larger than usual. The armoire, the chest of drawers, and our beds had disappeared.

As if to answer my thought, my mother said, "I had to raise money to bribe the officials for your release, so I sold everything."

The rest of my family, seated in my grandfather's bedroom, didn't hear us come in because of the loud rain. The house was gloomy, with little light penetrating the windows. My grandfather, stretched on his mattress, seemed lost in his Buddha's scriptures. A pipe hung forgotten at a corner of his mouth.

His bed frame and my uncle's altar were also gone, leaving a faded imprint on the gray cement. The room was bare, except for some of my grandmother's belongings. On her pillow lay the copper mortar and pestle she used to grind betel nuts with, and next to it was a basket of her garments.

With his back turned to us, my brother was giving my grandfather a foot massage. A few paces away, my sister played with Lou, who was curled up beside her pillow. While one of her tiny hands kept him still by his collar, the other caressed the dog's fur and stroked the folds of his chin.

Lou was the first to detect our presence. He sprang up from my sister's hold and barked, waving his tail. Jimmy ran toward us, pale from excitement. In the glimmering dimness, his face looked as if it were carved from marble. I embraced him, feeling his body quiver in my arms.

My grandfather was first stunned, then overcome with happiness. He got up from his bed, reached out his hands, and beckoned for me to come over. "Thank heaven you are saved," he said, his voice thick with emotion. He shook his head in disbelief. "Come to Grandpa, my poor boy."

AS WE SAT DOWN for lunch, my aunt entered the kitchen from the back steps. In just a few months, she had aged ten years. Her face, thin and exhausted, appeared starker than usual. Even her hair, once long and thick, was now as lifeless and dull as a mane of horsehair. She narrowed her eyes, which were swollen from crying, and awkwardly said to me, "I am glad that you made it home." She shifted her eyes to her feet. "Do me a favor, please. My daughter wants to see you."

I looked up to my mother, who remained quiet and stared at her bowl of rice. My grandfather patted my shoulder and said, "Go ahead, Kien. Moonlight has been waiting for you. Go and say good-bye to your cousin. Your mother and I will join you in about fifteen minutes."

My aunt covered her nose with a handkerchief and blew noisily. Obeying my grandfather's wish, I got up from the floor and followed her.

The black divan in their den, where Moonlight had spent most of her sick days, had been moved into her room at her request. Fresh lotus blossom and a glass of condensed milk sat on a counter nearby. The light from outside created a ghostly collage of black and white shadows on her heavily made-up face, making her look like a Japanese doll.

The moment she saw me, Moonlight coughed violently. Her body doubled over in my uncle's arms as she gasped for air, clutching her hands across her chest. Her family, scattered outside her room, watched silently. The attack grew increasingly severe, until she threw up blood onto the divan. Her blouse was also soaked in the thick red liquid, some of which spilled over to the floor below. At last, the cough subsided, and she waved at me.

I approached her bed. My aunt was standing beside me. I picked up Moonlight's hand and held it in mine, feeling her fingers as cold as ice. Her father instinctively pulled her away from me.

Moonlight lifted her head. Her lids hung heavily over her dark irises. "You made it home," she whispered to me. "At last I got to see you. I am running out of time, Kien."

I blinked away a tear.

"Daddy, may I have a private moment with him?" she asked.

My uncle's bushy eyebrows furrowed tightly over the bridge of his nose.

Moonlight repeated, "Please, Daddy. It will only take a few minutes."

He stood up and said to me, "Sit down. And hold her. If anything happens, just call us. We will be right outside."

I sat on the edge of her bed and she leaned back, pressing her shoulder against my chest. Her body was so bony it seemed as fragile as glass. Her lips were lavender as she tried to smile, but instead, a corner of her mouth just shook slightly. A trace of blood slowly oxidized with the air and became a dark brown mark on her pale skin.

Once we were alone, Moonlight whispered to me, "The postman came this morning, but there's still no letter from Ty Tong."

"I am so sorry," I said.

"Hey, I've got something for you," she said.

I waved my hand. "No, Moonlight. You don't have to give me anything. Just get better."

"Trust me, you'll want this," she said. "But first, help me. I need to lie down."

I laid her gently on her bed and stepped back to give her some room. Slowly, she reached inside her pillowcase and fumbled around. When her hand found what she was looking for, she pulled it out and held it protectively inside her palm. A sad smile returned to her face. "I would trade anything just for another day at the beach, swimming in the water and playing in the sun. Do you know the feeling? Of course you don't. Why should you? You can do any of those activities whenever you want. But don't ever take it for granted, Kien. Life is precious."

I nodded.

She looked up at the ceiling to recover herself, and then she continued. "I remember your wish that day at the Spirited Mountain Temple. Your prayer was about your father."

"Well," I said bitterly, "I also prayed for Grandmother's health, but she died. And now, look at you. Miracles don't always happen to poor people, Moonlight."

"Please don't lose your faith!" she urged. "At least not in humanity, Kien. I know you are angry, and I know the feeling of being ostracized. Look at me with this disease! People are afraid of getting close to me —" She stopped and gasped for air.

"You'll get better soon. Just slow down, Moonlight."

She shook her head. "It isn't important anymore. I want to apologize to you about my family. I want you to forgive them."

I looked away from her fervent face. "I don't know what you are talking about."

"Please, forgive them. I am going to tell you an important secret. Promise me that you will apply this knowledge for your own good. Don't use it against my family. You can hate them for what they did to your family, but I don't want another war in this house."

I held her hand. "Whatever you want, Moonlight. I promise you."

"You must swear by my death bed —"

I cried and nodded my head. Relieved, she raised her hand and opened her fingers, revealing a small piece of paper. Every crease on its surface had turned dark brown, and the ink was faded. I took it from her hand. It appeared to be part of an envelope, scribbled in some foreign language with my mother's handwriting.

"What is it, Moonlight?" I asked her.

She said, "It's your father's address. You can write to him now if you like."

"How did you get this?" I stuttered in shock. "All of the letters were buried and lost years ago. We dug the whole lawn upside down to search for it."

Moonlight choked in her own fluid. Suddenly, her cheeks turned from pale to pink, then to crimson, but she soon collected herself and took in several deep breaths. My aunt stuck her head in to check, but Moonlight waved her away.

"I am so sorry, Kien," she said. "I don't have an explanation for you. Nothing I can say will justify my family's behavior. You know why I couldn't give this to you earlier. For my sake, don't tell anyone, please."

I examined the paper in my hand. "Is it really his address? Half of his name is missing."

"I know. But that's all I have. I wish you a lot of luck finding your father. And when you do —" She paused.

"Yes, Moonlight?"

She sobbed, "Find Ty Tong for me. Tell him my heart is broken. Tell him I waited like he asked, but the postman never came."

I wiped the tears off her face and kissed her forehead before I withdrew from her room. Her mother pushed the door open and ran inside. My grandfather accompanied me back to my house, lit a candle for the kitchen gods, and then prepared tea. I could hear my aunt's weeping, faintly echoed in the rain.

CHAPTER FORTY-ONE

That night, after dinner, I helped my mother with the dishes by the well. My aunt's family clustered inside Moonlight's room with a doctor. On the ground next to us, a candle dripped its red, waxy tears onto a bronze dish. Its weak light sputtered in the thick darkness, showing just enough contrast for my mother to see what she was doing. The rain had stopped and the water inside the well was like black ink. Each time I dropped the bucket to scoop up some water, it made a wet sound. As the pail moved upward, pulled by old ropes on squeaking wheels, the noise reverberated like a moan. After filling up the basin, I sat down beside my mother.

"Mother, can I ask you something?"

"Sure," she said.

"Do you remember anything about my father?"

She paused. Her long hair covered most of her face, hiding her expression from view. "I remember some," she said, turning back to the dishes.

"What is he like?"

My mother wiped her hands with the rag she kept on her side and looked up. In the dim light, her eyes were as dark and mysterious as the well. "It has been so many years," she said. "Why do you want to know now?"

"I don't know," I said with a shrug. "Just wondering. Everyone has a father. I want to know whether or not mine exists, that's all."

"He exists just fine, somewhere in America."

"Does he know about me, mother?"

"Yes, son. You were three months old when he left."

"Mom, how did you meet him?"

My mother stretched her arms upward and moaned softly, complaining about a dull ache she felt on her back. In the shadow of the night, everything around us seemed calm. At the same time, the temperature was dropping. In a soft, whispering voice, as though she were talking to herself, my mother told me her story.

"I was supposed to get married to a son of your grandfather's friend. In those days, there was no such thing as marrying for love, and matches were prearranged. The night before the wedding, I sneaked out to see the groom's face, with the help of your late uncle, of course. We hid behind a bamboo bush outside his house for two hours before I could get a good look at his face for the first time. Good heavens, was he ugly! I cried like my Daddy had just died. It was awful, the thought of living with that man for the rest of my life. So, that same night your uncle, barely your age then, took me to the bus station and sent me off to Saigon."

"Mother, weren't you afraid?"

"Afraid? I was terrified, but I was also determined. Your grandfather was so mad, he beat the tar out of your uncle, and then went to Saigon to look for me. By the time he got there, I had a job in a jewelry store working as a hand model. I refused to go home, so your grandfather had to apologize to the groom's family and call off the wedding. It was a real scandal, and I was lucky that he didn't disown me for what I did. Then, a couple of months later, the Americans came to Vietnam. Everybody in the south took English classes so that they could get a better job working for the foreigners and getting paid in dollars instead of dong. I was inspired by their sophisticated culture, so I went back to night school and learned English. I met your father in Saigon, through an ad in a newspaper. Your daddy was looking for a translator, so I came for an interview and ended up spending the night. He was tall, dark, and handsome — just like a movie star. He swept me off my feet. You know the rest of the story. We moved back to Nhatrang and I got pregnant. The following year I gave birth to you."

In front of us, the dishes had been washed, dried and stacked on a tray. She went on, her voice low and mournful. "Three months after you were born, he left Vietnam. Your father was very upset that he had to leave you behind. In fact, he offered to take you with him, but I refused. You have a good father, Kien, just like everybody else. And for the short time that he was here with us, he loved you very much."

"What's his name?"

My mother sucked in a deep breath. "I don't remember."

"How could you not? You were living with him."

"He was my boss," she explained. "I called him by his last name like everybody else in the company, Mr. Russo this, Mr. Russo that. Have you any idea how many years ago that was? I am forced to forget about these things."

"I bet my father would remember your name," I said sarcastically.

My mother burst out laughing. "I seriously doubt that. He never knew my real name. He used to call me Nancy Kwan. Names weren't important to us. It was the sixties, for god's sake."

"Do you believe that he thinks about us sometimes?" I asked.

"Sure he does."

"Does he still want me?"

My mother furrowed her eyebrows. "I don't know, son. But if I were he, I certainly would. Any parent would be proud of you, Kien. You are a good son."

I got up and touched her hair gently. "Thanks, Mother."

THAT EVENING, after everybody else had gone to bed, I got up and poured some oil into the old lantern. On my new bed, which was made out of discarded rice sacks Tin had brought back from his company, I drafted a letter to my father. Even with the help of an English-Vietnamese dictionary, and with my limited knowledge of English grammar that I learned in school, the foreign language was more difficult than I had imagined. Under the dim light, I struggled to convey what I wanted him to know, wondering whether or not he would understand.

> *Dear Mr. Russo,*
>
> *I am your son from Vietnam. You don't know me yet. My name is Kien Nguyen, and I am fourteen years old. I was born May 12th, 1967. You left Nhatrang, Vietnam on August, same year.*
>
> *It was an exciting time this morning when I found your address. I have looked for you many years before. I think of you everyday and I want to meet you.*
>
> *Please take me to America. I have nothing to live for in Vietnam. I am always hungry, and unhappy. I don't have new clothes, or blanket. I am sleeping on two rice sacks because I have no bed. After many rains, lots of mosquitoes around, and the weather get very cold at night. You may remember about that since you lived here before.*
>
> *Please write. I want to hear from you. I can't send you any picture, because I don't have yet. Nancy Kwan says hello to you. She also said you love me, and you will take care of me. I want very much for her to be right.*
>
> *Your son,*
Kien Nguyen

I read the letter over and over again, trying to correct as many mistakes as I could before I put it in an envelope. Then, exhausted from my euphoria and hope, I fell asleep holding the letter close to my chest.

The next morning, I woke up early. I jumped out of bed, intending to show Moonlight the letter. On my way to my aunt's house, my mother stopped me at the kitchen. She was holding a pair of wooden chopsticks. Behind her, a pan of fried rice sizzled over the kiln. From inside my aunt's house, someone struck a gong three times and the sound echoed through the morning air. Monks in yellow robes appeared at her front steps between the rose bushes.

"Where are you going?" my mother asked.

"I am going to see Moonlight."

"Don't! Please stay here," she said sadly. "Moonlight passed away last night. Do not disturb her family."

I staggered to sit down, dizzy and numb from the news. Outside, white clouds and beautiful morning sun had replaced the rain. Lights sparkled on the soggy ground as if to announce summer was here at last.

Sometime later, I got up from the floor and stepped out of the kitchen. Sitting at my aunt's dinner table, my grandfather seemed lost in thought. In front of him, a cup of tea was left untouched. In the garden, my uncle, with the help of the monks, released the latch on his birdcage and let go about a hundred sparrows. Their wings fluttered under the bright sun before they disappeared from sight. Outside Moonlight's room, my aunt collapsed on the floor, hitting her head against the cement threshold in frustration. Her wail was blood-curdling and painful as her daughters huddled next to her. The moment she saw my face, my aunt stopped crying, got up and lunged at me. "I want to know what she said to you last night," she said.

"Who?" I lied. "I don't know what you are talking about."

"My daughter, Moonlight," she pressed. "What sorts of things did she tell you last night?"

"I can't tell you, Auntie," I stammered. "It's confidential."

"Why not?" she wailed. "I am her mother. Tell me."

"I can't. I promised her. Besides, it isn't important anymore."

The anger crept back in her eyes, and Pink pulled her away from me. "Not important?" my aunt cried. "How dare you? She hung on for weeks, waiting for your return so that she could tell you something. How dare you not confide in me what my daughter said?"

I shook my head and ran away.

IN THE GARDEN, I encountered Mr. Qui Ba on his way to my aunt's kitchen.

"Hey, congratulations," he said. "You are back."

"Yes, sir."

"Great, I got news for you. I talked to your dean the other day. He wanted me to tell you to enjoy the summer. Next semester you can go back to school. There will be no penalty after the faculty has evaluated your conduct."

"Thank you, sir." I looked at his face. "Or should I ask my mother to thank you for me?"

His smile disappeared. "You ungrateful mongrel," he snapped. "Your mother is a nobody. Who do you think she is, Queen of Sheba? And you, stay away from my daughter. She is out of your league. You are a smart boy — don't make me one of your enemies, son."

"If not because of my mother, why would you help me?"

He waved his hand. "Get out of here. I am sick of you."

I walked past him and headed to the post office to mail my father the letter.

THREE MONTHS LATER, one Saturday morning, the postman came looking for me. He handed me an envelope, which I recognized immediately. The letter had returned to me unopened, after traveling around the world. A red stamp slashed across my father's address, accompanied by the words, "Return to sender, address unknown."

1984

CHAPTER FORTY-TWO
Nhatrang, April 1984

When the letter to my father was returned to me unopened, any last shred of hope for a better life finally abandoned me. I grew to accept the disappointment, convincing myself that such misfortune was a part of my existence. With the deaths of Moonlight and Mrs. Dang receding into the past, and the tortures I had endured at the hands of the police still fresh on my mind, I focused my attention on leading a normal, less turbulent life. I did my best to block the horrors from my recollection.

In 1984 I was seventeen, Jimmy was fifteen, and BeTi was nine. Our clothes were ragged from years of wear, and no amount of patching or letting out seams could make them presentable. My mother bought second-hand garments from the thrift shops and altered them by hand to fit us. At school, the way we dressed drew a lot of attention from teachers and students. Their teasing was cruel, though perhaps inevitable. Jimmy and I got into fistfights with other children almost as often as we had lunch. Neither one of us confided the problem to our mother. We knew she had too much stress already.

By now, my mother had sold everything that could possibly be sold from our household. One item at a time, we parted with our blankets, the window frames, the marble thresholds, and part of our tin roof that covered the kitchen area. When she ran out of things to sell, my mother went back to the market. This time, with very little capital, all she could do was clean out a small area at the market entrance and sell fish soup by the sidewalk. Her customers were mainly the local housewives who came to the bazaar to shop for groceries.

Every day at dawn, my mother woke up before anyone else in the house. In the kitchen, she re-boiled the soup broth that she had prepared the night before, fried the fish cakes, steamed the noodles, and arranged lettuce into a container of salad. Once the soup bubbled and the smell of fried fish penetrated our mosquito net, my mother placed everything inside a glittering black lacquered basket. Into another basket she loaded clay bowls, chopsticks, spoons, and spices. When the grandfather clock in my aunt's house chimed six times, she left the house, lifted the two heavy containers on a bamboo rod over her shoulders, and headed to the market.

On weekends, when we didn't have school, Jimmy and I would help haul her burdens. Most days, my mother took my sister along for company. BeTi walked slowly behind her, holding the salad bowl in one hand and a broom in the other as they passed through the villages and rice paddies. Once they got to the bazaar, my mother set up her business on the ground under an oak tree. BeTi sat on the dirty pavement and played with her pillow, while my mother prepared to receive her first customer, keeping the pot's temperature up with the extra coals she carried in a tin inside her thin jacket.

Around noon, after she had sold her last bowl of soup, my mother closed her little shop and got ready for her next job. While BeTi waited under the oak tree, keeping an eye on the baskets, my mother took her broom and swept the sidewalk, moving up and down the street until she had cleaned up the entire market's entrance. The shop owners whose stores faced the street paid her a small service charge to keep their path clean. My mother used to tell us that this was how she had swept away the summers and winters of her life.

On stormy days, as the wind howled through the trees, it was painful to watch her bending down, her head hidden under a torn conical hat, struggling to keep the trash from being blown across the avenue. She grew thinner. Her skin was brown, leathery from the sun. Her hair turned mostly white, fuzzy, and unkempt, covering her head like cotton. The sparkle in her eyes, once so bewitching, had long since given way to a colder, more sullen look.

I was lucky enough to land a steady source of income. Through a series of writing contests given by the Communist Board of Education in Nhatrang, I won a scholarship that provided us with thirty-five pounds of rice and a hundred fifty dong a month. It also helped me find a position in the young writers' club, a prestigious organization. From then on, instead of going to regular school, I earned my education through attending the club's activities.

For a few golden months, I felt relief. Then, during my eleventh grade, while the other students prepared for the coming college examinations, the president of my club refused to endorse my college application. As a member of the "reactionary class," he advised me, I had gone as far as I possibly could with my education. My future options were limited: I could be either a substitute teacher or a private tutor. My training could take me no farther in our society.

With my college dream shattered, I was forced to reevaluate my options. No matter how hard I had tried, I could not escape my unfavorable past. The urge to leave Vietnam once again took root in me. However, this time, my mother did not have the financial backup or the contact with other boat people to help me escape. And even if she did, I would be too terrified from the last experience to try again. In desperation I scrawled letters to the United Nations and the U.S. Embassy in Thailand, asking them for help. No replies came back. It was as though my pleas dissolved into thin air the moment they left my fingertips at the post office.

Then one sunny day in April, I received my first correspondence from Bangkok. With shaking hands, I tore open the envelope and inhaled the fresh, foreign smell that came from within. The letter was printed on one page of brown, recycled paper.

Joint Voluntary Agency (J.V.A.)
U.S. Embassy Refugee Section
Bangkok, Thailand

Dear Kien Nguyen,

You have written to us several times in the past, requesting an application to resettle in the United States of America. Based on the information you have provided in your letters, we would like to explain to you the favorable probability of your case. In accordance with the Refugee Act of 1980, the United States of America has signed an agreement with the Vietnamese government relating to Amerasian children that were left behind after the Fall of Saigon in 1975. Orderly Departure Program (O.D.P.) provided that anyone who is an offspring of an American father can and will be found eligible for resettlement in the United States. Once you are granted permission to leave Vietnam, which shall be done in an orderly fashion, we will help you find a sponsor in one of the voluntary resettlement agencies. The announcement of this Act should be posted in your local county, together with the application. For your convenience, we enclose four copies of the application with this letter.

However, you cannot send the application back to us. The process must be carried out through your local government. Once you receive a laissez-passer (permission to leave) from your authorities, our sponsoring agency will arrange for a sponsor or will itself provide initial resettlement services for you and your family.

Your cooperation is appreciated.

Sincerely,
Richard C. Cooke
Deputy JVA Representative

Attachment: A/S

As I stood on my front stoop in the sultry afternoon, my jaw dropped. My throat tightened, incapable of making a sound. The letter was short, but the information it provided was like an earthquake in my soul. I relived my family's years of hardship, my wretched attempt to escape the country, the many painful paths that I had walked since paradise lost. There had not been a moment of happiness since the day I was taught the word *half-breed*.

My fingers ran over the black ink as I thought frantically to myself, "Who are the people that typed this letter? How do they live? What do they like?" They seemed so far away, yet a part of them was here, enclosed in the message that was addressed to me. Thousands of images raced through my mind and coalesced into one big question: How much of this could be true? Despite my past disappointments, I wanted to believe what it said, so much so that I would eat every word until it became one with me. This letter came just in time to give me the strength and encouragement I needed to keep on living. Without this news, I could not imagine what would happen to me. I sat there, my eyes blurred with tears, until the sky turned mauve.

That night, when my mother came home from work tired and cranky, I greeted her at the front gate with a cheerful smile. After taking her baskets into the kitchen, I hung up her coat and hat and served her a basin with fresh water so that she could wash her face. Jimmy pulled out the only chair left in the house for my grandfather. He sat under the wan light, looking out the window, waiting for the midnight cactus to bloom.

When it was time for dinner, I showed my mother the letter, translating as much as I could into Vietnamese. She stared at me with large, frightened eyes, as if the news were too much for her to handle. Jimmy clasped his hands together in excitement. I walked over to the window, joining my grandfather. Outside, the garden sank into an unfathomable darkness. A few steps away from us, the cactus shrub bathed in the dry and cool air, adding its aroma to the perfume of the rose bushes. Its white and pointed buds, as delicate as a lady's fingers, reached out toward the light from my room, waiting for the moon to help it blossom.

"What do they want us to do next?" my mother asked.

"We need to fill out the applications. After that we take our pictures, get our community leader to sign, and turn everything in. Then we sit back and wait some more."

"Do what you must," she muttered. "It sounds too uncertain and complicated to me. Just don't expect too much from this."

Pulling me close to him, my grandfather whispered, "Try it, child. What do you have to lose?"

THE NEXT DAY, I got up early. It was still dark when I headed for the community hall. After three hours of waiting in front of Mr. Qui Ba's office, I got my applications stamped and signed by his secretary. Next, I proceeded toward the emigration center — a tall building located three short blocks from the old Nguyen mansion. The salty wind rushed through the busy streets, reminding me that the ocean and its familiar beach were just a short distance away.

The emigration center was packed with anxious people clutching thick stacks of paper. At first, I thought I had gone to the wrong address and ended up in a busy doctor's office, since the construction was of a similar type. At the far end, where a glass panel divided the room, floor-to-ceiling shelves were packed with folders. Some of the files had sat forgotten for so long, their edges were brown and dusty. Behind the glass door, a receptionist slouched in her chair reading a translation of Victor Hugo's *Les Misérables*. Without losing her place in her book, she handed me a number. Her nose wrinkled indignantly as she told me to take a seat and wait.

I looked around the waiting room for an empty chair. There were none left. Most people were settled on the floor eating their lunches and gazing at each other with nervous fascination. It was a solemn, important day for them all, and the prospect of migrating brought hope to their faces. I went out to the hallway, joining the crowd waiting outside.

A man about thirty years old leaned against the wall and lit a cigarette. He cocked his head and examined me with undisguised curiosity. His thin, delicate face and brown eyes seemed European, yet the rest of his features wore the same beat-up, ragged, and tired appearance of any other Vietnamese. I stood near the entrance, listening to the numbers that were being called from inside.

"Hey," the man said as he waved at me. "What is your status?"

"I beg your pardon?"

"Why are you here?" he rephrased his question.

"I'm not sure." I stumbled for an answer. "There is a program called O.D.P., and I just want to get more information about it."

"Yes, I know about that program." The man blew a cloud of smoke in an exaggerated way. "It serves the half-breeds. I applied for it six months ago. Today, I am just coming to check on my status. I want to know if my file has been sent to Hanoi."

Curiosity took hold of me, and I asked him, "Was it difficult to apply?"

"Not really," he said, shaking his head. "You just fill out the form and give it to them. The difficult part is the waiting."

"Thank you," I said.

The man inhaled deeply from his cigarettes. As he exhaled, his words accompanied a white fume of smoke. "Hey, would you believe from looking at me that I am the son of an American soldier?"

"I don't know, are you?"

"Well, not exactly," he said, scratching his chin. "My father was a Frenchman. I hope I can fool them at the interview. What do you think?"

"I don't know, sir. But good luck."

"Thanks," he said, "You, too. Did you bring anything for the deputy chief?"

"No, I didn't know that I had to."

The man nodded his head knowingly. "You don't have to, but you should. He'll send your case out faster." He squashed his cigarette against the dirty wall and stepped back inside the waiting room.

MY MEETING THAT DAY with the deputy chief of the emigration center was short and awkward. In the large office, which
was full of bouquets of flowers and boxes of gifts, he sprawled on his
large office chair. Through a large window a beautiful view of the
blue ocean spread behind him. He was a hugely overweight man of
forty. The collar of his white shirt and his tie seemed to be gripping
his thick neck too tightly, making his large face a deep shade of
plum. His round cheeks pushed his eyes upward into two thin slits,
like the dark strokes of a Chinese ideogram. His feet remained
propped on his desk as I entered the room.

"What can I do for you?" he shouted over the crash of the waves.
His voice bounced off the walls, magnifying his powers of intimi-
dation.

I held the applications protectively across my chest. "I am here to
inquire about a program called O.D.P."

"You want the application?" He reached for a pile of papers on
his desk.

"No, sir. I think I've gotten the same ones through the mail."

"Then fill them out."

"I did."

"Then hand them over to me."

I handed the folder to him. His eyes met my stare, shifted to the
mountain of presents on the floor, and then returned to me. A few
seconds crawled by, and he terminated the meeting with a loud sigh.
His eyes turned icy.

"Here is your receipt. Your case is number three-fifteen." He
handed a small piece of paper to me, then threw my file on the floor
on top of the others.

"How long should I wait, sir?" I asked.

"I don't know, and I don't care. It's already out of my hands."

CHAPTER FORTY-THREE
Nhatrang, September 1984

September brought another monsoon season. For over two weeks the sky was obscured behind a layer of dark clouds. The wind bellowed, whipping violently against the coconut trees. All I could see from the window of my classroom each day was an endless sheet of water, falling over the flooded city.

On wet days, my mother found it difficult to sell soup at the market. Even if she managed to cover her pots, the customers could not enjoy their meals as the wind tore through the muddy streets, driving bullets of rain into them. The moisture saturated her clothes, and the cheap dyes that tinted her outfit washed down her body in a dense, black flood. Many days, she brought home a full pot of soup. Behind her, my sister chased bubbles across the wet ground, clutching her soggy pillow. As my mother's meager assets melted away, we could see signs of a devastating end.

One afternoon after the last period of my classes, I left the writing club in a hurry, holding a broken umbrella over my head. Outside, behind the school's large iron gate, Kim huddled inside an oversized yellow raincoat that covered half her face. As I pushed through the gate to join her, dead leaves scattered on the brick path.

"Ah, Kien, I found you," she said, looking directly at me.

I was surprised to see her outside my school. In the months since I
ad returned from my incarceration, I only saw her secretly as we met
t night, either under the magnolia tree near my house, or in the rice
eld behind her family's kitchen. "Is something wrong?" I asked.

She took a step closer. Her eyelashes, long and thick, fluttered
ike butterfly wings. I could see her round pupils open up like doors,
eckoning me to gaze deeply into her eyes. Everything about Kim
eemed so fragile my instinct was to reach out and protect her. Yet I
ould never forget everything her family represented. Conflicted, I
tood statue-like in the downpour.

"It's about your grandfather," she said. "I just saw him in town
attending the People's Court. Today the Communist Party is holding
trials to eliminate the 'negative phenomena' within the city government. Your grandfather was in the crowd watching as I was leaving.
There are so many people, I am a little worried for his safety." She lowered her voice and went on, "Why do you ask if something is wrong?"

"I was shocked seeing you here, that's all."

"Why would I need a reason to see you?"

Her last sentence caressed me like a warm touch. I forgot myself
and the incessant rain. All that mattered to me was the slender girl
with velvet eyes, and the way she was looking at me.

"Shall we go?" she asked.

"Go? Where to?"

She smiled. "To find your grandfather, silly."

I nodded dumbly and reached for her hand, leading her through
streets overhung with the thick branches of oak trees. Her fingers
rubbed tenderly against my palm. The combination of Kim's touch
and the anxiety of walking with her on Nhatrang's largest avenues
in broad daylight sent a shot of electricity through me that nearly
made me swoon.

We walked through the main market. Kim took me to the square
where she had spotted my grandfather. The open piazza, where the
six major boulevards of the city converged, was blocked with police
barriers and teeming with curious spectators. Police officers in brown

uniforms were everywhere. Despite the rain, hundreds of people thronged the street, ready for the demonstration that the Communist government had announced in the last few days. The spectacle had not yet begun, yet the crowd was shrill with anticipation. Across the square I saw my grandfather standing under a lamppost. His hand rested on his walking stick. He was soaking wet from the rain, but he paid no mind to the weather. His eyes were fixed, and I could tell he was deep in thought.

I pulled at Kim's hand. "I see him," I said. "How do we get to the other side?"

"Come with me," she yelled over the noise.

It took us twenty minutes to push through the mob to get to a policeman. From a distance, I could hear the marching footsteps. Kim tapped on the officer's shoulder to get his attention. He turned around and looked at her, his eyes bloodshot from the sting of the rain.

"We would like to cross the street," Kim said to him. "Can you let us through?"

The policeman raised his hand to stop her. "Wait a minute, the prisoners are coming."

As if to emphasize his statement, at the turn of a street, the band appeared, led by a troop of police. Their banners flapped in the wind, proclaiming slogans like "rectification campaign against the guilty members from within the Communist Party," and "erroneous thinking and nonsocialist behavior among the traitors deserve a severe punishment from the People's Court," in trails of dark ink scribbled across white fabrics. The deputy commander of the police sat atop a moving jeep, reciting Communist rhetoric into a loudspeaker. After each motto, he paused to allow time for the crowd to cheer. The prisoners, at least thirty of them, staggered in two rows, their heads bent downward, their hands tied behind their backs. Conical paper hats, the kind worn by the fool in Chinese operas, identified them with derogatory labels: betrayers, reactionaries, and antisocialists.

As the condemned passed through the crowd, people on both sides pelted them with rotten fruits, bricks, and stones, while at the same time chanting phrases like "long live the Communist Party," and "beware of the sinister schemes of the Chinese expansionists and the U.S. imperialists." Angry fists pounded the air, and hoarse voices demanded justice.

From across the street, I saw my grandfather. He stepped forward clumsily, dropping his walking stick on the ground. His hands reached out, shaking. Followed his stare, I looked among the prisoners and saw a beloved face. It was Loan.

As soon as she recognized my grandfather, Loan halted. Her knees wobbled and she fell to the wet pavement. The foolish hat dropped from her thick river of hair and was lost under the feet of the crowd. I saw that a rope was wrapped around her neck, making an X across her chest to dig at her hands, which were bent tortuously behind her back. In her bare feet, she appeared diminutive, almost like a little girl.

My grandfather limped over to Loan. He touched her shoulders, pressed her face against his waist, and stroked her hair. His mouth moved, but I could not hear his words above the street noise. At a corner of the street, a policeman noticed the affectionate display. He strode in between them, using his rifle to shove my grandfather back. The officer's strength and aggressiveness knocked both Loan and my grandfather to the ground. He fell backward, landing hard on his hip.

"Grandpa," I screamed out.

My grandfather didn't hear me. I dropped the torn umbrella, pushed aside the policeman who was holding Kim and me in place, and plunged into the crowd. My grandfather hoisted himself on his elbows and looked around, disoriented. I helped him up, brushing the filth from his clothes. Suddenly, Kim was beside me. The officer who had hit my grandfather stood a few steps away, blocking Loan from our view. I recognized him as one of Mr. Qui Ba's personal guards.

"Grandpa, are you okay?" I asked him.

"I am fine," my grandfather replied. "Get me to Loan. I want to say good-bye."

The officer held up a hand to us warningly. "It is forbidden to show affection to the criminals. I advise you two to get out of here, and take the old man with you." Someone yelled a taunting comment to the prisoners, and the policeman turned to investigate.

I straightened up and said to Kim, "Please stay here with my grandfather. I will say good-bye to Loan for him."

While the policeman was distracted, I rushed to Loan. Kneeling beside her, I noticed Mr. Tran for the first time. On the front of his chest hung a big cardboard sign that said, *"I was once a member of the cadre, but I dishonored the Party and betrayed my own country. I am now beyond redemption."* He seemed to recognize me, and a rush of shame washed over his face. His upper lip was swollen and curled upward, revealing the black gap where his long, repulsive incisors used to be. Quickly he looked away.

Loan remained on her knees on the ground. Her rain-soaked hair fell over her face, and a few strands caught in her mouth. Remnants of egg yolk and tomato seeds adorned her clothes. My head felt dizzy, as if I were in a nightmare. The noise of the angry crowd faded away. I reached out and touched her cheeks.

Loan buried her face in my hands and cried, her shoulders shaking. Suddenly, I could feel her tongue dart out of her mouth, soft and wet, brushing against my skin, as she expelled something into my palms. Then she lifted her head to look at me intently. In my open hands, a gold necklace and a piece of green jade the size of an old Chinese coin sparkled against the gray afternoon. I closed my fingers instinctively.

"Put it away, Kien," she said. "Your grandmother gave it to me when I first moved in with your family. Tell your mother I am returning it to her."

A blow exploded against my back, knocking me forward. I looked up to see the police officer looming above me, his eyes wide with rage.

"Get away from the criminals!" he screamed, whacking me again with his rifle.

"No!" Kim cried out. She left my grandfather on the pavement and ran to seize the officer's arm.

The moment he saw her, his anger changed to fear. "I'm sorry, Miss Kim," he stammered. "I didn't recognize you."

Kim took my hand. "We're leaving, right now. We don't mean any trouble."

We rejoined my grandfather and as quickly as possible, the three of us disappeared into the crowd.

NIGHT FELL over the square and the rain stopped. Outside the Tan Tan Theater, a large stage strung with colored lights faced the large piazza. A wooden bar on the left served as the defendant's stand. At the center of the platform, three male judges sat on a bench, looking down at the front row, where the prisoners were assembled. Since it was a People's Court, there would be no need for jurors or lawyers. Furthermore, the defendants weren't allowed to speak at any point during the trial. The People's representatives had already predetermined their guilt. It now was time for the officials to announce the verdicts.

We stood in the dark, watching the proceedings from behind hundreds of bobbing heads. People moved in and out of their rows, talking loudly to each other, fighting for better seats. Snacks passed from hand to hand, as though everyone were watching a performance. I stood transfixed, gazing at Loan among the prisoners. She sat with her head bent and her shoulders hunched, hiding her face between her knees. Her arms were tied behind her back, and it hurt my eyes to look at her.

When it was time for the trial to begin, a policeman on the stage fired his gun three times. The shots echoed through the square, and the crowd hushed. One of the judges stood in front of a microphone, holding a sheet of paper. Everything became a blur to me until I heard Loan's name called. Two policemen pulled her, kicking and screaming, to the stand. One of the policemen shoved a rag in her mouth to quiet her.

A judge denounced Loan and her husband for their degenerate conduct, which he called "a demonstration of an extremely dangerous kind of peasant Communism: subjectivism, rollback of socialism, and Maoism." They had betrayed the country, joined hands with the reactionaries. They insulted the honor of the Communist Party. And for that, he said, "They must be punished!" Loan was sentenced to fifteen years' hard labor with no chance of parole. Her husband's punishment was life imprisonment. After the ceremony, both of them were shoved down the stairs and driven away.

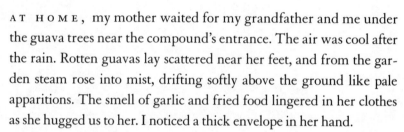

AT HOME, my mother waited for my grandfather and me under the guava trees near the compound's entrance. The air was cool after the rain. Rotten guavas lay scattered near her feet, and from the garden steam rose into mist, drifting softly above the ground like pale apparitions. The smell of garlic and fried food lingered in her clothes as she hugged us to her. I noticed a thick envelope in her hand.

"Guess what?" she cried. "We got our visas. In three months, we'll go to Saigon to be interviewed at the American Embassy. Kien, at last, those countless hours you spent at the community center for their signatures have paid off. Tonight, we'll celebrate our good fortune with a decent meal."

Lightheaded from the unexpected news, I handed her the necklace. My happy tears tasted bitter at the tip of my tongue.

My mother examined the chain. "What is it?" she asked.

"It's from Loan. She said to return it to you. We just came back from her trial."

My mother looked at my grandfather and said sadly, "Oh, Daddy, I am so sorry —"

My grandfather raised his hand to interrupt her. "Please, don't be," he replied, limping away into his room. "It isn't anybody's fault."

"Mom," I said. "What are you going to do with it?"

She replied without hesitation, "We'll sell it to raise money for the trip to Saigon. What else would you want me to do with it?"

"You can sell the necklace," I suggested. "But can I keep the jade? It's the only thing left for us to remember Loan."

My mother frowned. "Are you sure that it is what you want?"

I nodded.

"Okay," she sighed, separating the jade from the golden chain and handing it to me. "Take it now, before I change my mind. But if you lose it, may the gods help you, because I won't be so understanding at your excuse."

CHAPTER FORTY-FOUR

T hat night after dinner, I stole away to bed to examine the passports we had received from Hanoi. Each permit consisted of a four-inch-by-twelve-inch sheet, folded into four sections, as thin and fragile as an ordinary piece of paper. The front page was white and stamped with the Vietnamese national symbol — a circle of red on a flag with a yellow star in the middle and bordered with long grains of ripened rice. At the bottom of the image, the golden rice strands were tied together in a red ribbon, and the phrase "Socialist Republic of Vietnam" was printed across its surface. Underneath, it said, "Laissez-Passer, No. 40783ATH1." Inside was my picture looking straight at the camera, along with a space for my signature. The rest of the passport was dyed a pale green color and covered with red stamps, most of them dated May 30, 1984. Most exciting was the line that read, "The bearer of this ID is permitted to leave the Socialist Republic of Vietnam before May 30, 1985, to final destination: The United States of America." I repeated the line over and over again, trying to absorb its meaning.

Outside, my mother's voice called me to help with the dishes. I folded the passports away, got up, stretched, and walked out. The roofless kitchen had almost dried from the earlier rain. Still, puddles of stagnant water lay here and there on the floor, reflecting the iridescent, cloudless sky. My mother stood in the dark, watching my aunt's house, waiting. The chilly air howled through the empty dining hall, playing with her thin clothes. My footsteps startled her.

"Shhh." She put a finger to her lips, signaling for me to be quiet, and whispered, "Don't make a sound. I am waiting for her."

I halted in my tracks. The whooshing sound of water in the bathroom vibrated through the long hallway. Soon after, I heard the opening and closing of the door, and then the familiar clapping of my aunt's clogs echoed closer. She emerged into the frail glow of the kitchen's light, her hands at the side of her pants, tying the waist strings.

My mother cleared her throat. "Hello, sister," she said.

She looked up with a gasp. "Oh, hello." In the shadow of the corridor, her eyes formed two large spots on her face that made her look like a raccoon. "I didn't see you standing there. You scared me half to death."

"I am sorry. You must have heard about the news. Our passports came today."

"Yes, I did," my aunt replied, fixing her clothes. "Congratulations."

"Thank you. There is something I want to discuss with you. I am thinking about selling my house and moving to Saigon. We are leaving soon for America and I want to raise some cash to pursue this —"

My aunt interrupted her. "Wait, don't tell me this now. We need to discuss it with my husband."

"Why? It's my house and I am going to sell it. I just want you to know about my plan since you are my sister. I don't need to check with your husband."

My aunt yawned loudly. "I think you should. I'll see you tomorrow morning."

"Okay," my mother said, nodding. "If you insist — what time?"

She turned away from us. "Nine o'clock, my living room."

THE NEXT MORNING my mother woke up early even though she didn't have to prepare for the market. In the kitchen, she sat quietly on a small stool, boiling a pot of water to make ginger tea for my grandfather. I lay in bed, awakened by the frosty breeze that gusted through the big gap in the wall where my window used to be. The rough rice sacks felt prickly against my skin. I reached in between their layers for the hidden passports and read the fine print once more time, wondering whether we would actually leave Vietnam by the deadline of May 30, 1985. Jimmy got up from his bed. He walked noisily outside, into the kitchen, scratching his head. My mother handed him a cup of water and a toothbrush packed with a mixture of salt and baking soda. He brushed his teeth and spat out the excess liquid into the garden through a hole in the wall.

Outside, the neighborhood came to life. Houses rang with voices. Cocks crowed, doors squeaked open and closed, and children recited their poems one last time before school. Everything seemed clean and bright after the rain, and the smell of wet soil filled the air.

The grandfather clock in my aunt's house struck nine times, resonating through the garden. My mother wore a silk blouse that was so blue it was almost black, with tiny, faded gardenia flowers printed on it, and a pair of black nylon pants. They were the only decent garments she had left, and they were reserved solely for important occasions. Her hair was pulled back into a simple bun. Her body was stiff, and her eyes stared straight ahead, hard and chilly. She took a deep breath and walked out of the kitchen, heading past the garden. Jimmy and I waited by the window. We watched her disappear behind the tall column covered with thick patches of green moss that led to my aunt's house.

No more than two seconds later, she pushed their door open and stormed out angrily. She raised her fists above her head in frustration as she screamed out, "Daddy, where are you?"

My grandfather poked his head out of his room with a look of bewilderment on his face. His tangled hair stuck out from his head like porcupine quills. "What is going on?" he asked.

My mother stomped through the kitchen door. She kicked the stool out of her way and yelled, "Daddy, there is something I need you to settle for us. Would you please come with me?" She turned to my brother and me and ordered us in the same voice, "You two, get dressed, and follow me."

Before we could finish putting on our clothes, my mother grabbed Jimmy and me and strode back to my aunt's living room. My grandfather followed us a few steps behind. Waiting for us at the coffee table, my uncle sat with his back to the Buddha's altar. His arms were folded against his chest. Through his thick glasses, his eyes glared at us with a look that spelled trouble. Behind him, like a platoon of soldiers ready for combat, his eight sons stood still, echoing their father's unyielding expression. On the small section of the wall behind the Buddha hung Moonlight's picture, mounted neatly in a black frame, and next to it my grandmother's. Clouds of incense from the altar permeated the tense atmosphere. In the electric silence we could hear the relentless ticking of the clock.

My mother raised her voice, addressing no one in particular. "Where is that awful sister of mine?"

My uncle replied, using the same tactic to counterattack. "My wife can't attend the meeting. Something came up unexpectedly."

"What can possibly be more important than this? Is she afraid to face me?"

"My wife is not important in this matter," my uncle said. "You made us meet you here for a reason. Why don't you just say what you need to say and leave?"

My grandfather spoke up. "Aren't you going to invite us to sit down?"

"Forgive us," he said. Turning to Le, his oldest son, my uncle ordered, "Pull out a chair for your grandfather."

Le moved out of his rank like a robot, but my mother waved her hands to stop him. "Forget the phony formality," she said. "This is going to take only a minute. I want you all to know that I am planning to sell my house."

"I'm sorry," my uncle said, "but you can't do that."

My mother raised an eyebrow. "Why not? It's my house, isn't it? I hold the title deed."

My uncle turned to his oldest son and signaled to him with his eyes. Le opened a small door behind the Buddha's altar and pulled out a stack of folders, giving it to his father.

"Well?" my mother prodded him.

"Miss Khuon," my uncle began, turning the pages before him, "you are right about the ownership of your house. However, you can't sell your property, because I am the owner of the land that your house is standing on. It is documented in here. When you calm down, you may examine the papers if you don't believe me."

Anger darkened my mother's face. "I bought that land from you years ago," she said. "Your first son just turned fifteen years old the day you brought him to my mansion. I remember giving him his first bicycle, and I gave you the money to pay for the estate and the renovation. My parents and your son witnessed the deal between us. How dare you change the story now? Besides, I practically bought this entire compound for the price that I've paid you through the years."

My grandfather nodded pensively. "I am not senile yet. I remember that day clearly. Do you remember, Le?"

Le avoided my grandfather's stare. My mother drew a hand to her chest in her struggle for composure. Then she said to my uncle, "What am I supposed to do now? I need to raise money for our trip. Do you have any suggestion as to what we should do?"

My uncle pounded his fist on the glass surface of his coffee table, enunciating each word as though he were talking to a stubborn five-year-old child. "I don't care what you do. You are not selling my land. That is my final answer." He slammed the file shut, making a loud snap with his hands.

Silence returned to the room.

Finally, my mother tossed her hair out of her face. "Very well, you damnable thief. In fact, you are all thieves. If I can't sell my house, I am going to break it apart, brick by brick. You will never get that house, not while I am alive. This is not over yet." She stormed out, beckoning with her hand for Jimmy and me to follow. My cousins' laughter chased us through the garden.

FIVE MINUTES LATER, Tin showed up at the entrance of our kitchen. The sun peeked through the openings of my bedroom wall, shining on his pimpled face. His crossed eyes blinked apprehensively.

My mother walked out of her room and snapped at him, "What in hell do you want now?"

Tin stammered, "I am here to take back the rice sacks. My father needs them for storage."

"Take my bed away?" Jimmy protested. "Where will we sleep?"

"Don't argue, Jimmy," my mother said. She turned to Tin and said in a hoarse voice, "Take them away. Get those godforsaken things out of my house."

"Mommy, the cement is cold," BeTi cried.

My mother held her face in her hands, sobbing. "Then get some newspapers, lots of them. We don't need those stinking rice sacks."

1985

CHAPTER FORTY-FIVE
Saigon, January 2, 1985

With the money we got from selling Loan's necklace, my mother took us to Saigon one week prior to our appointment with the American interviewers. We took refuge at the home of the late Mrs. Dang's parents. The older couple lived within walking distance of the infamous Doc Lap Palace in a small shack that once had been their kitchen. The big house next door, where we had met with Mrs. Dang ten years ago on our way to the helicopter, had been subdivided several times and sold to different people. The kitchen and a tiny bathroom were all that they had left. The cabin was extremely small, even for two elderly people; nevertheless, Mr. and Mrs. Hom welcomed us in with open arms.

Saigon had changed a great deal since the end of the civil war. Like most of its disgruntled, tired citizens, the city showed signs of a difficult course of living. Once-fine houses were crumbling, gnawed by termites. Paint had peeled from walls and been replaced with moss. Through the holes that previously held windows, dirty faces of children peeked out at passersby with blank looks. Bicycles and rickshaws filled the narrow streets, contributing to a constant and deafening noise. In fact, the loud cacophony was difficult for us to get used to in this ever-zealous hive of activity.

I walked numbly through the unfamiliar streets, preoccupied

with the complicated departure procedures. I was afraid to face my fears. I did not know where fate would lead my family and me. Our future was a mystery. Whether I was going to leave or stay was being determined by faceless strangers I would never know.

Saigon in 1985 was cramped, congested, and swamped with filth. In the blazing temperature, dirt particles floated in the air and trickled down onto everything like an endless stream of black snow. I quickly learned not to wear anything light in color outside. Things got dirty fast, especially around the center of Saigon, where everybody scrambled to get from one polluted place to the next.

The letter that accompanied our passports gave the address of the emigration office as 4 Duy Tan Boulevard, a street well known for its tall, healthy, and lustrous tamarind trees. These were familiar tropical fruit trees with branches that had whorls of fish-scale leaves and jointed stems entwining together to roof the road like a canopy. Doc Lap Palace and the former U.S. Embassy were just a few blocks away, hidden behind those green curtains of leaves. At six-thirty in the morning, my family and I gathered outside the emigration office's gate with twenty other Amerasian children and their families. All were waiting for a bus that would take us to the interview site, an hour away.

At that time, the embargo between the U.S. and Vietnam was strictly enforced. In order for the American Council of Voluntary Agencies to work in Vietnam, its staff had to fly in from Bangkok every morning to a secluded town outside of Saigon, and leave before night fell. We came by bus to meet with the representatives during those designated hours.

Their place of work was located inside a mansion that had probably belonged to a rich entrepreneur in the past. Remnants of the former owners' expensive taste were still visible. The house sat on one side of a hill, overlooking a forest of rubber trees. Two enormous wings joined together with a much bigger central house in a U shape, embracing a wide, red marble veranda. Large rooms with oversized glass windows on the second and third floors had been turned into offices.

Through the sheer glass, I could see foreign people moving back and forth with folders and pens in their hands. Any of them could have been the one who typed the first correspondence to me. And they now would determine my fate. From a short distance, their faces looked so beautiful, so bright, and yet so alien. How I wanted to be one of them. And for the first time in many years, I was not ashamed of my American features. Watching them made me realize where I came from, and where I should belong. Their presence stirred up in me a surge of anxiety.

As if reading my thoughts, my mother pulled at my arm. "Look, Kien," she said, pointing at the Americans. "Do you know what that means? The eagle has come for her young."

Waiting for our names to be called, we gathered around a large rectangular table on one side of the veranda. Each of us was dressed in the nicest outfit that he or she could afford, according to the latest fashion of the city — blue jeans and silk blouses or striped shirts. Most of the Amerasian children in my group ranged in age from twelve to nineteen. They stared at one another, straining to conceal their curiosity with a mask of polite indifference.

Standing apart from the group was a family of sixteen, clad in beautiful clothing and expensive jewelry, and shining like a flock of peacocks. They huddled under a casuarina tree, eating green bean cakes from a picnic basket. A young girl of about fourteen, with straight blond hair and blue eyes, stood shyly among them. In her hands, she held a big pitcher of iced tea made from condensed milk and black tea. The oldest woman in the group, who was so fat that she seemed to swallow the chair underneath her, called out for the girl in a clear, exultant voice, "Give me something to drink, my petite daughter." She repeated the phrase over and over again, laughing as if at some private joke. A thick coat of powder cracked at the corner of her eyes. Her family recoiled each time she called the girl her daughter. They grunted with disgust, hiding their discomfort in their overly enthusiastic conversations.

When my family's name was called, we ran to meet our interviewer at the foot of a staircase. She was a black woman, dressed in a dark blue business suit, as beautiful and alien as a colored porcelain doll. Her perfume hung in the air like the smell of a black rose in my uncle's garden after the rain. A Vietnamese translator stayed a few steps behind her. After a simple greeting and handshakes, they took us upstairs.

As soon as she opened the door to her office and invited us in, a blast of cold wind from the air conditioner swallowed me in its gentle, westernized embrace. I took in a deep breath, and suddenly, America was inside my lungs. Next to me, my mother began to cry.

SOON AFTER THE INTERVIEW, we left Saigon in a hurry. There was no chance for us to enjoy the view. The city was so expensive that we could not afford to stay too long. Besides, the place of Mr. and Mrs. Hom was too small to accommodate a large family such as mine. My mother assigned Jimmy to stay behind at Mr. and Mrs. Hom's place to monitor the airplane schedule and the list of departing refugees, which was posted every week at the emigration office. After we returned to Nhatrang, we communicated with him mainly through telegrams. My duty was to take care of the paperwork. According to the Vietnamese government, before anyone could leave the country, three essential documents were required: a signature from the Department of Real Estate, a debt-free statement from the Central Bank of Vietnam, and a certification from the Department of Taxation. The purpose was to prove to the government that those departing owned and owed nothing. For us, time was running out.

Rumors about my family's meeting with the American interviewers arrived in Nhatrang before we did. Greeting us in front of our door was a line of Amerasians. Most of these children were homeless. Their filthy clothes were torn, their skin was dull, and their faces had no traces of baby fat. They looked at us, their eyes sparkling with hope. Many of the children had brought along the application they had picked up at the local emigration center. I walked in side by side with my mother and BeTi, reaching for the latch of the front gate.

Two black girls, the first in line, grinned at me. One of them said shyly, "Mr. Kien, would you please help my sister and me? We need to fill out these papers, but we can't read or write."

Her sister added, "We saved up some money to pay for your services." She opened her hand to show me a wrinkled twenty-dong note. She must have held on to it so long and so tightly that the bill was nearly decomposed from the perspiration of her palm. Carefully, she laid it in my hand. Both girls were about the same age, thirteen or fourteen. Their hairstyles were enormous, like two thick pine topiaries.

I pushed the money back to her. "Keep it," I told them. "I can't take your money. But don't worry, I will help you fill out those forms."

My mother spoke up. "Where do I know you girls? Was it from the noodle shop at Le Chan Street?"

"Yes, madam," they said simultaneously.

"Dear heaven, all those years, you are still on the street?" she asked. "Where is your mother?"

One of the sisters answered, "She died last year. The doctors said it was from syphilis. We have been on our own since."

I took the applications from their hands. Curiosity overtook me, and I asked them, "How did you know that we were coming home today?"

The same innocent smile brightened their faces. "We heard about your lucky news at the market on Monday. And since then we have been waiting here for the past three days."

THAT DAY I filled out more than twenty applications. The next day, more children arrived, bringing with them more papers. Not until then did I realize the shocking number of abandoned Amerasians in my city. Each morning, I woke up to see at least ten faces peering from behind the barbed wire that encircled my front lawn. All wore the same frightened, uncertain, yet trusting expression. They all wanted to touch me, to feel the significant reality of the Americans that I had come in contact with. For most of these children, what happened to my family was the dream they aspired to live someday themselves.

CHAPTER FORTY-SIX
Nhatrang, March 21, 1985

Jimmy's telegram came on Wednesday, March 21, 1985. *"Our family was first on the list this morning,"* it said. *"We are scheduled to leave Vietnam next Wednesday, March 28ᵗʰ. I am going home to say good-bye to Grandpa. Please send Kien out here to replace me. Love, Jimmy. p.s. Kien, have you taken care of all the paperwork yet?"*

His last sentence overshadowed the exciting news, restraining me from jumping for joy. For over two and a half months, I had not been able to get the Department of Real Estate to sign a release for my mother's house. Every deputy commander that I met in that office had pushed my application aside once he saw my uncle's name on the land deed. Our case was too complicated and time-consuming for them to handle, despite the expensive cigarettes and lotus teas that I brought on each visit as "gifts."

The relationship between my aunt and my mother had reached a new level of friction. Arguments broke out almost every day, with my mother screaming, pleading, and threatening. In desperation, she even offered to give the house to her sister and brother-in-law in exchange for their signatures on the release form. Nevertheless, both my aunt and her husband were so worried about the possible inheritance tax that they turned away from my mother's woeful tears. As far as my uncle was concerned, once my family abandoned the house, it would routinely become his, since the land was in his name. Any action on his part might attract the government's attention, which he feared could pose a potential danger to his family.

"STOP RUNNING AROUND, you are making me dizzy," my mother shouted to BeTi as they walked through the garden. The loud clanging of her pots and the heavy aroma of fried fish cakes preceded them, pulling me to my feet. My mother sauntered into the kitchen, cursing loudly at no one in particular. The heavy load of her baskets pulled at both ends of the bamboo rod, which dug painfully into her shoulder. She dropped her burden to the floor, squatted down right beside it, and fanned herself with her conical hat. Sweat soaked in large blotches across her blouse, accenting her armpits. BeTi stood at the entrance, holding a half-empty salad bowl. As usual, my sister seemed lost in her own trance.

I sat down next to my mother. "Was business bad today?" I asked her.

"Awful," she retorted. "The whole block was filled with soup mongers competing with one another. I couldn't even give the food away if I tried."

I showed her Jimmy's telegram. She glanced at it, and her eyes quickly filled with delight. She grabbed my arms and hugged me tightly, screaming like a happy child. Then, we both leaped onto our feet as she waved the paper above her head triumphantly. BeTi joined us, even though she was unsure about the reason for our outburst.

"Mother," I said when we stopped to catch our breath, "I have to leave tonight. There is a midnight train leaving for Saigon I want to catch. Jimmy will be here early tomorrow."

She nodded okay.

"I will need some money for the ticket. And you have to handle the real estate problem on your own. Without that piece of paper, you know we cannot leave this place."

Just as fast as it came, the cheerfulness vanished from her face. She returned the telegram to me, silently picked up her hat, and stepped outside.

"Where are you going?" I asked her.

Without looking back, she said over her shoulder, "I am going to get you some cash before you leave."

"How are you going to do that, Mom?"

"I don't know. It doesn't concern you. Go spend some time with your grandfather."

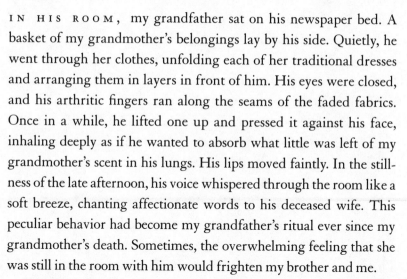

I N   H I S   R O O M, my grandfather sat on his newspaper bed. A basket of my grandmother's belongings lay by his side. Quietly, he went through her clothes, unfolding each of her traditional dresses and arranging them in layers in front of him. His eyes were closed, and his arthritic fingers ran along the seams of the faded fabrics. Once in a while, he lifted one up and pressed it against his face, inhaling deeply as if he wanted to absorb what little was left of my grandmother's scent in his lungs. His lips moved faintly. In the stillness of the late afternoon, his voice whispered through the room like a soft breeze, chanting affectionate words to his deceased wife. This peculiar behavior had become my grandfather's ritual ever since my grandmother's death. Sometimes, the overwhelming feeling that she was still in the room with him would frighten my brother and me.

"Hi, Grandpa," I called out, hoping that my voice would chase the eeriness away.

He looked up. Waves of the afternoon heat slipped through the openings in the wall, washing through his room, through his hair, and into the cement floor, as pungent as the steam off my mother's soup. The hot wind lured me closer to him. Upon seeing me, my grandfather's lips curled into a smile, and he patted the ground next to him.

"Come here," he said. "Come sit next to Grandpa."

I moved away from the entrance and sat down beside him.

"Grandpa, I am leaving for Saigon tonight," I began.

"I know, child," he said, nodding. "I heard you and your mother."

His attention shifted back to the array of clothing. Broodingly, his eyes softened as his fingers ran across a simple black velvet dress with large silver buttons and traditional high collar. Something had discolored the fabric, leaving a blotchy stain from its shoulders all the way down to the front of the skirt. On the elbows, the inside lining peeked through the torn fabric.

"Do you know that this was her favorite dress?" my grandfather murmured tenderly. "She wore it for every occasion. Shopping, dinner at Le Colonial Restaurant, my captain inauguration ceremony, our son's funeral, she was always in this dress."

"What caused the stain, Grandpa?" I asked him.

My grandfather chuckled, "The stain was from me. Good heavens, she was so mad at me that day when it happened."

"How could you make such a big stain, and from what?"

His chuckle turned into a healthy laugh as memory flooded his face. "Oh, it happened many years ago. And I don't think she would approve of me telling you this."

"Sir, you can't do this to me," I begged. "I am leaving soon. Give me something to remember about you and Grandma, please."

"Well, you are absolutely right," he said, smiling. "We don't have much time left together. Let's have some fun on her account. Okay, I'll tell you the story. It began one night. That evening was beautiful with a full moon, and we had just come back from dinner. I don't know if you are aware that your grandmother could become quite a dragon lady when she was jealous. And jealousy makes people do silly things —"

"Where was I?" I interrupted.

He leaned back against the wall. "You were just a little tyke, two or three years old. Your mother had just finished renovating the mansion for us. That night, I wanted to go out for some fresh air on the beach, to walk off the heavy dinner. Somehow, your Grandma didn't believe me. She decided to sneak out, spying on me a distance of about a hundred yards away. I knew she was there all along, but I pretended not to. On the sand, I waddled like a penguin, trying to embarrass her, but she kept on following me. Finally, I stopped, stretched, and said loud enough so that she could hear me, 'Oh, good heavens, where can a man go when he needs to relieve himself?' I could hear her plunging into a pine bush. I waited a while, then turned around, and walked over to the bush. I saw that black head of hers and I unzipped my pants and urinated, aiming straight at her hair. She didn't move once, not even a muscle, but I could hear her cursing me under her breath. So I whistled, finished, shook myself, and muttered as I walked away, 'That was a number one. I think I might have to do a number two very soon.' Still no word, she sat so still, waiting for me to get out of her sight —"

I burst out laughing.

My grandfather patted me on my shoulder. His eyes wrinkled thoughtfully. "Yes, that's good. Go ahead and laugh, child. You don't laugh enough for someone your age. I hope that may change soon."

And then he continued. "When your Grandma finally got home, your mother and I sat in the living room. We tried to act normal, but that lasted only a second once we saw her all wet and mad as hell. I fell off the chair from laughing so hard, and your mother got the hiccoughs for the rest of the evening. The dress was completely ruined. My urine was so strong that it ate through the velvet like acid. And because of that, your grandmother didn't talk to me for a whole week."

I commented, "That is a side of you I've never seen before, Grandpa."

My grandfather reached out to hug me. "I know, Kien. I am sorry we have grown so far apart. I am sorry you have never had a happy, jolly grandfather like you should have. And I am sorry I've kept you and your brother here in this godforsaken land where you don't belong. So many things have gone wrong, I don't even know where or when it all began. I just hope that it isn't too late for you, your brother, and your sister to have normal and happy lives, wherever you are going. Just remember, life is short. You have to enjoy every moment before it passes you by. Forgive me for all of my foolish decisions. I was behaving like a selfish and stubborn old bastard. Forgive your mother for taking your childhood away from you. What she did, she did the best way that she knew how. About your aunt and her family" — he sighed — "I don't know if you can forgive them for what they have done, but at least try to free yourself from them. Don't let this anger ruin your life any more than it already has. If you want to ever achieve happiness, don't dwell on the past. Instead, start living. What is the point of obsessing over something that has already happened, and that you cannot change? Live! And be merry. Remember Grandpa's advice when you have your own family someday."

I said over his shoulder, "Oh, Grandpa, are you going to be okay after we leave Vietnam?"

He nodded. "I am going to be fine. Don't worry about me. I have your grandmother's memory here to keep me company."

I hugged him for the last time. He kissed both of my cheeks. So many years had passed, yet my grandfather's breath still smelled like Jolly Rancher candy. I suddenly felt small in his arms, like the day I turned eight.

CHAPTER FORTY-SEVEN

Night fell over the city. The shade of leaves, the chirping of birds, and the loud motorcycles down the street all faded away with the dying sun. On the surrounding rice paddies, crickets and frogs blended their songs into an eerie, melancholy chant. The path to Kim's house was long and convoluted. Without a streetlight to show the way, I could not even see my own shadow as I made my way blindly down the pitted road.

The early summer heat was still intense, making the soil under my feet feel like the inside of an oven. Oily sweat trickled down my forehead, stinging my eyes. With little difficulty, I found her house standing across from a shallow stream of water. Cool mist from the brook evaporated like a natural humidifier, and I gratefully inhaled the fresh air it released. From a distance, every room in her house gleamed with fluorescent light, while the outside porch sank into the darkness. The closest neighbor was at least a hundred yards away, separated from her family's property by a desolate rice field.

It didn't take me long to find out where Kim was. Through a tangle of overgrown vines and thorn bushes that bordered her backyard, I saw her next to the well. She was wet from head to toe. The dim light from the kitchen bathed her body in a bronze glow. Her clothes clung to her like a second skin. With each bucket of water she poured over herself, I smelled the familiar fragrance of fresh lemongrass as it marinated weakly into the night. The kitchen door was open, and I could see her mother's tall silhouette hovering over a stove.

Carefully I climbed over the scratchy fence, making as little sound as possible and praying that my presence would not startle her. Then hidden in the dark, behind a thick rack of bamboo, I whispered her name, letting the wind carry that single syllable to her ear.

After my fifth try, Kim stopped bathing and peered into the dark garden in my direction. Her arms coiled over her chest in an attempt to cover herself as she walked closer to me.

"Who's there?" she said loudly.

I emerged from the shrubbery.

Her mother called out, "Is there something wrong, Kim?"

"Don't be afraid," I said to Kim. "It's me, Kien."

Under the pale light, I could see Kim holding her breath from nervousness. Several seconds passed, then she said to her mother, "It's nothing, mother. I just saw a squirrel." Then she whispered to me, "Kien, I didn't know you were coming to see me tonight."

"I need to speak to you."

"Give me a few minutes to get dressed, please. I'll meet you outside by the stream."

I shook my head. "I can't. I am leaving tonight for Saigon, then to America. I came to say good-bye."

She took a few steps further, and I reached out, pulling her toward me. We withdrew further into the rice field, away from her mother. Her wet body curved into my feverish embrace. No matter how many times I had held her in my arms, I could not get over how soft her body was. My heart beat wildly in my chest, threatening to burst. The thought of seeing her one last time gave me new courage to do what I had not dared every time we met. I grabbed her breasts. Kim let out a small cry, but she did not resist. I covered her mouth with kisses, keeping her body still as my flesh came alive with an overwhelming desire to make love to her.

In her ear, I whispered incoherent phrases. "I want you, your body — Everything about you is so beautiful. I need to see you alone, without your clothes —"

"I love you," she replied fervently. "Do you know that I loved you from the very first day I met you at the beach?"

I unbuttoned her shirt, peeling it off her body. She trembled like a sparrow caught in a trap. Her eyes rimmed with tears. I didn't understand why she cried; yet I didn't want to find out. One thought reverberated over and over again in my head: I had to get revenge for my mother, and for myself. Revenge required a price. I wondered what would be my price? I reached for her nylon pants, took them off and threw them on the ground next to her shirt. Intoxicated with my newly discovered power, I took off my own clothes as I watched her naked body shiver.

"I love you," she said. "Even if I never see you again, I will always love you, Kien."

I covered her mouth. "Stop talking," I told her.

We lay together on the grass and slowly I entered her. It was difficult at first, but I drove myself inside her. Her body shook more violently in response to the lovemaking, and for a moment, I got frightened. The images of her father, Mr. Tran, and many other Communist policemen temporarily disappeared from my mind.

"Am I hurting you, Kim?"

She didn't respond. Instead, her silent sobbing grew stronger.

Overcome with guilt, I begged her, "Please, let me know if I am hurting you."

"No, it doesn't hurt," she answered. "But I am scared."

"Of what?"

Wild grass entwined with her wet hair. She looked as if she had melted into the soil. Turning her face away from me, she whispered, "I am scared that you are making the same mistake that your father did. Look at us! You will be leaving this country soon. What will happen to me if I get pregnant? What will happen to the baby, unwanted before it's even born because its father is a half-breed?"

Her words stabbed me, penetrating the agony that I had buried so deep inside my soul. I shrank away from her and fumbled for my clothes. Kim grabbed my arm.

"Please," she said, wiping her tears away with the back of her hand. "Don't leave angry. I love you. Do what you want with me, but please be clear to yourself about why you are doing it."

I snapped at her, "Stop talking! Why do you have to be so smart all the time? Can't you just shut up and spare me your feelings? You want to know why am I doing this? Just look at yourself, and look at me. Do we look like we belong together? You with your stupid Communist accent, it sickened me from the very first day we met. I hate you and everything that you stand for. I hate your father and the way he treated my mother. I hate your people, how they robbed me of everything I ever got. If I could hurt one of you, I can leave this place satisfied."

"Don't go!" She gathered her clothes in front of her, sobbing. "That isn't why you came here tonight. Tell me you are here because you love me. You promised you were never going to hurt me, remember?"

I walked away.

Her wailing rose sharply in the dark, a foreign sound among the crickets' chirping. "Tell me just one time, before you leave me forever."

I froze in my tracks, dizzy from the conflicting thoughts that raced through my head. My lower lip quivered so much that I had a difficult time talking. "I can't say that, Kim. I can't love you. I don't know how."

I escaped her property like a thief, closing my ears to her desperate pleas.

BY THE TIME I got home, the whole neighborhood was submerged in a deep sleep, and the sliver of moon hung like a piece of fingernail across a bottomless sky. My mother sat in BeTi's bed, waiting for me. She ran her hand though my sister's hair and softly sang one of BeTi's favorite lullabies. A candle burned weakly in a tray nearby. Its light reflected on the wall created a host of distorted, dancing figures. Even wearing full makeup, my mother appeared haggard, tired, and old. Her eyes were sunken, encircled with droopy, wrinkled lids. Her facial skin sagged downward in the expression of a sad clown.

"Where have you been?" she demanded.

I ignored her question, searching the room for my backpack. "What time is it?" I asked her.

"Eleven o'clock. Where were you?"

"I stepped out to say good-bye to a few friends of mine. Mom, have you gotten any money for my train ticket?"

"Yes," she replied unenthusiastically.

"Excellent," I said. "I need to go through the documents with you. I will take everything with me, but I'll leave you one copy of the real estate papers. You must try to get them signed here, in case I can't get my set approved in Saigon. Right, Mom?"

"I'll try all I can. Everything is in my room," she said.

"By the way, how did you get the money?"

She looked straight at me. "It isn't important how I got it. You don't need to know, understand?"

I walked into her room, taking the candle with me. After we sold the kitchen's roof, the water had leaked into my mother's bedroom every time it rained. On the wall, the black and white pictures of my family in their cellophane covers — some of my mother and me, others of my mother and Jimmy — all were damaged from the constant moisture. They were peeling, torn, and yellow at the corners like fifty-year-old snapshots. On the floor, where her makeup desk used to be, our family's documents were gathered into stacks of paper, arranged in rows two feet high and four feet long. Three years of pursuing the visas had resulted in this mountain of records.

My mother followed me. She sat against the wall, watching as I went through the papers. I came upon a thick stash of hospital receipts wrapped together in a rubber band.

"What are these, Mom?" I showed the bundle to her.

"They are from me," she replied matter-of-factly. "Every time I sold my blood at the hospital, I got a receipt."

I uttered a small cry. "There must be at least fifty vouchers here. Why did you do it? And why wouldn't you tell us?"

"Oh, forget it." She waved aside my concern and said, "I had to put you, your brother, and your sister through school. Every semester, you needed books, clothing, shoes, and other stuff. Ten years of having no steady job, no income, what other choice did I have? I just didn't want you to worry, that's why I never told you."

I sighed deeply, overcome with guilt. My mother pulled at my arm. Her face relaxed, and the deep creases around her eyes pulled upward as she smiled.

"Listen, honey," she said gently. "You know your education is very important to me. I don't have anything to give you, except to show you a way to better yourself. And you know something? I didn't make a mistake. You've learned a great deal in school. You found a way to get us out of this miserable existence. On top of that, you have been a very good son to me. I promise you, it is going to get better soon from this time on."

"We may not get out of here, Mother," I said bitterly. "If those bastards refuse to sign the paper, we'll get stuck in this place forever."

She put a finger over her lips. "Don't speak like that. Think positively and the gods will help us work things out."

I got up from the floor, shoving the documents into my backpack. The moment had come for me to say good-bye to her, and I stood awkwardly in the room, searching for words.

"Are you ready?" she asked me.

"Yes, Mom."

She handed me three one-hundred-dong bills. I grabbed both of her hands, pushing back her long sleeves to reveal her veins. Under the flickering candlelight, I found a bandage on her right forearm. Beneath it, a large bruise had begun to form.

"You did it again," I cried. "You just sold your blood this afternoon."

"Like I said, it isn't important. Go now if you want to catch that train."

I grabbed my mother in my arms and hugged her. Her body felt so thin in my embrace.

"Take the money," she said.

I took two bills and handed her the last one. "I only need this much. You should go out tomorrow and buy something nice for yourself. Maybe you should take all the white out of your hair for the big trip."

"Okay," she said, nodding.

"Good-bye, Mother. I'll see you in a few days."

CHAPTER FORTY-EIGHT

As I walked through the empty streets in the middle of the night, a few rays of moonlight peeked out from behind the thick purple clouds, cracking the darkness open with their pale light. From a distance, I could hear the weak but distinct noise of a train, its pitch descending as it came to a stop. The station rested on the bank of a river that was black with the scum of the sewers from the neighborhood nearby. A fog of gas exhaust flooded the air as I ventured closer. Its burnt odor mixed with the stench of garbage.

An old woman, holding a teapot and a ceramic cup, sat on a large rock. Behind her, the glass window of the train station mirrored my reflection as the moonlight hit it at an angle. I touched my oily, life-less hair, trying to improve my appearance. The old lady looked at me with puffy eyes, red and swollen from a chronic infection. Cautiously, she guarded her teapot.

"Want some tea? It's fifty cents per cup," she said. Enthusiasm filled her voice. "But for you, it's free."

I shook my head to decline the offer, searching over her shoulder for the ticket salesperson. The booth was empty. There was no other soul in sight, except a bored policeman, who nodded drowsily at the far end of the station ground. In his hand, the hard leather of a black nightstick gleamed in the dark.

"Where are you going?" the old lady asked.

"To Saigon," I answered. "Where can I buy a ticket?"

She shook her head. "No one is here at this hour to sell you a ticket."

The thought of staying another day in Nhatrang struck panic in me. "Do you know of a way for me to get to Saigon tonight? I can't afford to waste any more time here."

A lamppost cast eerie shadows on her creased face as she looked at me. "Do you know how to jump a train?"

I shook my head no. "I am afraid that I don't."

"It's easy," she explained. "Wait till the train starts to move, then jump up into the last car. I could show you exactly where to hide so that you won't get caught. Once it gets to Saigon, wait until the train slows down before it reaches to a stop, then hop off. Just try not to break your legs on the way down."

"It's too risky," I thought out loud. "Is there any way I can get a ticket?"

"You won't get caught if you follow my directions. More than half of the people riding the train have no ticket. Just keep calm and blend in, you'll be fine."

"Okay." I saw no alternative. "Thank you very much, lady."

She held out a serving of black tea. The cup was stained with some unknown substance, the same shade as her black fingernails. "Do you want some?" she asked. "It's on the house."

I shook my head politely. In front of a stop sign, people began to form into a cluster, waiting for the train to depart. They seemed to materialize from out of nowhere. I turned to bid the old lady good-bye.

"I know who you are," she whispered. "Thank you for helping my grandson fill out his application."

I turned around to face her. "I am not sure I know who your grandson is."

"It's doesn't matter," the old lady said, waving her hand. "I know why you are going to Saigon. What you did for us, I couldn't repay you, but I could pray for the gods to bless you on your journey.

Someday soon, it will be my grandson's turn to be on this train just like you."

The engine shifted on the shining track, shrieking loudly. The policeman woke up from his nap and looked around. Carefully avoiding him, I walked the opposite way into the dark shadows. Fifteen minutes later, after everyone else boarded the train, it began to move. Once it got past me, I grabbed onto a small handle that stuck out from the wall of the last car and jumped up, just as I had been instructed. The wind whipped my hair wildly. I pressed my body against the cold steel of the door and closed my eyes.

The memory of Kim flooded my mind. Her female scent, still heady on my fingertips, stirred in me the mixed feelings that I felt for her. I remembered her tears when she held me in her arms and kissed me, and the emotion that gripped my heart. My face flushed with frustration and shame. Now I understood the price that I had to pay for my revenge. Whether Kim forgave me or not, I had broken her physically and emotionally. I was no better than Lam, or her father, or any other loathsome creature that ever crossed my path. Worst of all, I had to live with that knowledge. That was my price. As the train shot further into the dark, I realized the growing distance between us.

Half an hour later the train stopped at the next station, just long enough for the passengers to stretch their legs before it continued its journey. Moving from car to car, I found an attached wagon filled with farm produce. At the entrance, two women leaned against each other, deep in sleep. Carefully, I stepped over them. Hugging the knapsack in my arms, I chose a giant rice sack and dusted off its dirty surface. Lying on my temporary bed and rocking to the motion of the train, I soon fell asleep.

The trip took another ten hours to reach Saigon. As soon as the scenery became familiar, I leaped off the train, using the side of my body to break the fall. Down the hill, the city curled up along Saigon River, seeming miniscule like a child's toy. Houses clustered at the bottom of a valley, reaching out into the water. Their red tile roofs, scattered among the bougainvillea plants, gleamed like fire under the hot rays of sun. At the turn of a dusty red road, I hailed a rickshaw to Mr. and Mrs. Hom's cabin.

FOR THE NEXT FIVE DAYS in Saigon, I struggled to get the last piece of paper signed at the main Department of Real Estate. With each deputy mandarin that I encountered, I faced another rejection. Day after day, my presence in their waiting room became the center of jokes and laughter, yet I refused to give up. The application crumbled in my hand, smudged by my own sweaty fingers and yellowed from the harsh sun. Each word, each line was now part of my memory.

My mother's telegram came two days before our scheduled flight. It said, *"Grandpa passed away last night. Don't come home because we are leaving for Saigon. I'll see you soon. Love, Mom."*

I didn't have time to grieve. There were so many errands to do before my mother's arrival. In the course of one day, I picked up the airplane tickets, acquired proper vaccinations, and received a complete physical examination.

That night, from the window, I watched my mother walk in from the dark and slippery alley. Jimmy and BeTi followed, tired and cranky from a long trip. Along the walls of the neighboring houses, the shadows of my family danced like string puppets from a children's show. Rose petals littered the wet ground, rotting among the rocks and broken glass. From the way they smelled and the dirt on their clothes, I knew instantly that my family had taken the train to get here.

I turned on the porch light, waiting for them to stumble into the house. Mrs. Dang's parents sat quietly at a table playing cards. A pot of tea that had long lost its steam sat untouched in front of them.

My mother moved across the threshold. An eerie, golden stream of light washed over her face. Her features grew distinct under the light, and I saw that her eyes were full of sadness. A black cotton band, wrapped around her right arm, served as a reminder of the departed. The expression on her face was the same as it had been on the day she lost her mansion. All of life's injustices suffused her gaze as she stared into a void past my face.

I broke the silence to ask her, "Mother, how did it happen?"

"I don't know," she replied. "I woke up yesterday morning and found him dead on his bed. He must have gone in the middle of the night. Maybe he died from a heart attack, or maybe he just didn't want us to worry about him anymore."

My poor grandfather! Even in his death, he was being considerate of our future.

A couple of teardrops fell down my mother's cheeks. Soon we all wept with her.

Suddenly, I remembered my brother's dog, and I asked him, "What happened to Lou, Jimmy?"

Jimmy answered, "Duy Tong adopted him. He seemed happy in his new home."

"What is going to happen to Grandpa's funeral?" I asked my mother.

"Your aunt's family will arrange for the funeral," she replied. "We'll be on our way to Thailand that same day."

"We may not be allowed to leave, Mother," I said. "I can't get them to sign that paper for us. Unless you got somebody to endorse it for you in Nhatrang, I don't see how we can get out."

She wiped her tears and cleared her throat. The hoarseness vanished from her voice, making way for a sudden determination. "Don't worry, son. We came this far. We just have to keep going. There is still one more day for us to try."

CHAPTER FORTY-NINE

Explain your case to me one more time. Did your mother own that house?"

I sat at the edge of my seat across from the chief of the Real Estate Service. He bent his head, scanning through my file. A pencil spun maddeningly in his hand. Outside the two windows of his office, the city bathed in a serene and casual afternoon light. On a windowsill, a bug crawled toward a branch of a lemon tree and fluttered its wings.

"My family owned the house," I explained, pushing a pack of expensive cigarettes toward him. "My uncle owned the land."

He furrowed his eyebrows. "Why isn't his signature on this paper? Who inherits the house now?"

"I assume it now belongs to my uncle, sir. We abandoned it two days ago."

The chief shook his head and sucked his teeth disapprovingly. Closing my file, he slid it across the desk back to me. "I can't sign this paper," he said. "It is useless and illegal. Go back to Nhatrang, get your uncle to straighten out this mess, and come back to see me."

"But sir, I can't do that," I protested. "We are leaving tomorrow."

The officer burst out laughing. I closed my eyes, expecting another rain of tasteless jokes.

The chief leaned closer to me until his face was inches away. I noticed a few strands of untrimmed hair protruding from his nostrils. They trembled every time he breathed, like the bug's wings on the windowsill. "How badly do you want me to sign and stamp this paper?" he whispered. "Would you trade your soul for it?" A trace of humor appeared in his eyes.

I turned away from his stare, unable to answer. The officer continued to laugh. He threw the folder in my lap and waved his hands. "Get out of here," he said. "You are wasting my time, dumb half-breed."

"Please, sir," I begged. "Find it in your heart to help me. I will forever remember this act of kindness."

The chief leaned back into the leather chair, throwing his feet up on the desk. His lips tightened as he regarded his perfect manicure. In desperation, I sank to my knees and crawled around the desk to his side. "Please, have pity on me," I begged again, kissing his hand. "You are my last hope. I promise I will be out of your life forever."

He shook me off and wiped his hand quickly with a white handkerchief. He got up, poured himself a cup of tea from the pot nearby, and drank it slowly. I remained on the floor, waiting. Finally, he threw me a look of disdain.

"Come back tomorrow," he said. "And bring a gift with you. I don't do anything for free."

"But, sir," I protested, "the airplane will leave tomorrow morning."

"Like I said, I'll sign that paper tomorrow when you bring a substantial gift with you. Otherwise, we'll have nothing to do with each other."

His gaze shifted toward the windows where the lemon tree shimmered in the sunlight. I picked up my folder and left.

THAT NIGHT, except for BeTi, no one in my family was able to rest. On the floor, my mother lay still, deep in thought. Next to me,

Jimmy tossed and turned. All the doors and windows of the cabin were open to provide relief from the humidity. Rose petals followed the wind into the house and scattered on the floor like droplets of blood. The night was shrouded in fog, and on the table, a clock ticked loudly.

On my side, I curled up with my knees in my arms. Emotions paraded through me: sadness, pain, regret, and desire. Outside, a weak moonbeam shone its silver light through the window. I watched a wave of moths twirling in the field of light, crashing into one another as if suicide were their ultimate goal. I wondered how long it would take before I burned the last of my energy.

"Kien, are you awake?" Jimmy whispered to me.

I turned to face him.

"What is going to happen tomorrow?" he asked.

"You will go to the airport with Mom and BeTi. I'll meet up with you later, after I get the paper signed."

My mother spoke up, her voice filled with worry. "The airport will be closed at eleven o'clock in the morning. Make sure that you meet us there on time, with or without the signature."

"Yes, Mom," I promised. "I'll get there before eleven."

MORNING CAME with a sudden burst of cold air. My mother got up first. Noiselessly, she disappeared behind the bathroom door with her toothbrush while Jimmy, BeTi, and I got dressed. My brother and sister dressed in their new outfits that my mother had bought recently for the big day. Dapper in a white shirt and blue gabardine pants, Jimmy looked as shiny as a brand-new penny. His black sandals were also new. My sister wore a purple dress a size too big for her thin body. Nevertheless, it made her happy. She smiled, showing her two large front teeth like the famous Bugs Bunny.

I picked out an old shirt and a pair of torn khaki pants. For my last meeting with the real estate officers, I wanted to convey my impoverished condition. A strong and unsettling angst stirred up inside of me, making my heart race and my head reel as if I had the flu. My clothes were not thick enough to shield me from the cold. I huddled back under the sheet to keep warm.

Soon, my mother emerged from the bathroom. She too had changed into her nicest outfit, the familiar blue blouse with tiny gardenia flowers and a pair of black nylon pants. At the table, she placed a bottle of cognac, two cartons of cigarettes, and a few packages of dried squid jerky into my knapsack. Handing it over to me, she ordered, "Take these things to the chief deputy in exchange for his signature."

In the kitchen, Mrs. Hom appeared, bringing with her a pot of sticky rice and mung bean. The sweet smell of breakfast woke Mr. Hom. He got out of his bed and yawned loudly, groping for his slippers in the dark.

"Have some food before you go," the old lady invited.

WHILE MY FAMILY headed for the Tan Son Nhut airport, I walked over to the Department of Real Estate for the last time. My mother handed me four hundred dong and her watch so that I could keep track of time. The waiting room of the office was empty, draped in a sickly green light. I sat on the wooden bench, in the same crude, unfriendly spot where I had spent the past five days. Outside, the sun was rising. Its golden light filtered through the wood panels of the windows, dappling the walls of the room in tiny dots.

An hour later, the officers began to arrive in groups, discussing the latest soccer scores noisily among themselves. The moment the chief of the Real Estate Service appeared at the door, I shot up from my seat. Holding a cup of coffee, he walked past me without acknowledging my presence. Before I could greet him, he disappeared behind a closed door.

A secretary pointed at me and laughed out loud to his colleagues. "Take a look at that boy," he said. "Still here, kid? I thought your flight to America was scheduled today. Why are you still mopping my seat with your half-breed ass?"

I looked away, choking back a lump of frustration.

Time ticked slowly by. People came and went, bringing with them large sacks filled with presents. Some would leave in a few minutes, happy. Others who shared my ill luck stayed behind and waited. Finally, at nine-thirty, I gathered my courage and approached the secretary's desk.

"Excuse me, sir," I said, pointing at the chief of the Real Estate Service's office. "May I see the officer now?"

"No," he answered without looking up at me.

"Please, sir?" I waved a carton of cigarettes in front of him and added, "It will only take a second."

He grabbed the gift from my fingers. "Hurry up," he growled.

I hurried past the array of desks that filled the room, and knocked at the officer's door.

"Come in," a familiar voice answered.

I entered. The chief sat on his leather chair facing the windows. His nimble fingers swirled a pencil so fast it made a visible circle around his hand. He turned around and looked at me.

Reaching inside my knapsack for the gifts, I set each item on his desk carefully. His half-shut eyes moved from my face to the presents. The bored look never left his face.

"Please sign my paper," I stammered. "I have to catch a plane soon."

He picked up the cognac bottle and examined it. "Go outside and wait," he said.

"I have to get this paper signed as soon as possible, sir. I can't miss my flight."

He leaned back in his chair and stretched out his arms. "Hey, don't you have any faith in me? Have a seat and wait. Outside."

I left his office reluctantly, returning to my seat. Another half hour went by. The urge to scream or to break something mounted in me with each second. Finally, I shot up from my seat and stormed outside.

The secretary's voice echoed in my ear. "See you tomorrow, half-breed."

On the street, I looked around for a taxi. My watch indicated I had forty-five minutes left to meet up with my mother at the airport. In my head, an incendiary anger burned so intensely I could hardly see straight.

At the corner, a rickshaw pulled over to my side. "Can I take you somewhere, mister?" the driver asked me.

I nodded and hopped in. "Tan Son Nhut airport," I told him.

"Definitely, for a small fee of forty-eight dong," he chirped and began pedaling his three-wheeled vehicle into the middle of the street.

I sank back into the fake leather seat, too crushed to make a sound. The city passed in flashes of blurry images. Passersby stared at me as if they had witnessed all the indignities I had just gone through. Houses with red tile roofs and alleys that I had walked by so many times all pressed up against my eyes. Then everything faded away. The rickshaw carried me out of Saigon as the wind brought fresher air, diminishing my anxiety.

"We're here," he announced.

A hundred yards in front of me, the airport's entrance was jammed with taxis, buses, and motorcycles. Across an immense field of wild reeds, a couple of gray buildings huddled close to one another, receding into a haze. The road that led to them was interminably long, baking under a hot sun.

At the front gate of the airport, a policeman stopped us. After examining the rickshaw driver's ID carefully, he said, "You don't have a permit to take your vehicle inside." Turning to me, he scanned my passport. "Young man, you have to either walk or find another way to get to the waiting room."

"How far is it from here?" I asked him, at the same time paying the driver his fare.

"About two miles," the policeman said. "They are closing the door soon, so you better hurry."

My watch showed ten minutes to eleven o'clock. "How am I going to get there in ten minutes?" I cried.

Crouching among other drivers near the entrance, a young man in a striped shirt got my attention. "Hey," he yelled, grinning from ear to ear. "You want to hire me? I can get you inside."

"Okay," I said quickly.

"How much money do you have?" he asked me.

I reached inside my pocket, pulled out a wad of bills, and counted. "Three hundred and fifty-two dong are all I got," I said to him.

Swiftly, he grabbed the bills from my hand. "It's fine. Wait right here."

The sun rose higher, roasting anything that lay under its reach. The coachmen withdrew inside their vehicles to escape the glare. When the young man reappeared, in his hands, a rusty motorcycle rolled along the road like a faithful pet.

"Here she is," he said proudly, patting the seat. "We are all set to go. By the way, there is a tiny problem with this vehicle. You need to help me push-start the engine, because she can't start by herself. Once she gets going, you can jump up behind me."

I sank to the ground. With each new obstacle that I encountered, the level of difficulty grew. This one, I was sure, exceeded my capacity. The young man hopped on his bike, turned around, and beckoned for me to start pushing. An electric current pushed me to my feet.

I ran down the searing road. The motorcycle moved slowly in front of me, screeching like a sickly old person. Then, the engine crackled, expelling a cloud of dark gas in my face. Suddenly, the vehicle slipped from my fingers and shot ahead in a red cloud of dust. I stopped, watching it go in disbelief. Feeling like a complete fool, I looked around for the policeman.

However, before I could do anything, the bike returned. It raced past me, made a sharp turn, then slowed down. Bouncing impatiently on his seat, the young man called out to me, "Hey, what is the matter with you? Why didn't you hop on? Hurry, we don't have much time."

I made a flying leap onto the seat. The back of my khaki pants split open, but I didn't care. I grabbed his waist, ducked my head, and held on for all I was worth. He drove me to the front entrance of the compound and screeched to a halt. I glanced at my watch. Eleven o'clock. Did I make it on time? A hundred yards away, the glass doors to the departure area moved slowly on their hinges in the hands of two guards.

The motorcycle driver turned around. His face was filled with warmth. "Good luck," he said. "You better run now."

I waved my visa in the air and screamed to the guards, "Wait for me, please."

Behind the glass, the guards stopped, looking at one another. I rushed through the crack between the doors, forgetting to thank the driver. His motorcycle roared down the street triumphantly. Then I heard the gates close behind me.

CHAPTER FIFTY

The departure area was deserted, except for a few civilians and policemen. Evidence of a busy morning registered on everybody's face and in the scattered piles of garbage littering the floor. The only furniture was a row of aluminum desks in the center of the room. Behind each desk stood a policeman. My family was nowhere in sight. Neither were the three hundred other passengers. In fact, I seemed to be the only Amerasian in the room.

A female guard approached me. The curious look on her face dissipated the moment I presented to her my passport.

"Where in hell have you been?" she snapped and ushered me to the first desk. There, I was searched quickly for hidden weapons. At the second table I got my passport stamped. Next I had to sign a release form. In the paper they offered to me I immediately recognized my family's signatures, scribbled beside their printed names. Relieved, I scanned the room. Closed doors led to mysterious and unidentified areas. However, somewhere in that building, my family was waiting for me. I took a deep breath and stepped to the last table, praying silently for a miracle.

The policeman looked up. "Where are your documents?" he asked.

I stared at him, petrified. "In my knapsack, sir."

"Take them out."

I fumbled in my bag, and pulled out the thick stack of papers. Years of hard work had culminated in a two-foot heap of paper-work. Cautiously, I slid the unsigned real estate form into the middle of the pile before I handed everything to him. I tried to maintain a poker face, but inside, I felt about to faint.

The policeman seized the pile of papers. In one swift movement, he tossed everything in the air without glancing at it. Sheets of papers flew into the open space, flapping around me like white butterflies before they landed on the floor. I uttered a small cry. My pictures, my family's pictures, and every other document that I had worked so hard to prepare in the last three years all lay on the ground, facing upward among other anonymous, forgotten families.

"You're all done," the policeman said. "Go in there and join your family." He pointed toward a small doorway at the end of the room.

"What is the point of making us get these documents together if they are insignificant to you?" I protested, unable to believe what had just happened.

He shrugged, pushing me toward the exit. "Get out of here and stop wasting my time. Nobody wants to keep trash like you in this country."

I grabbed my knapsack and straightened my clothes. His cruel words could no longer hurt my feelings. In fact, my anger gave me new strength to move forward.

From the entrance, a voice called my name. I turned around, and time seemed to stop. Kim stood between the two guards, wearing the same sleeveless red blouse that had made me tremble the first day we met. Her jet-black hair was shiny like the midnight sky, and her teeth were perfect like porcelain. I dropped my knapsack on the floor, feeling my knees weaken as emotion rushed through me like the crash of the waves against the sandy beach.

She ran to me. One of the guards seized her arm, pulling her away through the room. Struggling free, she turned to face me. Her hand reached out in my direction, waving.

I ran after them and yelled, "Please stop. Let me say good-bye to her."

They let her go. We ran toward each other. I squeezed her with all my strength.

"I am so sorry," I stammered. "I am sorry for hurting you. I shouldn't have done what I did. Please forgive me."

She looked up at me. "It's quite all right, Kien. I am glad that my first time was with you."

"I — I didn't mean that. It was my first time as well. What I want to say is that I am sorry for treating you badly. Because of who you are, my intention was not pure when I befriended you."

"Do not think too much about that, Kien." She smiled, tapping her temple with her forefinger. "I have only beautiful memories of you right here."

I breathed a sigh of relief. "Thank you, I am glad that you do. By the way, how did you get here? And who brought you?"

She nestled her head on my chest. "I am here with your aunt," she said. "She is upstairs, waiting for your family on the balcony. You'll see us again when you walk out on the runway. My parents don't know yet that I am in Saigon. I came because I just cannot let you leave my life on that awful note. If there is nothing else between us, at least I want your friendship."

I smothered her face with kisses. "I have thought about us a great deal," I whispered in her ear. "I will never forget you as long as I am still alive."

"Thank you," she said. A mischievous smile brightened her face. "There is still hope for you after all, Kien."

A guard nudged my back. "Let's go," he urged, pushing the knapsack into my hand.

We broke apart. I touched her face, trying to memorize her delicate neck, her unblemished skin, and the distinctive freckles on her cheeks. "I'll write to you," I called. "I'll tell you what happens to us every week. No, every day, until we'll meet again."

She grabbed her shoulders, as if she were cold. Her eyelashes were beaded with tears, but she smiled, watching me disappear behind a door.

"Good-bye, Kim," I said to her one last time.

THE ROOM WAS PACKED with hundreds of children, screaming and chasing each other between rows of chairs like the inside of a giant classroom. Two of the walls, made out of glass, overlooked the landing strips. Outside on the cement, three airplanes were parked within a hundred feet of each other, reflecting the sunlight. I searched for my family. On the floor near the exit, they huddled together, preparing lunch. Jimmy jumped up and down, waving his hands to get my attention. I waved back, pushing past a group of children. The adults stared at me, yet no one made any attempt to let me get across.

Sitting alone on a bench at my right was the blond girl I had met at the interview site. Her overweight mother and fourteen pretentious siblings were nowhere in sight. One of her hands clutched a basket. The other held a heavy sack that was slung over her shoulder. Her eyes were red and swollen from crying.

"Hey," I said to the girl. "Are you okay?"

She nodded, avoiding my stare.

"I saw you at the interview a few months ago. Where is your family?"

"Those people are not my real family," she replied. "My mother sold me to that lady last year so that I could take her entire family to America. But when we came in for the interview, the Americans figured out the scam. They issued only one ticket for me after turning everybody else down." She began to sob bitterly.

"Don't cry," I consoled her. "When you get to America, you can sponsor your real family. It only takes another year before you can see them again."

"I don't know where they are," she cried. "My mother moved away soon after I was sold."

I patted her thin shoulder. "I'm sorry," I said. "But don't worry. You are not alone. I read somewhere that once you get to America, a good family will adopt you. Would you like to come over and sit with my family and me? We'll keep you company in the meantime."

She nodded, wiping her tears and gathering her belongings. Together, we stepped over rows of people, approaching my mother.

BeTi sat on the floor. Banana cake crumbs covered her hands. She winked at me and smiled.

"I made it here in one piece, Mother," I said over the loud noises.

My mother put a hand over her chest. Her face was pale from anxiety. "I was so worried," she said. "I don't know what I would have done if you'd gotten stuck behind. I've been praying all morning." Her eyes shifted curiously to the girl who stood behind me.

"It's a long story," I explained. "She will be needing our company for a while."

My mother leaned back against the glass door. She looked tired. "In that case, sit your friend down," she said. "I saved you some lunch."

CHAPTER FIFTY-ONE

At two o'clock in the afternoon the airplanes started to move slowly on the runway. Behind the wall of glass, people bustled about, dividing their belongings among their families. Nervous smiles masked the apprehension everybody was feeling. Outside, the clear blue summer sky seemed to expand like the inside of a hot-air balloon, reaching for the distant, untouchable white-rimmed horizon.

My mother sat on the floor with her knees drawn up against her chest. Her hands were pushed together at the wrists to form a stand, supporting her chin. Most of her fingernails were deformed, thickened from the years of hard labor she had endured. Her wrinkled skin, cracked at each knuckle from excessive dryness, was covered with calluses and leathery from the sun. In the span of ten years, the Communists had successfully stripped away from my mother the ultimate pride in her life — the gracefulness of her hands. No longer would they execute their charming dance on the stem of a champagne glass or pose daintily for a photograph. These hands belonged to a much older, hopelessly crushed spirit that bore little resemblance to the mother I once knew.

Somewhere above us a bell rang, sending a wave of apprehension through the crowded room. We leaped onto our feet and rushed toward the entrance. Soon the doors opened, and I was the first one that stepped out onto the airfield.

On a second-floor balcony overlooking the landing field, relatives of those departing lined the railing. People craned their necks and shaded their eyes, trying to make out the faces of their loved ones. I could hear my aunt's distinct voice, braying over the others.

I looked up. My aunt stood among the strangers, waving her arms to get my attention. Behind her, harsh rays of light shone through her salt-and-pepper hair. The sun and its torrid temperature made her look as if she were on fire.

"Hi, Kien — your auntie is over here," she yelled. "Forgive me. I never could imagine that they would let you out of this country. I want to apologize. Go to America, make it big and don't forget us." Her words were lost as other families shouted their farewells.

I looked straight ahead, ignoring her. The aircraft door opened in front of me, and a tall staircase dropped into position. I climbed the steps eagerly. Inside, a blast of air conditioning welcomed me in its chilly embrace.

In the dense air, a gong reverberated. I wondered if it was to announce the end of my journey or the beginning of a new one.

EPILOGUE

If you want to ever achieve happiness, don't dwell on the past. Instead, start living. What is the point of obsessing over something that has already happened, and that you cannot change? Live! And be merry.

My grandfather said these words to me during our last conversation, the night I left our home in Nhatrang for Saigon in 1984. For years I thought about his wisdom and tried to live by his advice. But as much as I tried, I couldn't forget my past. The events that had shaped me continued to weigh on my soul.

In June of 1998, more than fourteen years after I came to America, I graduated from the New York University College of Dentistry. That summer, as I waited to receive my license to practice, the nightmares I had kept at bay during the hectic years of my education returned to plague me with renewed intensity. The dreams came in waves, once or twice a week. Sometimes they came in groups of two or three. Often, I dreamed that I was still on the streets of Saigon, trying to get the last of my documents signed. And across the city, the plane was leaving without me. Other times, I saw myself drowning in the middle of a vast ocean. Above my head, pale corpses wrapped their limbs together to form a shield of flesh, preventing me from reaching the surface. I would awake, unable to shake my terror. Even during the daytime, the frightening images haunted me. I came to dread going to bed at night.

Desperate to free myself from a deep depression, I decided to keep a diary of the dreams. Day after day, I sat in front of a computer, staring at its blank screen, and toying with Loan's jade, which I wore on a chain around my neck. So many conflicting thoughts raced through my head: the early memories of my childhood, the years of hardship after the fall of Saigon, and the desperate preparations to leave the country. From the window of the library in the house in SoHo where I now live, the Old St. Patrick's Cathedral across the street became an austere companion. Somewhere in the church's attic, a bell tolled according to a preset timer. Its relentless noise penetrated my sanctuary, making it difficult to focus.

One late night while I sat at my computer, something strange happened. In the stillness of the room, the world around me seemed to disappear into the distance, and time, too, faded away. As a silkworm transforms into a caterpillar, so the furniture around me changed shape. The walls of the library slowly vanished, giving way to a noisy, crowded street. Beneath my feet, the wooden floor shifted into a burning pavement. Light bulbs grew into an enormous sun. And the church bell from outside sounded more like a series of explosions, assaulting my ears with the familiar sound of bombs and gunshots. I looked around the room, and as if in a dream, I was standing on a street corner in Saigon, watching a little boy among the faces of people from my past. I knew then I was looking at myself. And through the eyes of this boy, I saw the events of my life unfold before me. I began to write.

My reason for writing this book at first was purely personal. I just wanted to heal myself. But, as the story progressed, I thought more and more about the other Amerasians I had encountered. I recalled the sadness of their desperate lives, which I had both witnessed and heard described in my early years. As dark as my memoir may be, it is not unique by any means. It's estimated that more than fifty thousand Amerasian children shared my fate, or worse. Their stories were all too common ones of terror and repression, abuse and neglect, strength, and ultimately — for the lucky ones — survival. I kept writing in hopes that these innocent victims' lost childhoods might finally be mourned, and their buried secrets at last revealed.

I COMPLETED *The Unwanted* on March 22, 2000, at the same time that the world observed the twenty-fifth anniversary of the end of Vietnam's conflict. I don't have the nightmares anymore.